Thursday, November 2

1944

The American oil tanker SS *Fort Lee* is sunk in the Indian Ocean. En-route to Brisbane, Queensland carrying 93,000 barrels of oil she was torpedoed by the German U-boat submarine *U-181*. A total of four lifeboats managed to safely get away.

Twelve days later on November 14 1944 the historic port town of Albany located on the southern coast of Western Australia receives ashore 17 sailors from the United States Merchant Marines and Navy Armed Guard. On the very same date a further 16 men are delivered at Fremantle in Perth. Ten days later another 17 American sailors are dropped off in Colombo, Ceylon. The last lifeboat with 16 men in it disappears and nothing is heard of it for 45 years.

They were all survivors. However little did anyone seem to know anything about it, such as who they were and where they came from?

70 years later Kevin Gomm author of the popular "**Red Sun On The Kangaroo Paw**" candidly delivers this intriguing true account of the events leading up to the sinking of the SS *Fort Lee* and the attempts to piece together the movements of her surviving crew. It traces their extraordinary odyssey from rescue at sea to their eventual repatriation back to the United States.

Lifeboat #6

The Sinking of the SS

FORT LEE

1944 - 2014
70th Anniversary
SS Fort Lee

In Solidarity

This book is dedicated to all good sailors
everywhere who served with honour.
Duty most nobly done.

DIGGER

Published in Australia by Digger Press
Western Australia

Website: www.diggerpress.com
E-mail: admin@diggerpress.com

National Library of Australia
Cataloguing-in-Publishing Data

Lifeboat #6
The Sinking of the SS Fort Lee

by Kevin Gomm

© 2014

ISBN 978-0-9872231-8-0

Includes Bibliography

SS *Fort Lee* (ship) – *U-181* (U-boat submarine)
Tankers-United States-History-20th century
World War, 1939-1945 – campaigns-Indian Ocean
World War, 1939-1945 – Naval operations, German
World War, 1939-1945 – Naval operations – submarine
World War, 1939-1945 – Search and rescue operations
Merchant Marine – United States – History – 20th century
United States Navy - Shipwrecks - History - 20th century

Dewey number: 940.5451

Cover design: Digger Press, Western Australia
Book design & Layout: Digger Press, Western Australia
Advanced Typeset: David Bradbury

10 9 8 7 6 5 4 3 2 1 0

Contents

Lifeboat #6

The Sinking Of The SS Fort Lee

I extend my sincere gratitude and special thanks to Joe Sherry pictured here with their family pet Roland. Joe is the son of Michael Sherry who was one of the 17 survivors in Lifeboat #6 from the *Fort Lee* rescued by the *Tumacacori* and brought to Albany, Western Australia on November 14 1944. Without his assistance, support and contribution, this book would have been just a little more difficult to write. By means of modern technology a wonderful cyber friendship has evolved. Joe served in the U.S. Air Force during the Korean War. He and his wife Neva live today in Pinehurst, North Carolina.

Kevin Gomm

From the Author

In February 2013 I received a written reply back from Arthur R. Moore. Now 90 years of age, Captain Moore is a United States Merchant Marine Veteran from World War II. In his letter he remarked "That we should have written about all these stories 60 years ago when everybody was still alive."

To all who enjoy their history, whether they are those who study it professionally or just consider themselves to be the average person in the street possessing only a mere fleeting interest in it, they would have to nevertheless wholeheartedly agree that this is indeed a very true and valid statement.

Captain Arthur Moore is the author of '*A Careless Word – A Needless Sinking*' and also the online article '*Never Seen Or Heard From Again*' two works, particularly the latter, that set a precedent and has greatly assisted the development of this book.

However to be perfectly honest this has not been an easy story to research and compile together. But then again a subject matter concerning a myriad of obscure events and whose complexity by nature involves a remote and distant historical theme never usually are. To get both behind and inside the story of the sinking of the SS *Fort Lee* commenced as one gigantic jigsaw puzzle with many missing pieces. Slowly, and stressing emphasis on the word *slowly,* over time, coupled with much persistence and patience, these so called missing pieces began to gradually fall into place.

A strong motivation to persevere with this book was just simply the overwhelming determination to document this fascinating and little known story. As an added incentive, time itself was not on my side being only too well aware that the very last handful of living survivors from the *Fort Lee* are now aged in their late eighties and or early nineties.

The historical town of Albany is actually my old hometown where a small but pivotal piece of this story was played out. Located on the southern coast of Western Australia, it is about a five hour drive south of the state capital Perth. On a mild Tuesday morning back in November 1944 seventeen American sailors were landed safely ashore here. However no one in Albany historical circles seemed to have known anything of this occurring, let alone of the ship itself or the incident of her sinking. Equally no one in Perth for that matter in both naval and or maritime historical circles was familiar with the story either.

Seemingly Australia wide it displayed the all too common diagnosis of being one of those historical incidents that simply 'fell under the radar' and had simply been forgotten. Therefore it was easy to presume that it would be doubtful to find somebody in Ceylon [today Sri Lanka] possessing any historical knowledge of it as well. In fact it was difficult to find anybody anywhere who had even the remotest inkling of it taking place at all. Scouring through hundreds of editions of old newspapers from the time, the press too, despite wartime censorship, was seemingly gagged, lacking even a mention. Apart from what could be 'Googled' and found on websites like Wikipedia...these days the often all too convenient 'go to' first point of reference, the search for more information was equally barricaded and extremely difficult to find.

The SS *Fort Lee* first came to my attention back in early 2007 when I was researching material for my second book. Then I had stumbled across a brief but obscure reference pertaining to her. For *In The Shadow Of The Eagle* I only ended up dedicating a few paragraphs to it...just for the time being. Twelve months later in my third book *Beneath Cold Waves* I similarly included her just as a brief one page entry. Throughout it all I full well knew that at some future stage a concerted attempt to chronicle this saga in more thorough detail was going to have to be considered and seriously embarked upon.

I commenced by posting a message on the noticeboard of the United States Merchant Marine and Armed Guard website requesting either living survivors, relatives and or just anyone with further intimate knowledge that they may have about the ship and its sinking. The people at the USMM are fabulous and have helped me before with research.

Many months went by until one day out of the blue Joe Sherry contacted me. He introduced himself as the son of Michael Sherry one of the 17 men that were rescued in Lifeboat #6 and dropped off at Albany. He pointed out that he did not know a lot of details about the story himself for his father, like so many, never spoke of the incident. Joe still had some of his father's souvenirs from his brief time in Australia all those years ago. He kindly offered to help and assist as much as he could in any way.

I knew that by having a direct contact in the U.S.A. like Joe, who obviously has a direct interest in the story, was going to be very handy, if not essential. It was simply a matter of geography where it was going to be somewhat difficult for me to conduct first hand interviews in America, without actually having to go and spend time there, of which the budget at the time did not permit. I am indeed very grateful for the contribution made by the Sherry family.

Before long, again by way of the USMM & AG noticeboard more relatives such as daughters, sons and grandchildren of other *Fort Lee* survivors began to make contact. They were all enthusiastic to donate information as much as possible. Shortly after I then received a reply from David Burch from the Navy League of the United States who informed me of an actual *Fort Lee* survivor residing in a Veterans Administration Medical Centre in Georgia. It turned out he was one of the 16 that were rescued and brought to Fremantle. Before long another survivor was discovered and contact was soon made. He had been one of those taken to Colombo, Ceylon.

This was closely followed by the discovery of one of the 17 survivors who was brought to Albany. Meanwhile the hunt gathered pace to track down more families and relatives of others from all across America. There was hope that there may still be more living survivors.

The USMM & AG website is obviously one that is very well patronised because soon enough I received another highly sought after reply. This time it was from the daughter of an ex-crewman from the SS *Tumacacori* the ship that had rescued the men in Lifeboat #6 and disembarked them at Albany. She confirmed that her father was still alive and well. Finally after many months of stalemate new information began to accelerate and materialise at a rapid rate.

The campaign to find more families of those who had served on the *Fort Lee* yielded further results. From Wisconsin to Florida, from Kansas to Minnesota, replies were received. It culminated with the response from family members of the men who were lost in the ill fated Lifeboat #4.

During the time of writing and researching material for this book I chanced upon also another vessel that is deserving of equal attention. The SS *Garoet* had been torpedoed and sunk several months earlier by the exact same U-boat that would later engage the *Fort Lee*. Here again is the classic case of one story interconnecting with another that led to another that led to another story and so on. Besides being one of those all too common forgotten incidents, the main difference here is that the *Garoet* distinctly holds a much more significant Australian connection, albeit a tragic one.

In 2014 it will be the 70th anniversary when most of the following took place. Since 1945 much has changed and altered in our respective societies. However the recognition to merchant mariners and those that served on board armed merchant ships the world over took much longer than necessary. In the past, issues had been raised concerning the benefits and acknowledgement, or lack thereof deserving of these men in all Merchant Navies.

American Merchant Marine Veterans for instance endured the long hard road for official recognition. Though merchant seamen engaged in military operations and served in war zones, they were still officially classed as civilians. So much so that the moment their ship was sunk, that's when their wages stopped, until they were able to sign onto another vessel. After the war Merchant Mariners, even though the Merchant Marine itself came under auspices of the U.S. Coast Guard, were not permitted to qualify for, nor were they entitled to receive GI benefits such as education, health care, housing or employment preference. It took another 43 years before they finally and just deservedly received final recognition as War Veterans in 1988.

Whilst I openly vent my support to these men I will purposely refrain from inciting any political debate and circumvent undue controversy concerning the above by just weighing in on the historical accounts only. Thus I prevent myself from making irresponsible comment and argument where I am clearly not qualified to do so. Having said that, the same sentiments are also extended to the gallant men of the United States Navy Armed Guard whose job it was to defend these merchant vessels. A common thread I found with the Navy Armed Guards on board these ships was that they were all so young – some only boys still in or just barely out of their teens. A lot were hardly any older than 18 or 19 years of age. Not that the Merchant Marine faired any different with an age range anywhere from 16 to 60....with considerably a lot under the age of 25.

Before the *Fort Lee* finally slipped forever down into a watery grave, a total of four lifeboats were successfully launched. I have chosen to title this book *Lifeboat #6* with the appropriate sub title *The Sinking of the SS Fort Lee*. It is intended as a mark of respect to not only those who were in this lifeboat but also because of the obvious Albany connection.

However this title is not meant to purposely underscore nor draw attention away from the significant and equal importance deserving of all the other lifeboats. In fact quite the opposite. It is intended to overall encapsulate every one of those who were in Lifeboats 1, 2, and 4 and also the unfortunate numbers 3 and 5.

Whilst careful attention and vigilance is at all times espoused, I stand corrected on everything that I write and always welcome notice to any error and or inaccuracy that the reader may feel inclined. To ensure that this has not occurred I am grateful to receive valuable advice from World War II navy veterans like Sid Henry an ex-RNVR Lieutenant DSC, twice wounded who saw active service at D-Day, the North Sea, Mediterranean, North Africa, Italy, Indian Ocean and Burma. A veritable wealth of knowledge at 92 years young, Sid has frequently been my 'go to man' where it has been necessary to clarify things nautical and naval.

I am equally grateful to Bill Hultgren a long time maritime historian and U.S. World War Two veteran from Erie, Pennsylvania. Specialising in Liberty and merchant ships, Bill at 90 years of age, has a marvellous collection and was always able to provide those really hard to get photographs of ships.

This is my fifth book and has taken the best part of seven years to research and compile together. With its fertile tapestry of interwoven stories and accounts it has become my own veritable odyssey. It has been a long road and somewhat of a mammoth task, but one well worth it. At first the reader may feel inclined that they have to labour through the first two or three chapters before arriving at the core subject of this book. However it was necessary to include them to so call 'set the scene' and understand why a lone American tanker and a German U-boat were there each both far from home, particularly in this late stage of the war.

A large amount of the following has been compiled from the written and recorded testimonies and interviews conducted from the small handful of survivors still alive today. Other inclusions are drawn from the diaries, notes, private letters, photographs and personal recollections left behind from survivors who have since passed on. Collectively this allows the story to be told as much as possible in their own words.

Some are verbal recollections submitted by close family members of survivors as it was told to them. The remainder is from hundreds of declassified documents, testimonials, papers and bibliography from a wide range of various archives, libraries and museums. As a combination from all these sources

I was able to unearth a whole lot of new information. Simultaneously I was also able explode some myths and misconceptions that had arisen about the *Fort Lee* since she departed Abadan all those years ago.

In addition, a lot of the photographs here have never been published before and come from private family collections. None of the following is made up or fiction. Where there is liberal use of adjectives and or the insertion of a colourful narrative, it has purposely been done so simply to add effect. Here I ask the reader for a little forgiveness as I still harness delusions of attempting to become a creative writer one day.

But more importantly I express sincere and grateful thanks to all the wonderful people who kindly contributed information and donated their time and resources to this book both here in Australia, from around the globe and especially from the United States. In particular I give special thanks to the handful of living survivors and the families of survivors. It is a long book, but it had to be if one was going to do a comprehensive and proper job of it. For my part I hope I have.

A sobering statistic is that that over 300 ships were sunk as a result of direct combat in the Indian Ocean during the Second World War.

The SS *Fort Lee* was one of them. This is her story.

Hotbed of Activity

It has been sometimes described as the forgotten battle-field. The vast expanse of water that is the Indian Ocean is still probably the least documented theatre of maritime conflict during the Second World War that has been examined. It has never quite really captured the same level of fascination or interest like that of the North Atlantic or Pacific. Perhaps because it has simply been a victim of its own geography, where her role has been largely overshadowed by the greater air and sea battles that occurred elsewhere.

The triumphs and successes, or conversely the tragedies and failures endured and experienced by both Allied and Axis combatants in this remote and isolated ocean often set a precedence for lessons learnt in other fields of combat, for many 'firsts' were carried out here.

The Indian Ocean between 1939 and 1945 was certainly no backwater. A dangerous war zone, it was primarily a sea war fought out predominantly between ships and submarines. There was only really three incidents resembling land based battles involving troops, that being the joint Allied invasion of Vichy French Madagascar, the British and Italian campaigns in Somalia and Abyssinia and the Japanese occupation of tiny Christmas Island.

Nevertheless the importance of the Indian Ocean as the eastern gateway to the Orient cannot be dismissed lightly.

As the world's third largest ocean it stretches all the way from the east coast of Africa to the west coast of Australia and from the southern cold waters of Antarctica to the tropical monsoon shores of the Indian sub-continent from where it bears its name. It is of substantial size at 73,556,000 square kilometres or 28,350,000 square miles consisting of an area covering 20 per cent of water on the Earth's surface. It is also deep, very deep where some depths are over 8,000 metres or 26, 300 feet. The Indian Ocean is one of the most unpredictable, capable of delivering violent cyclonic storms and devastating Tsunami's as seen in recent years.

But what it has always been though is an important trade route. Trade between China, India, Africa, the Arabian Peninsula and also among the scattering of islands mainly dotted around the rim, stretch back millennia. Throughout the 16th and 17th centuries the Dutch, Spanish, Portuguese and English all set about to exploit it. Established soon was new colonies to harness this wealthy and lucrative so called 'Spice Trade'. None were more important than the Dutch East Indies [today Indonesia]. A testimony to this is the large number 17th century Dutch shipwrecks scattered all up and down along the long coastline of the west coast of Australia. Pushed along by the 'Roaring Forties' the winds that blow eastward in the Indian Ocean, many of these early vessels simply overtook their turning point and literally crashed into the uncharted and unknown reefs, cliffs and rocks of 'Terra Incognita'.

Despite fleeting interest shown by both the Dutch and French it was the British that chose to take possession of this the Great Southern Land for themselves. Not to overlook that the indigenous Aboriginal population of it had already been here for 60,000 years.

After 1788 New Holland soon to become known as Australia, increasingly began to become vital to the British Empire. Despite being initially a dumping ground for the Empire's convicts, throughout the 19th century as the colony grew, so too did her agricultural and manufacturing industries. By the 20th century Australia, as a newly federated nation, began to contribute nearly half of what Britain required. Wool, meat, grain, dairy produce, to name a few, clearly indicated that the Indian Ocean lines of sea transportation were now more important than ever.

Following the declaration of war on September 3 1939 it did not take long for both the British Admiralty and German naval authorities to come to terms with the fact that the sea war was not going to be necessarily confined entirely to the North Atlantic. In fact the German *Kriegsmarine* had been planning and making provisions for such a likelihood from as early as 1936, that operations would eventually be conducted in far away sea traffic lanes and oceans.

Germany's own presence and influence in the Indian Ocean goes back to the middle of the 19th century. Embarking on a build up of her naval forces that commenced in the 1870's precipitated the need to protect her new found colonies in the Pacific Ocean and Africa.

However it was with the onset of the First World War in 1914 that would teach German sea power many lessons. None more so than the cruiser *Emden*. Part of Admiral Von Spee's Asian Squadron based out of Tsingtao in China the *Emden* under the command of Captain Karl von Muller chose to remain behind and cause chaos in the Indian Ocean. On November 9 1914 after a fierce gun battle with the HMAS *Sydney* she was cornered and trapped. Not wishing to cause further casualties than necessary Muller ran the now stricken vessel ashore on the North Cocos Keeling Island. For the fledging Royal Australian Navy established only three years before in 1911 it was her first ever sea battle and a somewhat significantly successful one at that.

The following year on the other side of the Indian Ocean was the incident concerning the German cruiser *Konigsberg*. Trapped in the Rufigi River, once again the Royal Australian Navy played a decisive role with the HMAS *Pioneer* thwarting her attempts to 'break out' in to the Indian Ocean. Throughout the remainder of the First World War German merchant raiders such as the *Wolf* continued to operate in both the Indian and Pacific Oceans.

But later came more peaceful interests. In 1928 ten years after the 'War To End All Wars' the old cruiser *Berlin* on a post war round the world good will voyage departed Fremantle after an two week stay for the Bay of Bengal to conduct 'soundings' and 'correct charts'. Another was a German scientific expedition that in 1929 launched a sealed bottle in the Southern Ocean off Tasmania. Nicknamed *'The Flying Dutchman'* it had a message inside that could be read without it being opened. Circumnavigating the globe several times, some six years, 26,000 kilometres [16,000 miles] and 2,447 days later it washed up on the west coast of Australia in 1935 becoming one of the longest monitored voyages ever undertaken by a bottle.

Britain's empire which dominated a substantial size of the globe had for the past 200 years enjoyed total command of the major seaways. This she needed to do so to transport all the goods and commodities vital for her ongoing existence.

In order to protect these sea lanes she needed a sizeable navy. This she had in the form of the Royal Navy. Just as much as it was greatly admired and feared worldwide, just as much many other nations were jealous of it and attempted to emulate her naval capability and size to match. Under the Kaiser, Germany was one. So too was Japan, of which the British with actual open handedness assisted greatly to the building up and establishment of the new modern Imperial Japanese Navy.

Russia, Italy and France for example all constructed fleets of battleships, cruisers and destroyers on the strength to try and match, or at least keep up with Great Britain and her commonwealth. So too the United States, though largely an unknown factor in modern naval warfare, despite her Civil War in the 1860's and the Spanish War of 1896. During World War I her impact was minor due to the late entry. However 25 years later her substantial naval force would rise to the challenge and establish its dominance, a position that she still admirably holds today.

In 1939, just prior to the outbreak of hostilities, Admiral Karl Doenitz chief of the German U-boat arm decreed:

"In order to defeat England we must sever her lines of sea communication and supply."

A realist, despite his beguiled support of Hitler and National Socialism, he knew that this was going to be the most practical way of winning any war against Britain. It nearly worked. It was first attempted during World War I of which

Doenitz himself was then a young U-boat commander. However the Imperial German Navy did not possess the numbers nor the tactical submarine technology which was still rather in its infancy. With the ascension of Hitler coming to power, throughout the 1930's Germany was busily re-arming and preparing for it though. Times were changing and so was technology. The attempt to starve Britain into submission by this renewed concerted U-boat effort was the factor that nearly won them the war.

Even today a certain curiosity is still held in the fact that these same German U-boat submarines actually operated in the Indian Ocean during the Second World War and so close to Australia for that matter. The traditional familiarity perhaps is the notion that these 'Grey Wolves' are more identifiable plying the cold waters of the North Atlantic and North Sea in 'Wolf Packs' hunting for prey.

Nevertheless after the North and South Atlantic, the Caribbean, and the Mediterranean Sea, the Indian Ocean itself was the next most important and prolific sphere of operations. Before long it became a hotbed of activity and increasingly more so as the war carried on.

Since 1940 disguised German merchant raider vessels began to infiltrate these waters. One of the more widely known is the *Kormoran*. After sinking several merchant ships she suddenly came to grief herself following the now famous sea battle with the flagship of the Australian Navy, HMAS *Sydney* on November 19 1941.

Off the mid northern coast of Western Australia near Shark Bay she went down with the loss of all 645 lives. The *Kormoran* lost some 79 crew and managed 317 survivors including her captain before they were captured and interned in Australia for the duration of the war. For his efforts the commander of the *Kormoran*, Captain Theodore Anton Detmers was awarded the Knights Cross.

The incident was mired in controversy for years until the two wrecks were finally located in March 2008. It was the only occasion that an armed merchant raider had successfully fought and sunk a conventional class warship. Normally these raiders, despite their impressive arsenal, were completely outclassed and out gunned when compared to a corvette or cruiser. But it is understood and widely accepted that the *Sydney's* commander, Captain Joseph Burnett ignored Admiralty protocol and permitted his vessel to come within too close of a striking range for the *Kormoran* and was overwhelmed with the element of surprise.

In all there were up to eight different German raiders that operated in the Indian Ocean from 1940 to 1943. The *Pinguin*, under the command of Ernst Felix Kruder had for months been running rampant in the Indian Ocean completely unchecked when it captured the tanker *Storstad* near Christmas Island. Renaming her the *Passat* and converting it to a mine-laying auxiliary, in tandem they proceeded to bring the war a lot closer to Australia.

Both the *Pinguin* with her captured accomplice laid several minefields in the immediate waters off New South Wales, Victoria, Tasmania and South Australia causing casualties and sinking and damaging over half a dozen ships.

One was SS *City of Rayville* sunk off Cape Otway in Bass Strait, Victoria on November 8 1940 after hitting a mine that had been laid by the *Pinguin*. Occurring some 13 months before Pearl Harbour, she holds the unfortunate title of being the very first United States merchant ship to be sunk in World War II. The one casualty on board was 50 year old 3rd Engineer Mack Bruton Bryan who became the very first U.S. Merchant Marine to lose his life in the war.

On May 8 1941 the *Pinguin's* reign of terror finally came to an abrupt halt when she was hunted down and sunk east of the Seychelles in the Indian Ocean by the HMS *Cornwall*. She was the first of these elusive raiders to be sunk.

Besides the *Kormoran* and *Pinguin* and her captured auxiliary *Passat* there was also the *Thor* and *Atlantis*. Others such as the *Orion, Komet* and *Michel* all made forays into Australian waters and had varying degrees of success in sinking shipping and laying mines. The last raider to operate in the Indian Ocean was the *Michel*. On June 15 1943 she sank the Norwegian freighter SS *Hoegh Silverdawn* after it had departed Fremantle. Two days later it sank the oil tanker *Ferncastle* about 1000 nautical miles south of the Cocos Keeling Islands.

The *Michel's* luck ran out when she was sent to a watery grave by a torpedo from the American submarine USS *Tarpon* as it was attempting to make its way back to Yokohama. It eventuated to be one of the few instances where a German ship was sunk by an operational U.S. Navy submarine in the Pacific Ocean during the entire war.

In between the activities of the raiders, the so called blockade runners ran the gauntlet with attempts to make the perilous journey back to Germany. When hostilities were declared many merchant freighters and steamers found themselves cut off and trapped in neutral harbours. Some decided to sit the war out. Those that were unfortunately not in neutral or friendly ports were seized. The remainder became useful as supply and refuelling vessels for the raiders. Three, notably the *Ramses*, *Coburg* and *Ketty Brovig* a captured Norwegian tanker, were all were hunted down and sunk as they raced across the Indian Ocean to make a getaway.

Whilst not too many conventional German Navy warships entered the Indian Ocean there was one, the *Admiral Scheer*. The 16,200 ton cruiser sunk three ships near the Maldives and captured one off Madagascar in early February 1941, before making a hasty retreat back around South Africa's Cape of Good Hope. Hot on her heels were no less than seven Allied vessels including our own cruisers HMAS *Canberra* and *Australia* along with the British aircraft carrier *Hermes* chasing her.

Where the raiders ceased the U-boats took over. The Indian Ocean was one of the few battlegrounds where operations were waged and carried out by all three principal Axis partners simultaneously. That is Germany, Italy and Japan. Mindful of having said that, it was only just the naval forces from these three belligerents that had the tolerance or patience at developing some form of cohesion or joint working co-operation amongst themselves.

In the Indian Ocean theatre Germany had her raiders and U-boats. Italy had her armed sloops [known as banana boats], several converted liners and UIT submarines and Japan had her submarines, destroyers and some limited success with her own raider vessels.

Upon her own entry in to the war, Japan enjoyed early successes in the Indian Ocean. None more so than the sinking of the battle cruisers HMS *Prince of Wales* and *Repulse* on December 10 1941 off Malaya. This was followed up by the sinking off the USS *Houston* and HMAS *Perth* in the Sunda Strait off Java in late February 1942.

Throughout the evacuation of the Netherlands East Indies ahead of the Japanese advancement and also the first strikes on Darwin, came the losses in the Timor Sea including the destroyers USS *Edsall* and the HMAS *Yarra.* Sunk on February 27 1942 was the United States first aircraft carrier USS *Langley* about 120 kilometres south of Tjilajap, Java.

Then later there was the attack on Colombo itself in Ceylon [Sri Lanka] where between March 31 and April 10 1942 the Royal Navy lost no less than two cruisers, two destroyers, a corvette, including the aircraft carrier *Hermes* as well as over 24 other merchant ships and sloops.

The *Cornwall* who had earlier accounted for the *Pinguin* became a victim of the Indian Ocean herself when she was sunk along with the HMS *Dorsetshire* at the hands of Japanese 'Val' torpedo bombers off Ceylon on Easter Sunday 1942. The *Dorsetshire* had already found fame by being the ship responsible for sinking the mighty *Bismarck* in the North Sea.

A fleet of Japanese submarines with their smaller midget submarines attached were deployed for an attack on the naval base at Diego Suarez on Madagascar. Off Western Australia was also the sinking of the Japanese raider *Hokaku Maru* after her battle with the armed Dutch oil tanker *Ondina* and her escort the Indian Navy sloop *Bengal*.

The first ship to be sunk by a Japanese submarine in the Indian Ocean was the Dutch freighter MV *Eidsvold* by the *I-159* off Christmas Island on January 20 1942. However it is with the torpedoing of the last Allied ship in the Indian Ocean by a Japanese submarine that still echoes with controversy and disdain as it bears the scars of a great atrocity.

In May 1944 the U.S. Liberty ship SS *Jean Nicolet* departed San Pedro, California loaded with a cargo of war material and supplies intended for front line troops in India and Burma. After crossing the Pacific Ocean she docked at Fremantle before making for her next intended port which was Colombo and then her final destination Calcutta. On the night of July 2 1944 she was torpedoed and sunk by the *I-8* at a position 700 nautical miles south from the coast of Ceylon. All hands and passengers managed to safely abandon ship in lifeboats and rafts.

The *I-8* then surfaced. It meandered about seeking out survivors using a powerful search light. They were ordered under threat of being shot by machine gun in the water to abandon their lifeboats and swim over and board the sub. Upon deck most were tied up and systematically murdered by being bashed, bayoneted and or kicked over the side. Others were shot through the back of the neck. Finally the submarine submerged washing the remainder off and leaving them to their fate. Many drowned or were taken by sharks.

Out of the 100 persons travelling on the *Jean Nicolet* 76 were killed in this way by the Japanese. Only 24 survived, including one who was captured and taken below deck. Despite suffering repeated beatings and other privations, he ultimately managed to survive the war. The remaining 23 were later picked up by the HMS *Hoxa* after spending up to 14 hours in the water, miraculously some still tied with their hands behind their back.

The commander of the *I-8* was Captain Tetsunosuke Ariizumi a sadistic psychopath and cowardly thug already well known to Allied authorities. He had committed similar offences previously on other merchant shipping including the Dutch SS *Tjisalak* where 98 of her crew were horrendously machine gunned in the water. Only five survived. Some three months later and only days before the *Jean Nicolet* atrocity on June 29 1944 the *I-8* sank the Australian merchant ship SS *Nellore* by torpedo and gunfire. Of the seven survivors captured, Ariizumi only permitted a Javanese mother and her young child to live, executing the other five.

Ariizumi reputedly committed suicide upon Japan's surrender. However this claim in some quarters is disputed and suspicion has been cast that he changed identity and ended up living in secret in Japan. Only a handful of former crew members of the *I-8* were ever brought to trial and of those indicted, they all received light sentences. It is a disgrace for a submarine that had earlier under an entirely different commander, Captain Shinji Uchino, once successfully made the 30,000 nautical mile round journey from Japan to Germany and back again.

However by 1944 Japan's sea power was virtually a spent force. Since the battles of both Midway and the Coral Sea in

1942 where she had lost the bulk of her carrier fleet, that resulted in carrier based planes now having no choice but to become land based. Similarly her submarine squadrons, despite their somewhat overwhelming physical size, did not relish success like their German counterparts. So much so, that by 1945 nearly all of her submarines had been sunk. But it would be from 1943 onwards that the playing field of the Indian Ocean would once again inexorably change.

The German U-boats arrived.

Doenitz, by now promoted to Grand Admiral and in command of the entire German navy itself was initially reluctant to send his submarines so far away. But to do so, particularly after 'Black May' of 1943 where the shocking figure of over 40 U-boats were sunk in that month alone, the impetus relied on two pivotal indicators.

Firstly, Germany had completely lost the initiative in the North Atlantic. The Allies had developed anti submarine sonar and radar technology, particularly HFDF simply known as 'Huff Duff'. In addition the so called Atlantic Gap had been closed. Land based aircraft could now cover the entire surface of the Atlantic Ocean from the British Isles to America. New fields of operations for the Germans were going to have to be conducted in shipping lanes much further away.

Plus was the necessity to address the ever increasing demand for depleting raw materials, particularly rubber, desperately needed for Germany's war effort. A trade route was required with Japan, which now dominated most of South East Asia. The German Navy embarked on a campaign where large sized U-boat submarines could be converted to underwater cargo carriers making the long journey exchanging advanced technology in return for necessities like quinine, rubber and other rare commodities.

The most common U-boat submarine in the German arsenal was the Type VIIC. However these were too small, too slow and not suitable to undertake the 15,000 mile journey to the Far East. To make the long and perilous journey were the larger Type IX submarine U-boats, mainly of the IXD2 variation. Due to their size these 'cargo carriers' were capable of transporting up to 250 tons of material.

Their mission would serve two purposes. Commence operations against enemy shipping in the Indian Ocean as well as bring back as much raw materials to Germany as possible. Shortcutting the journey through the Suez Canal was out of the question. Passage would have to be done taking the hazardous course down the Atlantic and rounding the Cape of Good Hope off South Africa before racing across to seek safety in the Japanese occupied ports of Penang, Singapore and Batavia.

In agreement with Japan the German Navy began to set up bases South East Asia. They became known as the *Monsungruppe* [Monsoon Group] named after the monsoon rains prevalent in the tropics. Up to 40 of these large 'Monsoon' U-boats were sent out to the Far East between 1943 and 1944. Most were sunk en route in the Atlantic Ocean. Only a handful ever returned back to Europe with their crew and valuable cargo intact and only one operated with any level of success in the Pacific Ocean.

Adding to these figures, the Germans and Japanese as supposed Allies never enjoyed the union of co-operation, trust and collaboration as experienced by their British, Australian and American counterparts. Their alliance was meted out with a cold reception of mistrust, suspicion and arrogance. The Japanese were eager to get their hands on advanced German technology and the Germans needed essential raw materials found in the lands that Japan now occupied.

However both members of the Kriegsmarine and private German citizens stationed in South East Asia remarked after the war that they always felt that their Japanese hosts were only acceptable of the Germans whilst the war was going in their favour. When setbacks and reversals began to set in, so did Japanese faith and support.

But there were considerable successes in the Indian Ocean. Some 385 Allied merchant ships were sunk here between 1940 and 1945 as a direct result of enemy action, amounting to more than 1.7 million tons. In immediate Australian waters alone up to 55 vessels were sunk as direct result of enemy action. A lot were at the hands of Japanese submarines operating up and down off the east coast. Others were to our north in the Timor and Arafura Seas.

But it was a heavy price to pay. Before long U-boat losses began to take shape. Their resting places extend from the *U-197* sunk off the coast of South Africa, the *U-198* off the Seychelles to the *U-533* bombed by R.A.F. aircraft in the Gulf of Oman, near the entrance to the Persian Gulf. Another four were sunk in and around the island of Java, including the *U-196* that disappeared without trace. Already joining them were two armed raiders and many more blockade runners.

In late 1944 Doenitz ordered the remainder of his Far East *Mosungruppe* U-boats home. On the whole, the campaign had been a failure, with very little to show. Of those that were seaworthy, they were to load up with as much vital supplies as possible and make their way back home to European waters as best they could.

The French sea ports had long been over run. Therefore Norway was considered the only safe option to make for, before attempting the short but extremely hazardous journey across the Baltic Sea to the northern German ports that were still in ever dwindling German hands. Nevertheless, Doenitz initially expected all the U-boats to make it back by the end of January 1945. However this target was always going to be optimistic. The situation for Germany had deteriorated dismally.

Due either to engine trouble, unseaworthiness and or being laid up in dry dock, for one reason or another most of the U-boats were forced to stay behind in South East Asia. Before they could ever consider undertaking the perilously long journey back home events would suddenly overtake them whereupon they and their crews would find themselves involuntarily trapped in this part of the world.

A U-boat submarine called the *U-181* would be one of them.

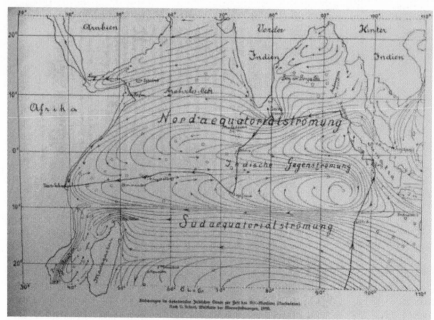

German nautical map of the Indian Ocean indicating wind currents dated 1899. Teutonic interest in the area extended back further well before the First World War.

The *Emden* beached and done for. The *Sydney* shelling the German raider in an artist's depiction from a rare tobacco tin card dating from 1916.

The Dutch tanker *Ondina* thwarted the attempts to be sunk by two Japanese raiders northwest off Western Australia.

The German raider *Pinguin* sunk by the HMS *Cornwall*.

The SS *City of Rayville* the first American ship to be sunk in the Second World War off Victoria, Australia.

Mack Bruton Bryant the only casualty on board the *City of Rayville* and the first U.S. Merchant Marine to lose his life in WWII.

HMAS *Perth* sunk in the Sunda Strait along with the USS *Houston* on March 1 1942.

The *U-198* sunk with all hands in the Indian Ocean not far from the Seychelles north off
Madagascar in August 1944.

The Australian merchant freighter SS *Nellore* another victim of the Japanese submarine *I-8* and her infamous commander Ariizumi, sunk only three days before the *Jean Nicolet* atrocity.

IN INDIAN OCEAN.

Enemy Claims Naval Success.

LONDON, March 11.—A communique issued in Tokio today claimed that a Japanese cruiser formation operating in the Indian Ocean west of Australia on March 2 sank the United States cruiser Marblehead (7,050 tons), "which was fleeing to Australia."

SUB SUNK IN INDIAN OCEAN

CAPETOWN, Tues—It is officially announced that the R.A.F. and R.A.A.F., in combined operations, destroyed a U-boat in the Indian Ocean.

A depth charge caused a terrific explosion, after which there was no trace of the submarine.

This is the second "kill" in South African waters announced within two months.

T2 Tankers

The main ingredient at achieving success to wage modern industrialised warfare especially since the turn of the 20th Century is oil. Without oil, the war machine simply splutters and grinds to an abrupt halt. Even Adolf Hitler knew this when he threw the bulk of his Wehrmacht across the barren steppes of the Ukraine in the now former USSR with the objective to capture the oil rich Caucasus region. Although this objective only became important after the failure to capture Moscow and grossly underestimating the diabolical harsh Russian winter. Then of course along came the all defining defeat at Stalingrad in February 1943.

Definitive also was Operation *Zitadelle*, the famous tank battle that took place near Kursk six months later. Still regarded as the largest combined tank battle in history, outside of Kursk as the Panzers foundered, coughed and then died for lack of fuel, they were then abandoned by their crews. The once all conquering but now retreating German Panzer Army found itself at the mercy of the equally well equipped if not superior Soviet T-34 tanks. With the Caucasus safely back in Stalin's hands the Red Army had the means to push the Fascist invader out of their country.

Another example was the failure of adequate oil supplies reaching Rommel in the North African desert. Constantly right up until and long after their defeat at El Alamein, the Afrika Korps was always one step away from grinding to a complete halt due to a lack of oil and basic supplies getting through. The seafloor of the Mediterranean Sea was becoming littered with the wrecks of German and Italian oil tankers that were being torpedoed and sunk by Allied submarines and bombers. In one week alone Rommel was robbed of 10,000 tons of fuel.

With Hitler screaming at his generals that they knew nothing of how to fight a modern war or possessing the necessary intelligence and economics to wage one, the Third Reich speedily precipitated its own irreversible downfall especially after losing access to the oilfields in Rumania in 1944.

Half a world away the earlier rapid southward advancement by the Japanese throughout December 1941 and February 1942 was crucial for them to secure the Dutch Netherlands East Indies and the oil refineries in British Borneo that was all going to be vital for their sustained war effort. Nevertheless, hurriedly ensuring the downfall of Japan and putting paid to her expansionist policies was the sinking of her oil tankers predominantly by U.S. submarines.

The United States luckily had most of her oil reserves in her own backyard. This constituted the wide plains of Texas, the Gulf of Mexico and the Caribbean. Then of course there was the Middle East where half of the world's oil production was under British control. Armies may march on their stomachs, but to keep the juggernaut of grinding machines and the wheels of war turning, it needs one vital thing - oil.

Since 1945 where some of the more innovative nations have harnessed the technological capability of nuclear power to run submarines and surface vessels, there still is no alternative or substitute to the 'Black Gold' coming out of the ground formed over millions of years from the breaking down of prehistoric matter.

After refinement, this is developed into various forms, primarily...fuel oil, diesel, aviation fuel, high octane gasoline, right down to just common grease and domestic oil. Then there are of course all the by-products of oil and other associated inflammable petroleum's such kerosene, benzene and turpentine.

War needs oil and securing and keeping it flowing is imperative. The 20th century was the century of oil. Without it everything very soon comes to a rapid halt. For any nation in the midst of conducting a war - no oil and you simply face the inevitable consequences.

Equally just as important is transporting it. One innovative idea following the successful D-Day operations was the equally successful and innovative PLUTO operation, or *Pipeline Line Under The Ocean*. These were a series of pipes laid under the English Channel to pump fuel from southern England over to France to keep the Allied war machine rolling.

Conflict has given rise to many inventions and has rapidly heralded new formats, interpretations and ways of doing things. Outlasting the Third Reich itself besides the Volkswagon *Beetle* motor car and the inception of running the Olympic Torch Relay from Greece, was the innovation of what we now colloquially call the 'Jerry Can'.

First developed by Germany for use by her Afrika Korps in the deserts of North Africa, the original concept was to carry water. However, it was soon discovered that it also equally doubled for, if not serving the purpose much better, to carry petrol. So much so that the Allies too were quick to grasp this convenient device.

As diesel slowly began to gradually replace coal as the preferred fuel to power warships, larger vessels were going to be needed to transport oil from far away distances, especially for countries like that of Britain and Germany that possessed no real backyard indigenous oilfields. One of the first countries to grasp the notion of constructing large heavy vessels to transport oil over long distances on masse was the United States of America.

The fundamental T2 type tanker design had been adopted from two earlier models namely the SS *Mobilfuel* and SS *Mobilelube*. Both had been built for the then Vacuum Oil Company, or known rather as the Socony–Vacuum Oil Company the forerunner to Mobil Oil. Socony actually stood for the Standard Oil Company of New York, which had been broken up in 1911. Renamed Mobil in 1963 it later joined forces with Exxon in 1999 to become ExxonMobil.

These tankers were 501 feet [153 metres] long from bow to stern with a beam or width of 68 feet [21 metres]. Rated at 9,900 tons gross with a deadweight tonnage of 15,850 tons, they displaced about 21,100 tons overall. Six of these ships were built by Bethlehem-Sparrows Point Shipyard in Maryland USA.

Interestingly the *Mobilelube* herself was actually later torpedoed by the Japanese submarine *I-21* some 97 kilometres east of Sydney, Australia on January 18 1943 killing three crew members. Badly damaged and heavily listing, she was towed back into Sydney by a salvage tug. Upon closer inspection the damage inflicted was deemed too great and therefore uneconomical to repair. As a result she was scrapped.

The most common variety of the T2 style tanker was the United States Maritime Commission type T2-SE-A1, a commercial design already being built by Sun Shipbuilding Company for Standard Oil Company of New Jersey. There were 481 of these built between 1942 and 1945.

The T2-SE-A1 type tanker was a variation of the standard T2 design. These ships were built by Sun Shipbuilding and Drydock Company in Chester, Pennsylvania for the Keystone Tankship Corporation and its affiliates in 1940. These particular T2 Type A tankers were slightly longer at 526 feet or 160 metres but still with the same 21 metre or 68 foot wide beam. Rated at 10,600 gross tons and coupled with a deadweight tonnage of 16,300 they displaced about 22,445 tons. Propulsion was provided by geared steam turbines driving a maximum rated speed of 16 and a half knots.

Both the SS *Fort Lee* and *Tumacacori,* two T2 tankers that feature prominently here in this book were of this design. The U.S. Navy took them over before construction was complete in 1942 to use as oilers.

The T2-SE-A1 types were designed with nine separate sets of tanks (*see diagram this chapter*). Tanks number 2 through to number 9 had a main centre tank carrying 391,500 gallons, and two side tanks, one port, one starboard, carrying a further 165,000 gallons each. Tank number one consisted of only two side by side tanks, divided by a common bulkhead, as this tank was only 13 feet 6 inches long. Tank sets 2 through 9 were 36 feet 6 inches long. Total cargo was about 5,930,000 gallons or about 141,200 barrels.

There was also a small dry cargo space of about 15,200 cubic feet located forward of Tank Number 1 above the deep tank for a very small amount of dry cargo. There were two pumprooms, one forward and one aft. The main pumproom was aft, and contained six pumps.

There were three large capacity pumps of 2,000 gallons per minute which were driven by electric motors located in an adjacent machinery space. There were also two 400 GPM pumps and one 700 GPM pump. In the forward pumproom was one 700 GPM pump and 300 GPM pump which were reciprocating pumps used for fuel transfer and stripping.

There were nearly 500 T2 type tankers constructed between 1940 and 1945. Later there were variants to the A1 with an A2 and A3 there was even a T3 type variation constructed. Like many vessels, including a lot of Liberty ships after the war they were sold off to various shipping lines where they were placed into peacetime service. Up until the turn of the 21st century there were still a handful of T2 tankers still in operation.

A T2 tanker at sea.

The SS *Mobilelube* torpedoed off the east coast of Australia by the Japanese submarine *I-21*.

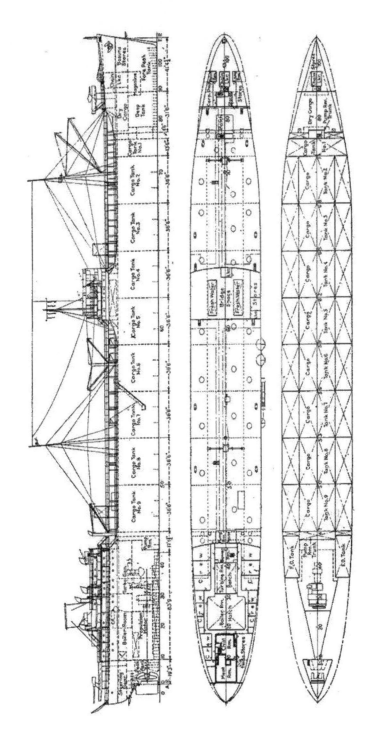

Schematic view of a T2 tanker.

U-181

It is unnecessary here to embark on a comprehensive narrative detailing and or chronicling the strategic operations of U-boat tactics conducted by the German *Kriegsmarine* during the Second World War. There are many hundreds, probably thousands of books, documentaries and publications available, along with the instant convenience of the internet that will methodically explain everything one ever needs to know about U-boats and U-boat warfare.

However the *U-181* herself would have to be one of the most remarkable submarines that conducted operations insofar that by the time she found herself in Far East waters she already possessed a colourful past. The *U-181* was a model known as a type IXD2. Most of the U-boat fleet that operated from 1939 to 1945 were of a type known as the type VIIC. However these type of IXD's were much larger both in length, width and beam and possessed more armaments and a heavier tonnage than their type VIIC counterparts.

The *U-181* itself known as 'werk' number 1021 and was laid down March 15 1941 at the AG Weser shipbuilding yard located at the northern port of Bremen, Germany. She was launched on December 30 1941 and commissioned four months later on May 9 1942.

At the forefront spearheading its intriguing war record, is her inaugural captain that came in the form of Kapitanleutnant Wolfgang Luth. Luth was already a U-boat hero and legend and went on to become one of the most successful and decorated commanders. Originally born to Baltic German parents in Riga which was then part of the Russian Empire on October 15 1913 he joined the German Navy in 1933. After serving aboard several surface vessels he transferred over to the U-boat arm in February 1937.

In July 1938 he was appointed 2nd Watch Officer on the *U-27* which went on to be deployed for a patrol in Spanish waters during the civil war there. However by October he was appointed the First Watch Officer to the *U-38*. In fact Luth was away at sea on board the *U-38* when Britain declared war on Germany on September 3 1939.

On December 30 1939 Luth took command of his first U-boat the *U-9*, a small Type IIB boat. He conducted six patrols, sinking nine vessels accounting for 16,669 tons. On June 27 1940 he transferred command to the *U-138* to which he sunk four ships on his first patrol for a total of some 34,644 gross registered tons. In October 1940 he was awarded the Knights Cross of the Iron Cross the highest German military honour. In this same month he was appointed commander of the *U-43* a long range Type IX U-boat.

In this he carried out a total of five patrols culminating in 204 days at sea and sinking 12 ships adding up to 64,852 GRT. On January 1 1941 he was promoted to Kapitanleutnant. His last command of a U-boat was the *U-181*. In September 1942 still with the rank of Kapitanleutnant, Luth departed Kiel for his first patrol with this boat. The intended operational area was the western part of the Indian Ocean, mostly in the area between Madagascar and South Africa. He commenced operations off Cape Town at the end of October and over the course of the next two weeks sank four ships for a total of 21,987 tons. Over the next two weeks he sank eight further ships for a total of 36,394 tons before arriving back at the U-boat base at Bordeaux, France in January 1943. During this time he was awarded the coveted Oak Leaves to the Knights Cross.

In March 1943 Luth departed Bordeaux again for another patrol off East Africa in the Indian Ocean. Again success followed him, sinking a further 10 ships with a total of 45,331 tons. During this patrol he became the very first U-boat officer to receive the Swords and Diamonds to his Knights Cross which was already adorned with Oak Leaves. In this patrol, which would be his last, the *U-181* completed an astonishing 206 days at sea [over six months] becoming the second longest patrol of the war conducted by a German submarine. During his career Luth sunk 47 merchant and naval ships for a total of 225,756 tons. In addition to this he damaged a further two ships for 17,343 tons.

However his ultimate fate was unfortunate. In January 1944 after five years of operational U-boat service, including 15 war patrols accounting for over 600 days at sea, Luth took command of 22nd U-boat Flotilla. Because of his experience like many other top commanders was tasked with training future U-boat commanders. Stationed at Gotenhafen it was a training unit for U-boat commanders. Promoted to the rank of Kapitan zur See, six months later in September 1944 he became the head of the Mürwik Naval Academy in Flensburg located near the Danish border.

Following the suicide of Hitler on April 30 1945 and the final surrender of Germany on May 9, Grand Admiral Karl Doenitz was named as the new successor. The Reich government was relocated to Flensburg where Doenitz had already established his headquarters at the barracks of the Murwik Naval Academy. British forces had actually occupied Flensburg since May 5 liaising with Doenitz's staff on a daily basis and permitting the formalities of government administration to still be enacted and carried out.

On the night of May 14 1945 Wolfgang Luth was accidentally shot in the head by young 18 year old guard Mathias Gottlob. Luth had apparently failed to respond when challenged with the password for the day which was 'Tannenberg'. Initially when senior officers were informed including Doenitz himself, it was thought that it was actually a practical joke.

Doenitz duly informed the new occupying commander of British forces at Flensburg of the incident and submitted a request to carry out a state funeral. Surprisingly permission was granted. It was conducted on May 16 with full military honours, a decision that was later heavily criticised by Allied authorities. This was especially where Germany, now as the defeated nation had already officially signed the document of unconditional surrender.

With the Nazi battle flag draping his coffin and six former U-boat commanders, all recipients of the Knights Cross them-selves forming the guard of honour, Doenitz, being Hitler's successor and now new *Fuhrer* delivered the eulogy. The final formal proceeding under the auspices of the now defeated Third Reich was played out at Luth's funeral. A week later on May 23 1945 Doenitz and his staff, making up the last gov-ernment of Nazi Germany were arrested by the British au-thorities and interned.

In itself it was acknowledged that the formality was not so much an attempt to give any credence to a disgraced regime that had espoused terror and destroyed their country, but rather fellow sailors and countrymen who wished to give one of their most respected and decorated officers a recognised farewell. Doenitz himself was afterwards tried at Nuremburg as a war criminal. Unlike Goering, Jodl, Kietel, and other leading top Nazis he narrowly avoided the death penalty and was subsequently sentenced to 20 years imprisonment. He died in 1980.

The *U-181's* second command would fall to 37 year old Kurt Freiwald. Holding the rank of Fregattenkapitan [Frigate Captain] he formally took charge on November 1 1943. Born on October 29 1906 in Berlin-Schoneberg he was no stranger to submarines. Too young for the First World War he joined the German Navy in the post war 1920's where the Treaty of Versailles had reduced Germany's once almighty powerful and formidable naval arm to barely a mere shadow of its former self.

In April 1931 Kurt Freiwald was a member of the Court of Honour assembled against one Reinhard Heydrich which was chaired by Vice Admiral Gottfried Hansen, the then commander of the pocket battleship *Schleswig-Holstein.* Making up the other members was Freiwald's former instructor, Lieutenant-Commander Gustav Kleikamp and Kapitanleutnant Karl-Jesko von Puttkamer.

Heydrich had fallen foul of the navy and was dismissed, a decision where he would always hold vehement resentment. Later with the rank of SS Obergruppenfuhrer, Heydrich would go on to become Himmler's deputy and the feared and notorious head of the RSHA [*Reichsicherheindienst* the SS Reich Main Security Office] and one of the most loathed men in Nazi Germany. He was assassinated by British trained Czech agents in 1942.

Following the ascendency of Adolf Hitler and the instalment of the Nazi party into power in January 1933, the German Navy was granted a new lease of life. Plans were quickly drawn up for the construction of new designs of battleships, destroyers, cruisers, incorporating an air carrier fleet and of course submarines. Known as U-boats from the German *unterseeboot* they would go on to become collectively one of the most effective weapons in the German war machine.

As a 26 year old Kapitanleutnant, Freiwald became the first commander of the *U-7*. Launched on June 29 1935 it was one of the smaller version Type IIB coastal submarines based out of Kiel. Later during the war, by which time Freiwald had long moved on as the commander, the *U-7* was credited with the sinking of only two vessels, the 2,694 ton British freighter SS *Akenside* on September 22 1939 and the Norwegian steamer *Takstaas* a week later on September 29. The *U-7* herself was sunk in a diving accident west of Pillau in the Baltic Sea on February 18 1944 with all 29 hands.

His next command was the *U-33* a type VIIA U-boat. Her keel was laid down on September 1 1935 at the Germaniawerft in Kiel. She was launched on June 11 1936 and commissioned on July 25 with Otto-Heinrich Junker in command. He was relieved in November by Freiwald. The *U-33* took part in Operation *Ursula* the German submarine operation in support of Franco's naval forces during the Spanish Civil War. It was from this campaign that Freiwald, as the boats commander for a short time, was afterwards awarded the Spanish Cross in Bronze with Swords in June 1939.

Promoted to Kapitan zur See [Captain of the Sea] he was appointed Adjutant to Grand Admiral Erich Raeder, the supreme commander of the German Navy. Thereafter he also became Adjutant to Admiral Karl Doenitz himself, commander of Germany's U-boat fleet and later the entire navy following Raeder's resignation in 1943.

Freiwald, appointed to take on the role to command the *U-181* was something that her crew initially reacted to with some scepticism. Where the balding Luth had been an abrupt, tough and a seasoned submariner, Freiwald presented himself as the intellectual...a gentleman type, tall with greying temples and expressing cordiality in line with that becoming of a traditional naval officer. Despite having some experience with U-boats before the war, along with being Adjutant to both Reader and Doenitz he was largely viewed as the officious 'paper shuffler'. He was to soon prove to be not only an innovative leader but also a highly skilled tactician and capable U-boat commander.

Joining him on board was the newly commissioned second watch officer, 29 year old Oberleutnant zur See Philip Otto Giese. An experienced sailor he had as a young sea cadet served with distinction aboard several sailing ships and merchant vessels. His last posting in the German Merchant Marine prior to the war was as a junior officer aboard the luxury liner SS *Columbus*. The ship was in the Mexican port of Veracruz when war broke out between Germany and England. In December 1939 the *Columbus* under the command of Captain Willibald Dahne was ordered, as best as could possibly be undertaken, to make her way back to Germany from Mexico.

Halfway across the North Atlantic they were spotted by the cruiser *USS Tuscaloosa* and even though the United States was still officially neutral, she shadowed the liner whilst constantly broadcasting her position to the British. Closing in was the Royal Navy destroyer HMS *Hyperion*. The German crew, knowing what was in store, practiced 'pulling the plug' in effect to scuttle the ship.

Faced with the inevitable, Dahne ordered the *Columbus* to stop dead in the water. She was then set afire and with the aid of explosive charges, went to a watery grave. In rehearsed orderly fashion the crew abandoned the ship and rowed over to the American cruiser which took them on board. The *Tuscaloosa* then made her way back to New York where the crew from the *Columbus* were placed ashore and immediately interned on Ellis Island.

Later the group, among them Otto Giese, were transported by train all the way across the length of continental United States to be imprisoned in a detention facility on Angel Island in San Francisco Bay. Here, across the water they could look out over to the famous prison of Alcatraz, where at the very same moment a gangster by the name of Al Capone was being held.

Shortly afterwards Giese managed to escape and find passage aboard a Japanese liner the *Asama Maru* bound for Yokahama. Once in Japan he was assigned to the German blockade runner *Anneliese Essberger* that was operating in the Pacific Ocean assisting raiders such as the *Komet*. It was on board this vessel that he eventually made his way back to Germany.

On arrival home after an absence of several years from the German Merchant Marine, Giese was invited to cross over and join the German Navy, specifically its U-boat submarine arm. After training he first served aboard the *U-405* throughout much of 1942 and 1943, before being posted to the bigger *U-181* where a lot of the existing crew were still the same that had previously served under Luth.

Finally the *U-181* was given new orders. Her mission was to the Far East, or what we more popularly call South East Asia. A hazardous 16,000 nautical mile journey, the destination was Japanese occupied Penang in Malaya, today Malaysia. Perhaps that is one of the reasons why Otto Giese was selected for this assignment insofar that he already had some experience of the Far East. En route the submarine was to target shipping both in the South Atlantic and Indian Ocean.

After loading up with as much precious cargo that she could carry deemed vital to Germany's war effort, she would embark for the return journey. In exchange for these materials the submarine would carry on board a cargo of crates containing advanced prototype designs of jet aircraft and aircraft engines for the Japanese.

The *U-181* would also carry with her the unique *Bachstelze* or 'Wagtail' as it is in English. It was a small one man gyro rotary helicopter. Known officially as a Focke-Achgelis FA 330, it was towed behind U-boats allowing the pilot to see far over the horizon and report back any shipping he may have observed.

Obviously only deployed when the submarine was surfaced, they were tethered by a 150 metre or 500 foot cable and allowed to be raised upwards to 120 metres or nearly 400 feet in the air. Equipped with a 7.3 metre diameter rotor, it was simply powered from being towed by the motion of the U-boat. When in flight it gave the pilot a bird's eye view seeing up to 45 kilometres over the horizon of the ocean in a 360 degree arc. When not used it was folded away and stored in two watertight compartments in the conning tower.

First developed and placed into service in 1942, the *U-181* was one of only three U-boats apparently to be equipped with one these contraptions. However its deployment resulted in only one known confirmed sinking ever occurring when the *U-177* used her *Bachstelze* to observe, intercept and sink the Greek freighter SS *Efthalia Mari* on August 6 1943. The other submarine that carried one was the *U-852* until she fell into Allied hands after capture in May 1944.

Despite the innovativeness and creative idea for their potential use, they were never popular with the crews and were considered to be more trouble than they were worth, thus they remained largely ineffective.

Kurt Freiwald taken after the Spanish Civil War and below on the conning tower bridge of the *U7* wearing the distinctive white commanding officers cap.

Oberleutnant Otto Giese who later became the 2nd Watch
Officer of the *U-181*. A sailor since his youth, after the
war he penned his autobiography.

Wolfgang Luth the highly decorated former commander of the *U-181* prior to Freiwald.

The last official formality of Germany's defeated Third Reich is played out at Luth's controversial funeral (*below*) taking place with full military honours, including his coffin being draped with the Nazi battle flag. The proceedings were heavily criticised for it actually took place two weeks after Germany's official surrender.

SS Janeta

After a farewell reception hosted by the staff of the 12th U-boat Flotilla, the *U-181* departed the French port Bordeaux on March 16 1944. Everybody on board had no illusions that it was going to be a long time before they would see Europe again. Accompanying her was the *U-196* another type IXD2 sister to the *U-181* under the command of Captain Eitel-Fredrich Kentrat. The *U-196* was also on her way to the

Far East where already under her current commander at 225 days held the record for the longest continuous war patrol at sea. Escorting them both out into the Bay of Biscay were seven minesweepers.

Submerging by day and surfacing at night to recharge her batteries, a curious observation noted was all the towns and small fishing villages dotted along the coastline of neutral Spain and Portugal with their streetlights and buildings lit up. It was in complete stark contrast to the rest of Europe where after five years of war things like streetlights were a distant memory. They had left a depressing climate where living in darkness from being enveloped in a constant blanket of black-outs had become the custom.

It was late in the afternoon of April 30 deep in the South Atlantic that the submerged *U-181* was first alerted to the distinct resonance of propeller noises coming from the surface. First Watch Officer Oberluetnant Otto Giese and his section were on duty at the time. Quickly they went up to periscope depth.

Steaming southbound was the unescorted 5,312 ton British cargo ship SS *Janeta*. Under the command of Captain John Cameron she had departed Algiers, Algeria on April 15 1944. Her destination, via Gibraltar was Rio de Janiero in the

River Plate, Brazil. With a crew of 60 she was sailing in ballast [devoid of cargo]. Built by Barclay, Curle & Company at Whiteinch in Glasgow, Scotland [Yard #634] she was launched in October 1929 and owned Maclay & McIntyre of the United Shipping Company, Glasgow.

The company was founded in 1885 by Joseph Maclay and Walter McIntyre who started with only six small steamers. By the turn of the century they had amassed a fleet of over 30 ships. At the outbreak of World War I that figure had increased to 51 ships, but by 1918 a further 16 had been lost. Post war throughout the twenties and thirties, MacLay & McIntyre ships were mostly employed in the coal and grain trades between the United Kingdom and South America and also transporting sugar from Cuba. During the Second World War another seven ships were lost leaving the company with only five. However by the 1950's with the downturn in freight rates, the last two were sold off and the company folded altogether in 1960.

The U-boat surfaced some distance away and commenced to chase down the *Janeta*. Suddenly without warning, an unidentified aircraft was spotted zooming in low from over the horizon. At once the alert to crash dive was ordered. The tension mounted in the hope that they had not been seen. Aircraft were submarines deadliest enemy.

A little over an hour later the *U-181* resurfaced. The coast was clear. The plane was gone. But she had to now make up lost ground and spent the next good 10 hours pursuing and getting ahead of the *Janeta*. Finally, they positioned themselves about 6,000 metres ahead of her just as clouds started to cover the moon.

At 04.11 hours in the morning of May 1 1944 the *U-181* unleashed two torpedoes that darted off to their quarry. Several minutes later they both accurately slammed into the starboard side of the vessel.

At a point about 900 nautical miles south by south west of Ascension Island the *Janeta* commenced to sink quickly. She went to a watery grave at the position of 18°14'S-20°00'W in the middle of the South Atlantic almost halfway between Rio de Janeiro and Luanda in Angola.

Of those lost were twelve British sailors including four gunners, and one Canadian able seaman. Initially, due no doubt to the speed of the vessel sinking, only a few managed to actually safely get away in the ships lifeboats. The U-boat surfaced and manoeuvred over to be close enough within earshot to question survivors, who were by now busy struggling in the water and hold onto to anything that was afloat.

With his good command of English this task fell to Otto Giese. He asked one of them for the name of the ship, her cargo and destination. When replied he mistook it somehow for the name *Benavon*. It was only later that this error was discovered.

Some 35 crew including her Master eventually survived and were later rescued and taken to Salvador, Bahia in Brazil arriving on May 14. Another 15 were picked up by the neutral Swedish merchant ship *Freja* approximately 300 kilometres south of Salvador and taken to Rio de Janeiro. A further 10 men were rescued by the USS *Alger* [DE-101] a cannon class destroyer on May 12 and taken back to Salvador. After the war The *Alger* herself was decommissioned and sold to the Brazilian Navy and renamed the *Babitonga* until she was broken up for scrap in 1964.

The name *Janeta* was not seemingly a lucky one. The first, launched in 1905, was sunk during World War One by the German submarine *UB-109* some 25 miles off Cornwall on April 4 1918. Twenty two years later a second *Janeta* was torpedoed and sunk by the *U-86* on January 18 1942. The sinking of this third *Janeta* however, being the first for Freiwald in his capacity as the new commander of the *U-181* would be just the beginning of a successful third war patrol.

The submarine carried on with her journey. It was here in the lower South Atlantic over the following week, that she also lost her *Bachstelze* – the small, single seat, observation helicopter. In its deployment the cable suddenly snapped, forcing the machine to come crashing back down to the surface again with an almighty splash. The tiny helicopter quickly disappeared.

Whilst the pilot survived with minor bruises and cuts, all of a sudden from everywhere, flights of Albatrosses and seagulls, obviously thinking that he was supper in being a wounded fish, began attacking him and attempted to constantly peck at his bobbing head. The incident created much amusement for the onlooking crew. Luckily they were able to rescue him out of the water and relieve him from his plight before any serious damage was inflicted.

However good riddance for the *Bachstelze* helicopter though, as it was not missed.

The SS *Janeta* sunk in the South Atlantic - the first under Freiwald's command.

USS *Alger* assisted in rescuing 10 survivors from the torpedoed *Janeta*.

Blue border and blue letter on a white background, the flag of Maclay & McIntyre from the United Shipping Company, Glasgow that owned the ill-fated *Janeta*.

The *Bachstelze* helicopter (*above and depiction at left*). Whilst innovative it failed to achieve the desired results. The *U-181* was one of only three U-boats that carried this device considered by the crew to be more trouble than it was worth.

SS Garoet

T here was now great elation for Freiwald and the crew. This was mainly championed on the back of having just sunk the unfortunate *Janeta*. On May 17 after rounding the Cape of Good Hope and keeping well away from the South African coastline, being mindful enough to avoid the prying eyes of Allied reconnaissance aircraft, the *U-181* finally entered the Indian Ocean.

For the second time in her operational life she found herself back in familiar waters again in an area some 400 kilometres southeast of Madagascar and south of Mauritius. As Luth had previously done, the *U-181* commenced to hunt in the shipping lanes between both Durban and Colombo and the line of traffic between Aden and Australian ports. For the rest of May and into early June weather conditions at this time were described as almost perfect with gloriously coloured sunsets followed by clear balmy and temperate moonlit nights.

As the submarine now turned north it followed a course up off the east coast of Madagascar. But there was no sign of any enemy ships. Luck seemingly started to turn against her in attempting to find the next victim. Adding to the irritating boredom and frustration that faces many submariners, the entire crew had just been inoculated by the U-boats resident doctor Dr. Klaus Buchholz against cholera, of which fever and cold shivers were the unfortunate reactionary side effects.

On Tuesday June 6 1944 the crew received news of the massive Allied landings which had taken place on the Normandy beaches in France. An immediate reaction in an attempt to keep up spirits and morale was prompted in a message from Doenitz's Headquarters. With conviction he ordered all U-boats everywhere to now brandish and wield themselves gallantly to the highest expectations.

It was nearly two weeks later at a position northeast from the island of Mauritius that the *U-181* finally met and intercepted her next quarry. Smoke from a lone freighter was sighted in the distance. Sadly this encounter would engender itself to become one of those tragic and classically little known, or in the very least, diminutively written about events of World War II of which there are decidedly countless.

In the late afternoon of Monday, June 19 1944 the 7,118 ton Netherlands steam merchant and cargo passenger freighter SS *Garoet* came into *U-181*'s view. Owned by N.V. Lloyd Rotterdam she was not what could be called a good looking ship, but nevertheless had been in continuous loyal service since being launched 27 years earlier. This was in August 1917 at a time when the horrors of trench warfare still raged across the muddied and bloody battlefields of Flanders during the height of the Great War.

The *Garoet* named after a provincial town in west Java, was constructed by the Dutch Scheepsbouw – en Werktuigen-fabriek 'De Schelde' [shipbuilders and tool factory] Vlissin-gen in Rotterdam. Throughout the 1920's and 1930's the North Atlantic sea routes were regularly plied until several forays over to Asia saw her eventually become a mainstay throughout the far reaches of the Indian Ocean, particularly in the Arabian Sea and Bay of Bengal area.

As a shipping line, the origins of N. V. Lloyd [Koninkijke Rotterdamsche Lloyd] go back to 1883. After the Second World War it merged with four other Dutch shipping lines. After 1977 it became known as Nedlloyd. Twenty years later in 1997 Nedlloyd, the liner shipping division merged with British P&O Containers to become P&O Nedlloyd [the P&O originally stood for Peninsular and Oriental]. However that too was ultimately taken over in 2005 by Danish giant Maersk. Thus the Nedlloyd trademark with its pedigree in facilitating Dutch colonial trading from a bygone era, thereafter ceased to exist.

On the morning of Sunday, June 11 1944, the *Garoet* had departed Marmagao, the harbour of what was then the Portuguese colony of Goa on the west coast of India. Carrying a cargo that included 1,000 tons of crushed peanuts, her destination was Durban, South Africa. Although owned by N.V. Lloyd she was under charter to the British India Steamship Company.

On board were a total of 98 crewmembers made up of a veritable melting pot of nationalities. The Master was 55 year old Pluen de Raadt an experienced seaman and long time N.V. Lloyd employee. Of the 12 officers they were made up of a various mixture of mostly European and British dominion nationals. The remainder of the crew consisted of 19 Dutch deck ratings and cooks, 13 Javanese stewards and 44 Indian Lascars. A Persian word, Lascar is the title given to those coming from primarily the Indian subcontinent employed as sailors on board European ships from as early as the 16th century.

The vessel was indeed armed, being classed as a DEMS or *Defensively Equipped Merchant Ship* with one 4 inch [100mm] deck gun mounted on the stern [rear], one 40mm gun and a further array of six 20mm machine guns. Manning these were nine Royal Navy gunners and one Dutch seaman gunner.

Holding the esteemed and valued position of 2nd Radio Officer on board was 22 year old Ronald Jeffrey Jacka. Out of all the officers and crew he was the only Australian. Known simply as Jeffrey or Jeff he had originated from the old gold mining town of Ballarat in the state of Victoria. Born on July 30 1922 he was the younger son and one of six children to Jesse Richard and Edith Jane Jacka. The family all lived and grew up in the Ballarat area until circumstances necessitated relocating to a modest house in Cooper Street in the northern Melbourne suburb of West Preston.

His father, a train engine driver, apparently left the family home and moved to Papua New Guinea while Jeffrey was still only a child. It is not exactly clear what he did there or what precipitated the break-up, however he reputedly returned back to Australia only once in 1934 to see his family before returning again to New Guinea where he eventually passed away aged 79 in 1966.

Described as a good, kind hearted boy devoted to his family, after completing school Jeffrey took up a position with the Victorian Railways in the rolling stock branch. Shortly after in 1941 at age 19 he joined the Australian Merchant Navy as a Wireless Telegraph Operator. Besides the formal training involved, he could often be heard in his bedroom spending hours on end tapping away practicing Morse code. Eighteen months later he now found himself in the middle of the Indian Ocean on board a foreign steam freighter and about to directly experience firsthand the personal tragedy of war.

The exact details of how this Australian Merchant Navy seaman came to be serving aboard a Dutch vessel are unclear. It is figured that he may perhaps have been part of some type of exchange programme where he was seconded, a practice common amongst the Allies during the war, or that he simply had signed onto the vessel where a Radio Officer was needed.

Since departing Goa eight days before the voyage for the *Garoet* had so far been routine and uneventful. The exception reportedly being an unidentified aircraft [thought to be friendly] that was sighted at a distance approximately some five miles away or so from the ship on June 17. However two days later, her fate was about to be decided.

As dusk was approaching at 17.55 hours G.M.T. [5.55pm] in the early evening of Monday, June 19 1944 the SS *Garoet* was steaming on a steady 180° southbound course at a speed of around 10 knots. The sun had already disappeared over the horizon off the starboard side ushering in a moonless night. Accompanying these conditions was a calm sea with moderate south easterly winds. She was sailing in a straight line and not following the usual zigzag path as prescribed by most vessels at sea during wartime.

Approximately two thousand yards away from the unsuspecting Dutch freighter, the *U-181* readied herself and proceeded to take up a firing position. Any vessel sailing alone, especially with an absence of an armed escort *sans* convoy was always too good a target to pass up. The submarine positioned herself in an east-west configuration, at right angles to the *Garoet's* course. From the control room known as *zentralle* through the periscope Freiwald's command to fire torpedoes echoed through the long narrow cigar shaped U-boat.

"Torpedo los!" [*Torpedo release!*]

In quick succession of each other they both raced off. After being dispatched from their tubes, the trim on board the submarine, due to the immediate loss in weight, now had to be quickly adjusted and re-balanced accordingly. Simultaneously speeding through the water, the two torpedoes impacted the port side of the unsuspecting *Garoet*.

The time was exactly 18.02 hours [6.02 pm] when the first hit the ship aft. Less than two minutes later the second collided into the hull, impacting into the No.2 hold. Neither the lookout nor any other member of the *Garoet's* complement apparently saw the tell tale incoming wake of the torpedoes.

In the radio room, fellow Wireless Officer Ross Treloar, who was on watch, attempted immediately to start the main radio transmitter. His efforts to do so were unsuccessful and in vain. Below deck water had already reached the dynamo in the engine room. It is reasoned that the batteries or the cables leading from them up to the radio room had either been damaged or severed by the resulting explosions.

The Chief Mate 29 year old Jan Kuijer, accompanied also by Radio Operator Sjoerd de Boer with Third Officer Johannes Quist quickly arrived and they too proceeded to check all transmitters without positive results. Consequently it was now not possible to communicate with the outside world and send a distress signal. Captain de Raadt gave the order to abandon ship as the *Garoet* was rapidly taking on water. She began sinking so quickly, given the abrupt surprise of the attack, that no time was granted to effectively lower any of the life boats.

With an inexorable groan, the ship slipped beneath the cold waters of the Indian Ocean at the position of 12°30'S-64°00'E at 18.15 hours [quarter past six] within fifteen minutes after the impact of the first torpedo. Out of the 98 persons on board only 10 survived.

One of the lucky ones was Radio Officer Treloar. The remaining 88 crew, including her master Pluen de Raadt either drowned or were killed due to the impact of the torpedoes striking.

It remains a matter of open conjecture whether those members of the crew who were still alive after the initial explosions and could reach the life boats, might possibly have manned them. But if so, they must have drowned when the life boats were taken down with the suction of the ship.

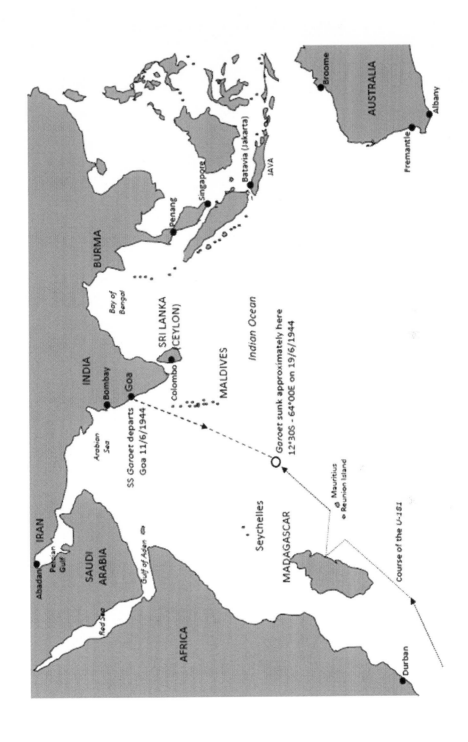

The N.V. Lloyd Dutch freighter SS *Garoet*

Ronald Jeffrey Jacka, at age 19 in Merchant Navy uniform. Three years later at age 22 as the 2nd Radio Officer he was the only Australian and one of 88 on the *Garoet* to lose his life.

Fellow radio officer Ross Treloar was one of only 10 survivors from the *Garoet*.

Indian Lascar sailors on board the *Viceroy of India*.

The N.V. Lloyd Rotterdam memorial in The Netherlands where Captain Pluen de Raadt's name (*inset*) from the *Garoet* is listed on the 3rd panel.

The British merchant ship *Daldorch* rescued the five Indian Lascars and took them to Mauritius.

The British India steamship SS *Nirvana* which rescued Wireless Radio Operator Ross Treloar along with four other crewmen and took them to Durban, South Africa, ironically the *Garoet's* original destination.

The badge of the Australian Merchant Navy.

This is most likely how 22 year old Jeffrey Jacka, the only Australian national serving on board lost his life. Ross Treloar testified afterwards when interviewed by the Red Cross in Durban that the last time he saw Radio Officer Jacka he was in a lifeboat along with several others.

Treloar recalled that he witnessed it going down, disappearing beneath the water. Young Jeffrey simply did not come up again. Of those who survived the disaster they owe their lives much rather to the circumstances that they were washed off the deck by the rapidly enveloping sea before they could reach any of the lifeboats.

Treloar along with another three Dutch crewmen and one Indian Lascar managed to climb onto a floating raft. On another piece of floating debris a further five Indian Lascars including greaser Jabed Ulla grappled for their lives. There were a great number of the crew swimming in the water. Surrounding them bobbing in the water was an equally greater amount the detritus and flotsam of a sunken ship.

Within five minutes after the *Garoet* had sunk, from the south, the dark grey U-boat, in a dramatic voluminous wash of seawater and spray suddenly surfaced like some menacing primeval monster from the briny deep.

Commander Freiwald, along with several other crewmen appeared on the conning tower. So too did Oberleutnant Otto Giese on the rear of the conning tower known as the *Wintergarden*. Cupping his hands around his mouth, in good, clear English with a distinctive Teutonic accent, but without malice, he called out over to the survivors in the raft containing the five Indian Lascars.

"Who is in command of your vessel?"

Silence.

"Who is the Chief Officer?"

Again silence.

"Is your Chief Engineer among you?"

Up to this point there was no immediate reply to any of Giese's questions. Giese then enquired after the name of the vessel, a description of her cargo, her departure port and destination. This time his questions were seemingly answered with more willingness.

In return, Giese issued to the survivors directions indicating the shortest route to the nearest landfall. No other assistance or help to those stranded in the water was apparently rendered or offered. Nothing is recorded nor mentioned that they were given any extra emergency rations. Satisfied that no more could be done for the survivors and leaving them to their fate and the mercy of the sea, the U-boat hurriedly exited the area disappearing away from the scene in a northerly direction.

Meanwhile, with the lack of other evident survivors, two rafts containing 10 survivors were lashed together. For the next 24 hours they drifted together until the one containing Treloar, and the other four men made the decision to go it alone figuring this way they stood perhaps a better chance. After severing the rope the two life rafts both farewelled each other and proceeded to separately float away.

For the next 16 days the five Lascars aimlessly drifted eastwards towards the African coast at the mercy of Indian Ocean currents. The poor devils became terribly sunburnt, dehydrated and hungry. Despite what bare rations they had managed to salvage, their physical condition was all much the worse for wear.

Suddenly smoke was sighted on the horizon.

At 5.00 o'clock in the morning of July 4 1944 in the position of 11°00'S–55°50'E almost half-way between the Seychelles and Madagascar, the lookout on the southbound British freighter SS *Daldorch* spotted something in the water. After 20 gruelling days since their ship had been sunk at last they had found rescue.

The *Daldorch*, under the command of Captain W. Thompson now commenced a quick course for Port Louis, Mauritius. They arrived there on July 9.

The 5,571 ton *Daldorch*, launched in 1930, was an old veteran of the Russian convoys having plied the cold Arctic waters to Murmansk. Built by W. Beardmore and Sons in Scotland, her original owners had been J.M. Campbell and Son until 1941when she was sold to the British and Burmese Steam Navigation Company. Under going three more post war owners the *Daldorch* ended her life flying under a Yugoslavian flag until she was scrapped in 1972.

Meanwhile Treloar and the other four men in their life raft had fortunately already found rescue a little earlier. They had been sighted by the southbound British India vessel SS *Nirvana* on June 30 1944 only 11 days after having been sunk. Though equally sunburnt, dehydrated and the worse for wear, they were taken to Durban, South Africa, ironically the *Garoet's* original destination.

In both Port Louis and Durban each of the two surviving groups made out their reports to the respective local naval authorities. Radio Officer Treloar and Jabed Ulla were interviewed and questioned by the Naval Officer in Charge.

Two months later the Victorian Division of the Australian Red Cross Society then located at the address of 289-293 Swanston Street, Melbourne, received a cable dated August 25 1944. It was a reply from their Red Cross colleagues in South Africa. Weeks earlier on August 7 Mrs Doris Brodtman the older sister to Jeffrey Jacka had visited the society headquarters on behalf of the rest of the family. Here she made enquiries requesting an attempt to gather as much as possible information concerning the fate of her now missing brother.

The Melbourne branch had cabled the South African Red Cross Society in Durban where representatives were able to interview Treloar. He gave his account as best as he could recall, describing that he never saw any sign of him again after the vessel sank. For the Jacka family in a letter addressed to Doris Brodtman from the Australian Red Cross Society dated August 31 1944 the news was disappointing. The correspondence, whilst attempting to be honestly helpful in an effort to be comforting, ended with the discouraging:

'This distressing information will, we know, cause you great grief, especially as it appears to leave little room for hope.'

After the war in 1946 Ross Treloar arrived in Australia and made a special trip to visit Jeffrey's mother Edith still residing at number 34 Cooper Street, West Preston in Melbourne. He offered his condolences and related to her his own firsthand account of what he knew concerning the disappearance and death of her son. Treloar also offered additional information and a slightly different version from what he originally provided in his official Red Cross account.

He said that Jeffrey may have suddenly remembered some important and 'classified' papers left back on board in the Radio Room. Conscientious of his duty in not wanting them to possibly float in the water and therefore potentially fall in to enemy hands, he made the brazen effort to go back on board the deck of the now rapidly sinking ship.

Then the boilers exploded.

Not long after Treloar's visit Mrs Jacka also received a letter from N.V. Rotterdamsche Lloyd's head office dated May 7 1946 which set about to confirm the circumstances as best known, involving his death.

Edith took it stoically but like so many other mothers and families, she clung to the distant hope that he may still be alive somewhere, washed up on a desert island or rescued by some other unknown passing ship just waiting to be found.

Without the evidence of a body, there is always that remaining and nagging sense of not knowing. Simply not knowing with absolute concise certainty to what exactly happened. This is only matched by the empty vexation of being denied some sort sense of closure.

For many years afterwards Edith tenuously held to the belief that her son would one day walk back in through the door again.

Today Ronald Jeffrey Jacka is rightfully remembered on the memorial dedicated to fallen members of the Australian Merchant Navy in Canberra. His name is also listed on the Tower Hill Memorial to Allied merchant seamen in London.

The two eldest Jacka children were his sisters Doris and Edna. His older brother and the third eldest Howard Robert served with the Australian Army during World War II. Enlisting in October 1939 he served for virtually the entire duration of the war itself until final discharge in September 1945. The next sibling was Valentine Clifford, who died shortly after birth at age three months in 1919. It is suspected that he may have succumbed to what we now widely identify today as SIDS or Sudden Infant Death Syndrome. Anecdotally it is thought that he was christened with this name for the initials V.C. represented the words Victoria Cross after his famous but distant relative Albert Jacka who received the coveted award in World War I. The two are remotely related as both Jacka families originate from the Redruth region in Cornwall.

Edith Jacka continued to live on in West Preston for many years afterwards. In later life she moved to reside with her youngest daughter Mavis and her family in Station Street, Dudley South, near Wonthaggi in Victoria. This is where her final years were spent until she passed away in 1973 aged 85. She is buried in the Wonthaggi Cemetery. Interestingly there is also a street named Jacka Street located in the Melbourne suburb of West Preston. However its origins are possibly un-related it may be named after another relative.

For this non-descript author and nouveau historian, gather-ing information on the *Garoet* originally commenced merely as customary routine research. However the attention very soon refocused itself when discovery was made concerning the fatality of Ronald Jeffery Jacka. Furthermore was the revelation that amongst all those who lost their lives on board this little known ship, he was the only Australian. It was de-cided that a concerted effort to investigate this individual commence in earnest.

The initial discovery making reference to him was found on a U-boat website that simply mentioned Jacka as being a victim lost at sea on board the *Garoet*. This was in addition to the mention of his name inscribed on two memorials dedicated to those who lost their life at sea whilst in the service of the Merchant Navy. His name is also listed on the Commemorative Roll at the Australian War Memorial in Canberra. But that that was seemingly it. There was nothing else.

A crusade to track down living family relatives, thanks largely to the wonders of modern technology by way of a myriad of emails soon harvested positive results. It transpires that there are in fact quite a few Jacka members in Australia, where some have done extensive genealogy research on their own family tree. Before long, contact was made with the wife of a nephew. Through their kind efforts they were able to inform and place me in contact with a niece who as a young girl vividly remembers Uncle Jeffrey.

Delighted that somebody out there after 70 odd years was interested enough in wanting to write about their long gone, but to them not forgotten uncle, their own co-operation became invaluable where soon, more than enough information and photographs were appreciatively forthcoming which were gratefully accepted with equal eagerness.

This story and the quest to actively seek out more information about Jacka mirror so many. Often armed only with just a name and little else, it can at first present itself as being a rather daunting task – if not decidedly a needle in a hay-stack. However generically speaking for any historical writer, if invariable success and pure blind luck permits itself, a snowball effect can sometimes be generated whereupon soon enough all kinds of wonderful information is in the offing. This is especially forthcoming if one explains the genuine purpose intended and displays an equally genuine appreciative and discreetly polite discourse.

Before one knows it, old Kodak Box Brownie sepia tinged photographs and faded letters still in their original envelopes from the wardrobes and drawers of private family collections and albums, are dusted off to reveal a long sought after and rich bevy of information. Not to mention both the professional and amateur historians 'Holy Grail' of perhaps finding some-body still alive who was actually there at the time and can who can still recall and remember first hand a certain particu-lar event or incident with somewhat enthusiastic vividness! The story here is a case in point.

These opulent rewards for any writer conducting research do sometimes, albeit with rarity come about providing one has acute adherence to patience, tenacity and commits themselves to highly organised homework. Not only is it something that I

have personally experienced many times over, but a phenomenon that I have seen occur with numerous other researchers and writers as well.

I speak personally that I may have in some small tiny way contributed to the preservation of our history. This is being in the fortunate position to write about it and indeed expand on further on it where hitherto little was known. Concerning the fate of the *Garoet,* Ronald Jeffrey Jacka was another young Australian serving his country in war. Like so many he gave the supreme sacrifice. It is not only highly rewarding, but also an honoured privilege to write about him.

Date: June 20 1944. The *U-181* made its way up past the Maldives following almost identically the same course that the unfortunate southbound *Garoet* had taken coming the other way. Freiwald had been duly informed of the busy shipping lanes in the Arabian Sea and the prolific amount of coastal steamers plying the waters off the Indian sub continent. The area held potential rich pickings where again the submarine would soon enough be rewarded.

Gone were the balmy moonlit nights though, replaced now with a sweeping monsoonal wind blowing with force from the south west. The conditions below, especially in the engine room reached temperatures of an unbearably hot 50 degrees. During one afternoon, as it began raining in blinding torrents, part of the crew including Captain Freiwald himself appeared on the bridge of the conning tower completely stark naked! The incoming gush of rain was proving itself to be a blessing at washing off their coats of blackened grime and dirt.

Thick, grey, heavy rainclouds were the order of the day in that July as the *U-181* made her way around the Laccadive Islands and through the stretch of water known as the Eight and Nine Degree Channel respectively.

Zigzagging her way up off the west coast of India was the 7,174 ton steam passenger and cargo vessel SS *Tanda*. Owned by the London based Eastern and Australian Steam Ship Company she was en route to Bombay via Colombo after having originally departed Melbourne. She was carrying 5,000 tons of general cargo and 800 tons of copra, which is the dried kernel from coconuts where the oil is extracted from. She also had a cargo of tallow. Tallow is a form of processed beef or mutton fat that usually does not need refrigeration.

The *Tanda* herself was an old tramp streamer completed and launched in May 1914 following construction by A. Stephen and Sons in Glasgow, Scotland. However soon after the outbreak of the First World War she was commandeered by the Admiralty and converted for use as a hospital ship.

Renamed HMHS *Madras* it was a post she went on to hold for the next six years from October 1914 until late 1920. With the end of official hostilities upon the signing of the Treaty of Versailles, her role as a hospital ship was not needed anymore and so she was accordingly returned back to the original owners and reverted to her original name.

The SS *Tanda* was certainly no stranger to Australian ports. For many years throughout the 1920's and 30's she was a common sight in these waters where she developed a respected reputation as a sound passenger and cargo liner. A little over three months earlier in April 1944 the *Tanda* was quarantined in Fremantle Harbour due to one confirmed case of smallpox being detected on board. The person in question was disembarked and transferred down to the Woodman Point Quarantine Station.

This facility has an interesting history all of its own. Named after Thomas Woodman who accompanied Captain James Stirling in the HMS *Success* that explored the upper regions of the Swan River in 1829, the site is situated on a headland jutting out into the Indian Ocean about 10 kilometres south of Fremantle. The facility was established in the mid 1880's to meet the needs of the growing colony with the ever increasing volume of vessels arriving from exotic ports around the globe with both confirmed and suspected instances of contagious diseases. Cases of those inflicted with bubonic plague, smallpox and the deadly Spanish influenza epidemic that followed World War I, were all kept here.

Already there was a Quarantine Station located at Albany however this facility was only able to cope with one disease at a time. During World War II the Woodman Point site was also used to accommodate Prisoners of War, mainly captured German and Italians from North Africa. There was also a series of underground bunkers constructed to store ammunition.

One noted wartime incident at Woodman Point occurred in April 1943 when four Fijian crewmen from the freighter SS *Suva* died of smallpox and were cremated. Their ashes were interred in a single grave where they are still there to this day. Another was the Chief Officer Arthur Waters also from the *Suva* who died there on April 1st 1943. His remains were originally buried in the Woodman Point cemetery but later exhumed and re-interred at Perth's Karrakatta Cemetery.

The four young sailors from Fiji were Ordinary Seaman, Samuela Waledau who died on March 30 1943 at age 23. The Ship's Cook, Eroni Builoto who died April 5 at age 25, ship's Steward, Rasaca Cigilau who died on April 9 aged 20 years and Ordinary Seaman, Osea Toqova aged 20 years who passed away on April 11 1943. Normally back then, any Oriental crew members who were even remotely suspected of harbouring a contagion were not welcomed. Supplied with a week's worth of provisions they were faced with the prospect of being placed in isolation on board an open barge anchored offshore.

The Woodman Point facility ceased as a Quarantine Station in 1979. The isolation required in treating patients could now be carried out in local hospitals. In 2002 the Western Australian Government Department of Sport and Recreation acquired the area and the old Woodman Point Quarantine Station was declared a heritage listed site. Today, with its buildings renovated and restored along with additional holiday chalets and a caravan park, it re-opened as a recreational reserve in 2007.

On the night of July 15 1944 the unsuspecting *Tanda* was steaming northbound some 85 kilometres [52 miles] off Mangalore on the western Indian shoreline. Bombay [today Mumbai] was only another day or two's sailing away. Under the command of Captain Thomas John Mills the *Tanda* was carrying a complement of 188 crew members including 12 gunners. Adding to the figure were a further 27 passengers.

She had first been sighted by the *U-181* at around quarter past six. However the submarine needed to manoeuvre itself into a more favourable position of attack. Remaining on the surface she spent the next two hours chasing to get ahead of the *Tanda*. However, this attack would also prove afterwards to account for almost the end for the *U-181* herself.

At around 10.00 p.m. the *Naxos*, the German acronym given to the on board radar warning system suddenly sounded. Despite this, the surfaced U-boat maintained her position. Not wanting to lose sight of the *Tanda* in the darkness, she fired off two torpedoes. They both impacted the port side of the ship, the first doing so at 22.13 hours [10.13 pm.] She sunk quickly at the position of 13°22'N-74°09'E.

Of the 216 persons on board, a total of 19 perished, eighteen crewmembers and one passenger, leaving 197 survivors. Of those who perished one was another Australian born Radio Officer. He was 49 year old Wireless Operator Robert Claude Vivian Humphery from Vaucluse in Sydney, New South Wales. Married to Mavis, he was the son of Robert and Maud

Humphery also from Vaucluse. A veteran of the First World War he was a 22 year old chemist living in Paddington, Sydney when he first enlisted in November 1915. He was posted to the 3rd Infantry Battalion, 21st reinforcements A.I.F where he attained the rank of acting sergeant. By the time the Second World War arrived he joined the Australian Merchant Navy. His body was never recovered and after the war in June 1949 his last will and testament was granted to his widow.

With the signal from the *Naxos* increasing in volume the *U-181* quickly submerged leaving the sinking *Tanda* behind. Of the survivors 195 were shortly rescued by the Indian sloop HMIS *Bihar* while the last two were picked up by the HMS *Monkshood* and taken to Colombo, Ceylon arriving there on July 18.

Meanwhile the *U-181* was having problems of her own. For the next 12 hours she continually surfaced and submerged as radar signals were still being constantly detected. In the morning of July 16 she was spotted by an aeroplane. The alarm was sounded and she crash dived. At a depth of 40 metres four explosions rocked the boat causing the electricity to go off. Oberleutnant Otto Giese recounted after the war in his published memoirs that a pipeline was also severed, fiercely blowing off compressed air in the control room. The hydroplanes were jammed forcing the U-boat into a forward list up to 35 degrees whilst she was still descending. Then the electrical engines ceased functioning as all the fuses blew. The gyrocompass too was badly damaged. And that was not the worst of it. The explosions had caused one of the fuel bunkers to crack and leak, losing an estimated 30 cubic metres of precious diesel in the process.

However submariners are highly trained and disciplined sailors. Those on the *U-181* were no exception. The damage was identified within minutes after the attack and temporary repairs commenced at once. At a depth of 80 metres [262 feet] the leaking pipe was isolated, the hydroplanes were operated manually levelling the trim. Fuses were replaced and the electricity came back on. The bunker was flushed out with seawater after the remaining diesel was siphoned off.

Following the attack by the airplane, Allied authorities now had their suspicions confirmed that a rogue U-boat was operating in the area. Later in the afternoon, the still submerged submarine suddenly came under another massive depth charge attack. After several hours at enduring this, the *U-181* was lucky to escape. However hot on their heels was the Indian corvette HMIS *Sutlej* and RAF aircraft out of India.

For the next 18 hours the *U-181* remained submerged, narrowly outwitting her pursuers until she cautiously resurfaced only to find an empty sea. Freiwald decided to make for the safety of the nearby Laccadive Islands to the south where many of the surrounding low lying atolls would provide good cover. Here they were able to continue carrying out repairs to the boat. Only four days after sinking the *Tanda* they were operational again.

On the morning of July 19 1944 the 5,265 ton British freighter SS *King Frederick* was making her way across the Arabian Sea. After originally departing Haifa in Syria she had called into Port Said, Egypt and Aden in Yemen along the way. Her next intended port of call was Colombo, Ceylon before carrying on to Calcutta, her final destination.

Under the command of Captain Richard Esslemont she was carrying 6,600 tons of salt and also mail for British troops stationed in Ceylon and India. Owned by Dodd, Thompson and Company of London, she had been constructed by the Hong Kong and Whampoa Dock Company Limited at Kowloon in March 1920. Launched as the *War Sceptre* she was later sold to a Greek line and renamed *Trialos* before sailing under her present guise.

At 10.45 she was sighted steaming on the horizon by the surfaced *U-181*. Rather than go in for the attack there and then, Freiwald opted to wait until darkness fell, giving the submarine also time to manoeuvre into a better forwarding position.

At 17.03 hours that 'better forwarding position' had been decided upon and two torpedoes were fired towards their target. Both collided into the starboard hull of the *King Frederick* at the position of 09°29'N-71°45'E in the Nine Degree Channel off the south west tip of India.

Esselemont knew he no option but to abandon ship as it began to quickly sink. Those that could, managed to launch several lifeboats. Out of a complement of 56 crew, 27 lost their lives leaving 29 survivors.

The *U-181* approached the lifeboats now bobbing in the water amongst the debris of wreckage. Once again Freiwald along with other officers and crew lined the deck and conning tower to inspect their handiwork. Again also it was Otto Giese assigned with the task to question the survivors. Asking the routine questions for the name of the ship, her cargo and destination, he was met with nothing but fearful silence. The lack of co-operation at replying was probably justified as the survivors thought the submarine to be initially Japanese and that their providence would now be at the end of a machine gun. The Japanese Navy's reputation of committing atrocities at shooting shipwrecked survivors in the water was widely known. Throughout the war documented cases had been all too common. It had only been barely three weeks since the notorious *Jean Nicolet* massacre.

Fortunately it was not for these survivors.

Despite receiving no response the *U-181* disappeared again into the night, leaving them to their lot. With good foresight, the lifeboats were evidently prepared for an emergency and were well stocked with rations of fresh water and food. Fortunately the 29 survivors did not need to rely on them for any extended length of time. Two days later they were rescued by the British ship SS *Samshee* and taken back to Aden in Yemen. Meanwhile Freiwald turned south of the Indian sub continent and plotted an easterly course for the final leg of their journey to Penang.

The day after sinking the *King Frederick* was July 20 1944. It is another date that would unfold its significance for the Second World War. A general alarm was sounded for all German forces on land, sea and air following the assassination attempt on Hitler at his *Wolfs Lair* headquarters in East Prussia. The Nazi Fuhrer survived the attempt where in following months it has been estimated that up to 5,000 officers and officials were executed, paying the price for either directly taking part in or having knowledge of it.

Nevertheless German soldiers everywhere were bounded by their oath. Whilst those who possessed any rational thinking secretly realised that the war was lost for Germany, the required duty was to still carry on fighting to the bitter end in the defence of the Fatherland.

With the initiative of the war now truly well held in the Allies favour, the remainder of the journey to Penang was going to be perilous as the U-boat approached closer to the war zone of the Asia Pacific region. Since her departure from France the journey had been actually quite successful at sinking four vessels en route in terms of tonnage. Freiwald radioed back to BdU informing of the four ships sunk so far. Despite this accomplishment, complacency at any time never had any place on board a U-boat.

With a link to Western Australia the SS *Tanda* was sunk off the west coast of India on July 15 1944 by the *U-181*.

An unidentified sailor from the *Tanda*

A pre-war image with KB bottles of beer and cigars. Judging by the way that two of the empty bottles are ignominiously turned on their sides and also the seemingly animated bonhomie of the discussion, this session had been passing all afternoon. The chairs that both men are sitting on are stamped SS *Tanda*

The SS *King Frederick*. Four days after the *Tanda* she was torpedoed and sunk on July 19 1944

Penang

O n the approach to Penang island the wireless operator aboard U-boat radioed on ahead her estimated time of arrival which was received ashore. She was expected. A reply was swiftly sent back from the office of Fregattenkapitan [Junior Captain] Wilhelm Dommes, the German Navy's chief officer in South East Asia issuing instructions for procedure.

Near the straits off Langkawi Island, situated about 30 kilometres off the Malaysian coast near the Thai border north of Penang, a Japanese pilot boat along with quite surprisingly a German Arado seaplane adorned with full Luftwaffe markings came out to greet her. A large swastika had already been painted on both sides of the submarines conning tower so that Japanese pilots would be able to identify her as 'a friendly German' thus avoiding any potential attack. Under a clear blue tropical sky the seaplane circled around the U-boat several times acknowledging the crew, of which most had now climbed up to line the deck. The Arado in return was greeted with enthusiastic waving and loud cries of '*Hurrah*'.

The Japanese escort boat, not exactly a corvette or minesweeper as expected, but rather something resembling a decrepit speed boat with a machine gun mounted on the bow, docked alongside. A German escort officer, a Lieutenant Kolln then transferred over. Following brief introductions he proceeded to present the crew with welcoming baskets of fresh bananas and pineapples which were gratefully received. Without hesitation he then quietly related, with a profound sense of candid honesty, the current mindset of their 'honourable allies' the Japanese.

"Don't believe the propaganda that the good Doctor Goebbels may tell you back home gentlemen. The 'glorious and all powerful' Imperial Japanese Navy has suffered devastating losses in recent months in dramatic sea and air battles in the Pacific" he abruptly announced superciliously.

"All the same I strongly urge and advise you to simply refrain from arguing with the Japanese."

He then held a private discussion just with Freiwald only. The two casually strolled together out to the bow of the sub and back again, away from the rest of the crew before he departed as quickly as he had arrived.

"Auf Wiedersehen meine Herren. Ich werde Sie sicher sehen in Penang"* saluted the Lieutenant courteously with typical Germanic conclusiveness before reboarding the Japanese escort. Without showing any emotion Freiwald and Giese briefly glanced at each other thoughtfully. In each mans mind it went without saying that not everything appeared to be as it seemed. Giese could not help that the rhetoric perhaps held some sort of disguised message, even a warning. Nevertheless orders were orders and so was the urgency to press on.

Following the pilot boat, finally, on a bright glittering sunny but hot, humid morning, the *U-181* with much fanfare entered Penang Harbour. It was August 9 1944. It had taken 92 long days to complete the journey from Europe to South East Asia. There to greet her on the pier was a Japanese admiral and his staff all dressed in pristine white uniforms. This was in stark contrast to the resident German naval officers dressed in their khaki tropical kit. A local Malayan brass band

*Goodbye gentlemen. See you safely in Penang

was in attendance playing dubious sounding versions of both the German and Japanese national anthems before following up with equally questionable sounding versions of selected marches. Despite the sense of adventure that the crew anticipated in this far away exotic part of the world, the reality of it under austere Japanese occupation would soon reveal itself. As will also in due course the true extent of Japanese and Germans relations.

The two never enjoyed the same camaraderie and or level of friendly and co-operative joint collaboration like that of the Allies. In particular the Japanese treated their Teutonic guests with suspicion and a degree of mistrust. Giese described the feeling as being 'cautiously friendly'. Other times it could be downright arrogant, even aggressive.

Despite these less than warm feelings, all throughout their stay on the Malay Peninsula it was seen to that the crew were given good conditions ashore. The accommodation was generous and there were available local markets to shop at. Social events including sightseeing were organised and a club set aside for them on shore where cold beer was in ample supply not to mention the Eurasian and Japanese girls.

Whilst still in Penang much of the crew were awarded medals including Freiwald himself who received a personal message of congratulations from Doenitz. Iron Crosses both second and first class, along many other honours were bestowed. It was also here that the crew were invited to attend a garden party hosted by none other than Captain Ariizumi, the same merciless submarine commander from the *I-8*. In fact several of the *U-181*'s officers later went on a hunting trip with him accompanied by other Japanese officers. Even here Giese describes him as being "quick witted, a slightly imperiously overbearing officer with harsh manners."

Although at the time he had his suspicions, Otto Giese admits that it was only after the war that he found out about the true long record of awful atrocities committed by this man.

In early September 1944 the *U-181* sailed down to Singapore. Kurt Freiwald was briefly called away for a series of meetings with the German Naval Attaché in Tokyo therefore the U-boat was given to the temporary command of Oskar Herwartz normally in charge of another *Monsungruppe* U-boat the *U-843*. Here off the coast of Malaya she ran aground on a sand bar that caused temporary consternation. Fortunately she was able to lift off with the next tide.

In Singapore Harbour further servicing and repairs were carried out in preparation for her return journey to Germany. By this stage Freiwald had returned from Japan resuming command where on September 25 with most of the cargo loaded on board, the *U-181* sailed for Batavia, known today as Jakarta, the capital of modern day Indonesia. One last change in this period was being informed of her transfer from the *12th U-boat Flotilla* to the newly created *33rd U-boat Flotilla*. Established a month earlier in September, it included many of the U-boats that had once operated out of the French bases and ports, now overrun by the Allies and all the current *Monsungruppe* serving in the Far East and Indian Ocean.

In Batavia the submarine was refuelled and replenished with some more last minute supplies, and the final instalment of her cargo was loaded up. In all it consisted of 130 tons of tin in the form of ingots, 20 tons of molybdenum ore, one ton of quinine and a small consignment of opium. Included also was 100 tons of raw rubber desperately needed for tyres for the Luftwaffe's newest jet aircraft. All this was squeezed in to every available nook and cranny throughout the submarine. Space was at a premium. Only *two* torpedoes were retained for the return journey.

For security reasons, lest the enemy find out, requests had been forwarded to the Japanese authorities asking that no news of the submarines actual departure date be made known. Leading up to it, there were several farewell parties and dinners - even a champagne breakfast, all indicators that could further tip the enemy off that the submarine was about to weigh anchor and leave.

To make the departure as clandestine as possible the Germans organised a 'false' boxing match for the following evening. A Japanese truck adorned with a promotional feature down its side was even commandeered to drive around the streets of Batavia advertising that the best of the Fuhrer's Kriegsmarine was taking on the local champions. The Batavia newspaper too picked up the event and inserted some last minute advertisements. It was all a cover and a purposely coordinated exercise in an attempt to silently sneak away unnoticed.

On the night of Thursday, October 19 1944 when darkness had descended, the *U-181* quietly slipped out of Batavia's Tanjong Priok harbour. It had been just over two months since she had arrived. Now she was going home, on what would be her 4th and as it would turn out, final war patrol. Sailing straight into a strong wind, those on watch did not bother to look back. Their objective was to make good speed for the Sunda Strait and then out into the Indian Ocean. The minds of every man on board were now occupied with thoughts of home.

As the swastika battle flag flutters the *U-181* enters Penang harbour, formerly British Malaya (today Malaysia). In a photograph taken by Otto Giese a large welcoming party can be seen in the background at left assembled on the pier. There to greet her dressed in white are Japanese officers and sailors.

Captain Kurt Freiwald attired in tropical summer uniform taken in Singapore in 1944. Crewmen can be seen behind him in the background.

Japanese and German sailors together at a group dinner. Despite the scene depicted here the relationship was uneasy and the alliance between the two countries never enjoyed the same benefits or close camaraderie in comparison to the Allies.

Oberleutnant zur See Johannes Limbach. Later awarded the Knights Cross, he was also the Third Watch Officer aboard the *U-181*.

On deck in the Indian Ocean facing back towards the conning tower.

The crew of the *U-181* in Singapore October 1944 with Captain Freiwald at centre dressed in their tropical uniforms.

The so called *Wintergarten* and anti aircraft gun.

SS Fort Lee

Her hull was numbered #327 and she was laid down on October 24 1942. Assigned to construct the vessel was the Sun Shipbuilding and Drydock Company located at Chester, Pennsylvania. It is located 15 miles or just under 25 kilometres south of Philadelphia on the banks of the Delaware River where it went on to become one of the largest ship building yards in the United States.

Originally developed by the Sun Oil Company hence the name 'Sun' in its title, the first vessel from here was launched in 1917 just as the United States was preparing to enter World War I. However by the early1920s it had progressed to become a major shipyard, building tankers for the Standard Oil Company.

At the start of World War II the site consisted of eight slipways, the onshore ramp by which ships and boats are launched and or are used for dry docking. Throughout the duration of the war a further twenty slipway ramps were added. At its peak, the company employed more than 40,000 workers at four shipyards, including one manned almost entirely by African Americans.

By the end of the war in 1945 Sun Shipbuilding had constructed over 280 T2 type tankers accounting for nearly 40 per cent of the total wartime output in the United States. Besides tankers the yard also built hospital ships, merchant freighters as well as her share of Liberty ships for the U.S. Maritime Commission.

After the war Sun Shipbuilding and Drydock continued as the foremost shipbuilder in America even though some of the yard facilities had been sold off for industrial development in the 1950's. Then in 1982 the company itself was sold to Pennsylvania Shipbuilding. It continued for another seven years until it finally closed altogether in 1989. Today much of the site has either been leased or sold, although a small section remains serving as an independent cargo terminal.

Most of the earlier type T1 tankers were named quite appropriately after oilfields in the United States. However the T2's began to take on names after national parks, lakes, forts, and historic battles. This one was christened the *Fort Lee*.

There are actually two separate locations in the United States that bear this name. However it is popularly thought that the vessel was named after the municipality of Fort Lee located in Bergen County, New Jersey. It was here that troops under the command of General Charles Lee loyal to General George Washington encamped on Mount Constitution for the defence of New York City in 1776.

Later Fort Lee also became the inaugural hub for the fledgling motion picture industry in America long before Hollywood. In the early 1900's small independent film studios with familiar names such as Goldwyn Picture Corporation, Metro Pictures and Selznick Pictures, including the Champion Film Company that would later become better known as Universal Studios, all had their start here. By the early 1930's for mainly economic reasons and lower production costs including a more hospitable climate, most of these major movie producing studios had relocated to California. Many would afterwards merge or be taken over by larger studios to become the film industry giants synonymous today the world over.

Alternatively there is also Fort Lee in Virginia named after the famous Confederate General Robert E. Lee. It is the centre for the Combined Arms Support Command and Quartermaster School for the United States Army and also the site for the U.S. Army Quartermaster's Museum as well as the U.S. Army Women's Museum.

Despite the small uncertainty of the origins of her name, the SS *Fort Lee* was launched on February 15 1943. At 10,198 gross registered tons she was a T2 tanker or in the full description a T2-SE-A1 type, constructed for the United States Maritime Commission. The War Shipping Administration assigned her to the somewhat diversified New York based company Bernuth, Lembcke Inc. located in premises at the Graybar Building, 420 Lexington Avenue, New York as the licensed operating agents.

Her displacement tonnage was 21,880 tons and the length of the vessel measured 159.56 metres or 523 feet 6 inches from bow to stern. Her beam was 21 metres or 61 feet and her draft 9.4 metres or 31 feet. With her two turbo electric diesel engines, the *Fort Lee* was capable of delivering over 7,000 horsepower giving her top speed of around 23 knots.

On board she carried six lifeboats and an equal array of life rafts. The lifeboats themselves numbering from #1 to #6 were constructed of a steel alumina. They measured a length of 24 feet and came equipped with gripping rails welded on the hull. These were designed that should it ever overturn or capsize, stranded sailors in the water could still obtain a suitable hold onto it. In the early 1940's U.S. Maritime Authorities had requested that all tankers were to be equipped with metal lifeboats. Most of these were constructed by the Globe American Stove Corporation in Kokomo, Indiana. In fact they were the first company to manufacture steel lifeboats for both Liberty ships and tankers alike.

The vessel carried a standard range of armaments to give herself some form of protection. Mounted on the stern was a 5 inch calibre gun and on the bow a three inch version. This was in addition to eight 20 millimetre anti-aircraft guns.

As far as a T2 tanker goes the *Fort Lee* herself was actually a sound and well constructed vessel that seemingly had no faults or obvious signs of bad workmanship. She was completed, ready for service and delivered to Sheepshead Bay harbour in Brooklyn, New York on March 15 1943.

Just barely two months following her launch she was already being put through her paces. Crews had been assigned and she was in service to do her part for the war effort. Initially the *Fort Lee* commenced plying the North Atlantic convoy routes between America and Malta before going on to operate largely in and around the Mediterranean Sea area.

Her maiden convoy that she participated in was Convoy USG 9 which consisted of 65 merchant ships and 14 U.S. Navy destroyers as escorts, some 79 vessels in all.

One of the first Naval Armed Guards to serve aboard her in these early days was 23 year old Seaman 1st Class William George Baltoumas from Peabody, Massachusetts. After joining the U.S. Navy in 1942 he served aboard several vessels before being posted to the *Fort Lee*. He sailed aboard her on her maiden voyage before being shortly transferred over to another tanker. Boultoumas stayed in the navy for the duration of the war going on to serve aboard several Liberty ships including the SS *George H. Williams* and the SS *Joseph Goldberg.*

The *Fort Lee* departed New York City harbour on May 28 1943 and arrived at the British enclave of Gibraltar on June 16 whilst the remainder of convoy continued on to Port Said, Egypt arriving there on June 25 1943.

A little over six weeks later convoy MKF 18 departed Malta on July 11 1943 where the *Fort Lee* joined it the next day on July 12 after departing Gibraltar. The convoy consisted of 13 ships mainly British and Dutch registered, carrying troops and other war material. A little over a week later the tanker arrived at Clyde in the United Kingdom on July 23 1943.

Of course this was around the time when all the Axis forces had only just surrendered in North Africa, bringing that campaign to an end there. For the victorious Allies the focus was now going to be on Italy and then later Normandy. In mid August 1943 the SS *Fort Lee* departed Liverpool for New York. She crossed the Atlantic alone and unescorted to arrive safely back there on August 28 1943.

Commanding this vessel was 54 year old Ottar Marius Andersen from Houston, Texas. An experienced, fair but strict master he was Norwegian by birth having been born in a small village on the outskirts of Oslo on April 2 1890. Andersen migrated to the United States before her hesitant entry into the First World War where he later joined the army becoming one of their famous 'doughboys' serving in France. It was only afterwards that he joined the Merchant Marines going on to forge a long and successful career at sea.

The complement of crew was numbered 75 in total, including the Master. This consisted of 49 Merchant Mariners who were employed to work and run the vessel. To protect her and ensure the safety on board were 26 members of the United States Navy Reserve [U.S.N.R.] Armed Guard who had their own Officer in Charge commanding them, Lieutenant James W. Milne.

Most were young, barely 20 years of age and for many of them this was their first time away at sea. In fact it was also the first time at sea for even some of the older ones like 38 year old former policeman Michael Joseph Sherry from Summit, New Jersey.

Born at Amsink Hill in Summit on July 28 1906 Michael was the youngest son to Timothy and Annie Sherry. After attending St. Teresa Grammar School he later joined the Summit Police Department in 1929 as a 23 year old rookie. Local Police Chief William Lambert himself a World War One veteran apparently played an influential role in securing the job for him when jobs, any job, were extremely hard to come by. It was the year of the crash and the advent of the Great Depression. In the U.S., Prohibition, that contemptible ban on alcohol was still in effect.

On June 2 1930 Michael Sherry married Nancy McCusker. Initially they rented an apartment before buying a house situated in Passiac Avenue, Summit in 1934. Soon, in quick succession three sons were born, Joseph, Donald and James.

By now war had arrived. The United States at first, due largely to public opinion, did her best to keep out of what she regarded essentially as a 'European war'. America jealously guarded her neutrality. However it was only inevitable with her omnipotent industrial might and wealth of resources that whether she liked it or not, she was going to be dragged kicking and screaming into this war. She did not have long to wait. Events played themselves out for her.

Sunday, December 7 1941. A day of infamy. Japan attacks Pearl Harbour in Hawaii paralysing the U.S. Pacific fleet. A couple of days later Nazi Germany audaciously declares war on the United States of America. Initially due to his role as a policeman and possibly also his age, Sherry may have had an exemption from service. But as the war developed and expanded, more men were needed. Patriotism and the irrevocable sense 'of doing ones duty' was the zeitgeist and became the catalyst to join and serve.

In 1943 with a wife and three children all under nine years of age, Michael Sherry chose to join the Merchant Marines. After completing his basic training at Sheepshead Bay in Brooklyn, New York, he was assigned to the new T2 oil tanker SS *Fort Lee* to work as a Galleyman and Steward in the mess.

On board he was affectionately known as 'Pop' a reference perhaps to his older age amongst some of the younger crew who viewed him as a type of father figure. With his quiet and friendly nature the married former policeman already had a wealth of life experience. He was always there to lend an ear, and to provide moral support. For most, especially the younger ones, this was not only their first time away at sea, but also their first time away from home. Some had only just graduated and left school. This resulted in feelings of homesickness for many. Adding to this was frightening prospect of never returning. One need not be reminded that it was war time.

For the remainder of 1943 the *Fort Lee* continued crossing the familiar routes of the Atlantic until she was re-assigned for duties in the Pacific and Indian Ocean theatre. In May 1944 the tanker sailed to the island of Curacao located off Venezuela in the Caribbean. In a letter dated May 30 1944 Michael Sherry wrote back home to his wife Nancy implying that the next leg of this voyage could possibly be through the Panama Canal.

In fact both the islands of Curacao and Aruba, the former Dutch Antilles, were pivotal to the Allied war effort. Oil rich, just like their mainland neighbour Venezuela, their refineries supplied oil for the Allies. From 1942 to 1945 they were placed under total U.S. protection. Despite their allure as a potential target, only once were they attacked when the *U-156* attempted to shell the refinery at Curacao without much success.

The *Fort Lee* returned briefly to the United States in July to replenish before sailing once more. It was here that she also took on a new Oiler in 26 year old Rudolph Broedlin from Bridgeport, Connecticut. A recent graduate of the Merchant Marine Academy at Kings Point he had his Seaman's Certificate stamped and issued on July 11.

By August the *Fort Lee* was in the Pacific Ocean off the coast of South America with a load of crude oil bound for the Marshall Islands. For much of the time life was fairly mundane. Around the clock it was just simply work; going on shift, coming off shift and sleep. Adding to this, especially for the Navy Armed Guards was the extra vigilance required especially when entering war zones. The awareness heightened to the ever present danger lurking below or even possible attack by air.

Americans and particularly her military forces are well known for setting the benchmark at providing above average conditions for her fighting troops stationed abroad. World War Two was no exception. The rations on board this ship were described as being very good, with every man having the choice of at least two entrees at the main meals. There were actually two separate mess areas on board, one for the Armed Guards and the other for the Merchant Marines that were divided by the galley and kitchen in the middle.

However to amuse oneself required patience. When off duty, some played poker or chess to pass the time. Others preferred to write letters or read magazines and books. Another popular pastime was observing sea life from gulls to albatrosses ducking and weaving near the ship; anything to while away the long hours and stave off the terror of boredom. But the most common was cards, especially double deck pinochle. Pronounced *pee-knockle* it is a card game consisting usually of four players where as partners there is an auction in which they bid the number of points their team will try to win. Pinochle was king. Everybody played pinochle, where games sometimes turned into marathons lasting days – even weeks.

Bradley Royce Pruitt from Mount Rainier, Maryland had joined the Merchant Marines the year before in 1943 at just age 19 and already was an old hand aboard ship. He signed on as the 2nd Cook and Baker. In his own words nearly 70 years later he vividly remembers this period of time in his life with alacrity. Brad Pruitt describes the *Fort Lee* as a good vessel and knew of no reason why anybody would not wish to serve on board her. Aside from being a newly constructed ship, the conditions were good, the crew were a good bunch and over-all the vessel was sound and reliable.

As an illustration of Michael Sherry's benevolence to the younger members of the crew, Brad Pruitt was once invited back to his family home in Summit, New Jersey just before they were to sail out again. 'Pop' Sherry introduced him to his wife and three young sons before they all sat down and shared a meal together, enjoying the delights of home cooked food one last time before shipping back out the next day.

Captain Ottar Andersen too is recalled with equal admiration.

"He was a good, experienced captain and an excellent seaman" recalls Brad Pruitt 70 years later in 2014.

"He was well schooled in shipping and able to control the running of a ship of this size. He was a master with fairness, treating his officers and crew below him with skill that kept maintenance and things running smoothly at all times."

After crossing the Pacific Ocean the vessel first anchored off Kwajalein, in the Marshall Islands. Here it refuelled several waiting cruisers. In the late afternoon whilst lying at anchor, a small boat filled with around half a dozen GI's raced out from shore wanting to buy sugar. Second Cook and Baker Pruitt knew that there were plenty of supplies of sugar down below in the hold, where most had hardened from being exposed to moisture. He had about 10 bags of the stuff and thought to himself this is a good time to offload this and perhaps get something for it. Before long, four 200 pound bags appeared on deck, the contents inside as hard as a rock.

A deal was struck that they could have the sugar in exchange for whatever Japanese souvenirs they could spare in return. It turns out the sugar was desperately needed back on shore to facilitate the production of a homemade brew of hooch. No matter what deal could be made, one way or another that sugar was needed!

With the aid of two other mess hands the first was tied up and carefully lowered over the side by rope down to the boat. About halfway down, the bag suddenly loosened itself and without warning hit the water with an almighty splash. Luckily it just missed the small lighter which had inadvertently drifted around parallel to the side of the ship. If it had directly hit it, no doubt an out of control 200 pound bag of rock hard sugar coming down at them would have either holed it or sunk it...or even injured or killed one of those waiting below. The next three bags Pruitt decided to tie up himself having had some previous training in the art of how to tie various knots back in Sheepshead Bay. The remainder were lowered away and were received without incident.

The GI's gleefully departed rest assured that their batch of moonshine could now be completed. Before they left they said that they would be back before dark, informing them that there was a movie being played that night if they wanted to come ashore and watch it. Sure enough they shortly returned and picked up half a dozen men, amongst them Brad Pruitt.

On shore a large crowd of troops had gathered on the side of a hill finding room to sit wherever they could in what could only be described as being like a natural amphitheatre facing downwards toward the screen. Whilst after 70 years the memory has dimmed only slightly to be unable to recall exactly what movie it was, only minutes into it out of nowhere, suddenly the air was cut by the quick rapport of rapid machine gun fire! It had evidently come down from the top of the hill above where all the troops had gathered. The shots were aimed at the screen. Immediately all the lights were shut off.

It seemed not all Japanese units on the island had surrendered or been cleared out yet and there were still small pockets of them holed up and unaccounted for. On this occasion they chose a bad night to cause mischief.

Brad Pruitt had found himself seated within earshot near a captain in the U.S. Marines. To this day he clearly remembers this particular captain call out four men by their name. In two words he simply said, "Get 'em!'

As it was rumoured afterwards, in no time these four Marines disposed of those Jap soldiers, not by shooting them or stabbing them, but by slicing and cutting in half the 'backstrap' muscle tendon of both their heels in their feet. In doing this one is largely disabled and unable to stand, let alone walk or run. At best one can only crawl and it was ruminated afterwards with much dark humour, minus any guilt, that those Jap soldiers had a long way to crawl back to Japan.

That's how they were left that way right up on top of that hill. After half an hour the four Marines reported back to the captain that the area was now secured, whereupon the movie recommenced playing as if nothing had happened. When it was finished Pruitt and the others were transported back to the *Fort Lee* along with their newly acquired souvenirs and an experience of a night out at the movies that they wouldn't forget in a hurry.

The following day the *Fort Lee* departed, heading south. The ship crossed the Equator, so it was here that Michael Sherry along with all the rest of the so called *shellbacks* on board underwent that age old initiation whereupon they became exclusive members of that 'Ancient Order of the Deep'. It is a ritual ceremony bestowed on sailors when crossing the Equator for the first time, a custom still observed by many crews from around the world today.

Finally the *Fort Lee* arrived in Sydney, New South Wales. The war against Japan in the Pacific ensured the strategic importance of Australia. It also set the precedence at cementing the relations still highly valued and regarded between Australia and the United States today. It was also here that Michael Sherry wrote another letter back home to his wife Nancy in Summit, New Jersey. Whilst censored and undated it exemplifies the first exposure for him and for most of the rest of the crew to Australia and the local inhabitants. He begins with the apt title:

"From The land Down Under

Dear Sweetheart

We arrived here safe and sound yesterday and everything is fine. We had a nice trip but very cool, it was hailing when we pulled into port but cleared up at noon and was very warm. I went to the city last night, it sure is a busy place. I wish you were here with me to figure out the pounds (lbs). I am having a hard time getting by as it is a lot of fuss."

This is obviously a reference to the old pounds, shillings and pence monetary unit of currency that Australia possessed until 1966 when it converted to dollars and cents.

"I get a kick out of it also, the way they talk, but they speak English! This is the first place we have been that they did. Our supplies just came and we are due to sail tonight. Our liberty is up at 3 pm so I am going back to the city to send your present."

Whilst Sherry is unable to exactly say due to wartime security where the next port of call is for the *Fort Lee*, he does provide a small, but vague clue.

"Our next stop is where they have very fine wool. I hope you can make out what I am mean, if so let me

know. I try the best to explain everything the best I can. Your mail is not censored so you can tell me all."

Michael Sherry goes on to wish his three boys '*health and happiness*' and hopes that they are fine and getting along well in school. He concludes;

"Well so long for now, with all my love to you as ever."

Before long, the tanker is issued with new orders. In late September 1944 her destination is Abadan in Iran to load up and bring back a full cargo of fuel oil for the U.S. Navy. After loading she would make the return journey sailing back across the Indian Ocean to Brisbane the state capital of Queensland.

The port of Abadan is situated on an island almost at the extreme western point in the waters of the Persian Gulf. Early cartographers first make mention of a settlement in the area as far back as 100 AD. Interestingly however it was not until the turn of 20th century that the rich oil fields, of which it is famous for, were discovered.

In 1909 the Anglo-Persian Oil Company built their first pipeline terminus oil refinery here. Completed in 1913 it was to become the largest in the world where even today it remains a vast facility for refining petroleum. Abadan's population in 1910 was only around 400. However with all these refineries springing up she needed workers to man them. Between the wars the population more than doubled, then tripled, so that by 1956 it had increased to more than 220,000 people.

In 1951 the now newly renamed Iran, formerly Persia, nationalized all oil fields whereupon refining simply stopped on the island. That is until three years later in 1954 when an agreement was reached permitting international oil companies to manage the production and refining facilities. During World War II from 1941 to 1945 Abadan, besides being a crucial port for Allied oil tankers, also served as a principal logistics hub where Lend-Lease material including aircraft from the United States were sent to the Soviet Union.

Forty years later the island city was in the direct line of fire coming under frequent attack during the 1980-1988 Iran-Iraq War. It was constantly besieged but never captured by Iraqi forces. In more relatively peaceful years an oil museum is in current development to celebrate the 100 years of refining, exploration and export of the lucrative 'black gold'. Today it still remains as one of the pivotal oil refining and exporting ports of the Middle East.

Since departing Sydney there was one strange incident occurring en route that led inadvertently to a promotion for

Brad Pruitt. From the time the tanker had left New York and throughout the entire journey across the Pacific, the Chief Cook had been placing amorous pressure on some of the younger crew in requesting sexual favours. As the voyage progressed, so too did his uninvited attempts become more demanding, virtually forcing himself onto some of these young boys.

Tiring of this unwanted attention, those who were on the receiving end duly reported his conduct to the Captain. Consequently upon docking for short stopover in Colombo, Ceylon, the Chief Cook was summarily marched off the ship personally by Andersen himself who gave him his money owed, on explicit instructions that he never set board on any ship under his command again. Whether it be wartime or peacetime the Master would not tolerate any kind of perversions of this type on his ship.

Back on board, Anderson summoned Pruitt to his cabin.

"So Mr Pruitt, I understand you work down there in the galley, but do you know how to cook?"

"Well Captain," he began slowly, "you're in luck as I had just finished cooking school before I signed on. As a matter of fact I went to school to become a 2nd Cook and Baker and also started training as a Chef. So yes sir you have got a winner on your side."

"Oh, really, is that right" replied the Captain thoughtfully. "Well in that case congratulations son, from here on in you've just been promoted to Chief Cook."

Despite the surprise promotion Brad Pruitt could not help but quip, "does the wage go along with it also sir?" To which Captain Andersen responded only with laughter.

So for the voyage from Colombo to Abadan the *Fort Lee's* crew was reduced by one and now stood at 74. But it would only be temporary.

William (Bill) Francis Mootz was only 16 years of age from Kansas City, Kansas. He had barely been in the Merchant Marines for seven months having only joined earlier that same year in April, lying about his age in the process. On completion of training on Catalina Island off the coast of California he was shipped out on the tanker SS *Charles S. Jones*. It was while it was docked here in Abadan he was discharged from that ship and sent to a military hospital on shore for a high fever.

After being laid up for almost a week, young Bill was then told to report to the American Consulate in Abadan. It was here that he was informed that there was a spot going on board another tanker called the *Fort Lee* which had only just arrived and docked in port. He wasted no time in signing on board her as a Messman thus becoming the youngest crew member as well. Now her number was restored to her original full complement of 75.

On the morning of October 21 1944 the 10,198 ton T2-SE-A1 class tanker SS *Fort Lee* departed Abadan. Loaded into her nine holds was a cargo of some 93,000 barrels of Navy Special Bunker 'C' fuel oil. The term bunker fuel derives its name from the storage units where it is commonly housed. Back in the days of steam power, coal was originally stored in bunkers. With the advent of diesel engines, instead of coal it is bunker oil that is stored in them and the name has simply stuck. Bunker oil is fundamentally the type of fuel oil used by ships. Bunker 'C' oil is a heavy residual high viscosity fuel oil. The term residual refers to the matter that remains behind after the more important elements of crude oil have boiled away.

Sailing through Straits of Hormuz the narrow entrance to the Persian Gulf, the *Fort Lee* made her way back out into the Arabian Sea. There was no escort. She was alone which was nothing out of the ordinary for these tankers were designed to potentially out run submarines. She had her Routing Instructions and code manuals.

Even though news was filtering through nearly every day that the tide had truly well turned and that the enemy were now facing overwhelming reversals, the shipping lanes were still not safe. All it would take is one lone unswept mine or a rogue long range submarine lurking about to extinguish immediately any thoughts entertaining a false sense of security.

The intended course plotted was following a south easterly path all the way back across the vast expanse of the Indian Ocean. Then continue further eastbound, passing well south off Cape Leeuwin, to enter the relatively safe waters of the Southern Ocean crossing the Great Australian Bight, then up along the east coast of Australia to arrive at Brisbane.

Two obscure accounts, both of them linked, ostensibly report that the tanker was first targeted for attack not long after departing Abadan. On October 26 in the Arabian Sea after only five days sailing 'the wake of an incoming torpedo was apparently observed aimed at the tanker which barely missed'. Even *The Washington Post* newspaper dated Wednesday, February 7 1945 incorrectly makes a brief reference to this.

Four days later on October 30 some Navy Armed Guard lookouts may have mistaken for what was perhaps a whale or a piece of floating flotsam for a submarine periscope that had 'surfaced some way off in the distance'.

Both of these reports however are completely bogus and false. Perhaps a sense of heightened alert plays tricks on the eyes and the mind. Records prove without question, that the *U-181* having just departed Batavia was the *only* enemy U-boat at sea in the Indian Ocean around these dates. But at this stage she was still a long, long way from the current position of where the *Fort Lee* was. Two U-boats, the *U-195* and *U-219 were* making their way for the Indian Ocean but were still in the South Atlantic at this time. Furthermore, two Japanese submarines the *RO-113* and *RO-115* had departed Penang on October 25 but they both never left the confines of the Bay of Bengal.

In the thirteen days from when she left Abadan the *Fort Lee* encountered no authentic contact with the enemy. She continued on her way without incident. However she was about to cross paths with a confirmed and genuine threat where that ineluctable kismet of history that sometimes so well defines, but also at the same time offers up strange twists of fate, was about to be unleashed. The only difference is that the two vessels concerned did not know this yet.

Two aerial views of the massive Sun Shipbuilding and Drydock facilities at Chester Pennsylvania circa 1940 where the *Fort Lee* was constructed in 1943.

A metal lifeboat similar to those on the *Fort Lee* as seen here aboard the preserved U.S. Liberty ship SS *Jeremiah O'Brien*. The knotted centre ropes can be seen at top.

The flag of Bernuth Lembcke & Co. Inc. – red border, white background, black lettering.

Seaman 1st Class William G. Baltoumas from Massachusetts, a Naval Guard who had served time earlier on board the *Fort Lee*. He had long transferred to another vessel by the time she met her fate. Discharged from the Navy in 1945 he passed away at age 90 in 2010.

U.S. Merchant Marine recruitment poster and a U.S. Navy poster warning of the perils of loose talk.

Lifeboat drill at Sheepshead Bay training station in Brooklyn for the Merchant Marines. Clearly seen suspended from their davits are the fore and aft falls (or ropes) that lower the boat into the water.

U.S. Navy Armed Guards practice drill on a 20mm gun (*above*) and a demonstration at being stationed on look out dressed in full foul weather attire (*left*).

U.S. Navy Armed Guard training Great Lakes Illinois 1943.

The massive oil refinery network at Abadan 1945.

Bellicose

The *U-181* was in the early stages of undertaking her long and dangerous voyage back to Europe. With every conceivable space and square inch packed tight with cargo and provisions, simple room to move about anywhere along its narrow long cigar shaped tube was at a premium. As the old saying goes 'there was no room to swing a cat'. For the crew, everything experienced and lived over the last three months was quickly becoming diffused as a distant memory. The endless cocktails parties, hunting trips, lovely Eurasian girls, balmy tropical nights and the exotic foods and smells typically resplendent of the Far East, were now behind them. Traded in its place were the harsh, bitter filthy sounds of war.

It had now been three days since the U-boat had surreptitiously slipped out of Batavia's Tandjok Priok harbour. So far the weather all the way had been foul, the sea rough. The usual procedure of submerging by day and surfacing at night was practiced. Whilst the ever present danger of Allied aircraft, submarines and or destroyers loitering about was constant, the journey so far had been uneventful. That is until now.

It was in the late afternoon of Wednesday, November 1 1944 shortly before 18.00 hours [6 o'clock p.m.] that the *U-181* first spotted the *Fort Lee*.

A single smoke cloud was sighted on the horizon. To Freiwald, Giese, Limbach and other officers taking turns to view her approaching outline through the periscope, it was agreed that it held further interest. Like a moth to a candle the submarine proceeded to close in for a closer inspection. Their discovery heralded the result that it was indeed a lone oil tanker estimated to be around the 10,000 ton mark steaming at approximately 18 knots. It was heading eastbound towards Australia.

Undetected the U-boat fell silently in behind her wake.

Initially it was not met with overt confidence that they should perhaps attempt to go after her. The Chief Engineer remarked that it will be a hard job, but soon thought better of it. However after brief consultation, senior officers agreed that although the vessel presented itself as a difficult target, any sense of doubt soon gave way to assured optimism.

"Let's give it a try" Freiwald looked around and nodded assuredly to his officers. He requested from the Chief Engineer "to give the best possible speed."

The die was cast. Once more the unfortunate tragedy of war was to revisit the Indian Ocean. At any other time but for the time of hostilities, on both sides of the fence they were all sailors who if they had found themselves in the company of each other would possibly have shared a joke, a drink, offered cigarettes, compared photographs of girlfriends back home, laughed and exchanged tales of seafaring and adventure. But here tonight, because of hegemony politics and belligerent principles espoused by their government leaders they were both deemed enemies and therefore they were bound by duty to destroy each other. That is the madness of war.

Sea conditions had by now dwindled to a more acceptable calm, especially since they had left the Sunda Strait. The wind, more rather like a soft breeze swathed over the surface of the Indian Ocean. The temperature for this time of year in the Southern Hemisphere was mild. It was summer. The visibility was good.

All the while the tanker's course was being plotted by the Third Watch Officer, Leutnant Johannes Limbach as all the crew remained alert and positioned at their battle stations. Limbach himself had just been awarded the coveted Knights Cross that was presented to him in Singapore. A long time crewman of the *U-181* where he had also had been a navigation officer previously under Luth.

All throughout the night of November 1st and in to the early hours of the 2nd the *U-181* persevered to race ahead of the *Fort Lee* in order to gain a critical vantage point for attack. Freiwald must have obviously considered the tanker to be a target well worth the risk, for the pursuit itself continued for over 24 hours – a tedious and wearisome exercise, but all part of the hunt that U-boats are accustomed to.

Captain Ottar Anderson was completely unaware that his ship was being surreptitiously followed and that malevolent preying eyes had been intensely observing her every movement over nearly the last 30 hours.

By the late afternoon of Thursday, November 2 1944, the *U-181* had edged her way forward to find itself in an advantageous position within proximity to the oncoming vessel. The evening had now progressed to the latter stages of dusk - that informal transitory period between sunset and moonrise. The *Fort Lee* altered to a new course, as anticipated by the U-boat which now found the best favourable forwarding position being close, in fact very close.

"So close that our powerful Ziess binoculars could not even cover the entire length of the ship" as Otto Giese later described.

With her outline silhouetted against the backdrop of a darkening sea and sky, the *U-181* approached the *Fort Lee*. Suddenly over the boats internal public address loudspeakers comes the announcement *"Bootsangriffe"* [boat attacks] as the alarm goes off.

Freiwald orders "Los!"

The first torpedo is launched. It is a G7e model - an electric acoustic type. It races off towards its unsuspecting victim. The only tell tale evidence left behind is its own wake. A minute later the sound of a dampened explosion like that of a dull thud reverberates.

The time is exactly 20.00 hours or 8.00 p.m. local Western Standard Time.

Back in Perth some 2,000 kilometres to the east the clocks had just clicked over to 11.00 p.m. For the summer of 1944-1945 there was no Daylight Saving time in the state of Western Australia.

Onboard the *Fort Lee* everything was normal and not out of place. For men that were off duty, most were in the mess about to shuffle a pack of cards – the usual nightly routine for many. Others were in the midst of finishing off that letter to a loved one and or family back home with the intent of posting it as soon as they arrived at the next port, that being Brisbane. But for most of the ship's crew they were at work. The Navy Armed Guards, that is those assigned on duty, were at their respective posts.

The *Fort Lee* was steering on course 119° true and doing a speed of 16 knots. The depth below measured approximately 2,800 fathoms [5,000 metres]. It is the middle of the Indian Ocean at a point roughly half way between Perth and Mauritius. Whilst the sea had been mostly calm since leaving Abadan nearly 13 days before, there was a current storm warning issued for a cyclone bearing well south of their position. However it posed no immediate threat and was actually travelling well away in a south westerly direction. In accordance with her routing instructions she was not zigzagging, but travelling in a straight line. There were no visible external lights showing. She was sailing under complete black out.

The radio was silent. In fact it had not been used at all for the previous 47 hours since 23 year old Chief Radio Operator William Hart from Hickory, North Carolina sent a coded message to Colombo, Ceylon reporting their position.

The conditions were clear. The sea moderate with a south west swell, the wind south east force 3 with approximate horizon visibility. The sun had already gone down and was setting in the west now generating a soft pinkish reddish glow. It is late spring in the southern hemisphere and the outside air temperature was still hovering around a comfortable 15°C [59°F] after a day that had reached the high twenties. The first stars were just beginning to materialise, where soon enough they would all be out in abundance with the last quarter of the moon due to appear soon. It was good sailing weather.

On board the *Fort Lee* keeping watch was one able bodied seaman manning the flying bridge with one Navy Armed Guard situated on each wing of the flying bridge and another two Armed Guards aft manning the 5 inch gun platform. The five watches were just about to be relieved. There were no lookouts stationed forward or at the main deck level. However it had been a customary practice for the relieving watch to proceed directly from the brightly lit crew's spaces to their stations and relieve immediately. No red glasses were used. The deck officer of the old watch always stayed with the new watch for at least 15 minutes. The deck officer on watch had available two pairs of 7 x 50 binoculars. However there were no binoculars available to the Armed Guards on watch.

One of these was 20 year old James [Jim] Marvin Wilson from St James, Missouri. He had been serving onboard the *Fort Lee* since February. Born on October 31 1924 in Frederick Town, Missouri he attended St. James High School before joining the United States Navy in 1943 whilst still only aged 18. At 19.47 hours [7.47 p.m.] fifteen minutes before the first torpedo collided, Jim Wilson was in his quarters located directly above the engine room.

"That night I was scheduled to go on the midnight watch," he recalls 70 years later at the age of 89.

"I tried to convince some of the other guys to come up to the mess hall with me to play cards. Nobody would come, so off I went up to the mess hall by myself. A few minutes later I sat down and was just about getting ready to play cards when the first torpedo hit"

It was 20.02 hours [8.02 p.m.] when it impacted the port side of the engine room directly underneath the boilers. Throughout the vessel it resounded with the shock of a heavy muffled explosion. The incoming track or wake of the torpedo was not observed. It is estimated that it struck the hull between 8 to 12 feet below the waterline.

Just coming in off his shift at 8.00 pm was 21 year old Armed Guard Joseph William Gorga from Paterson, New Jersey. "I went straight to the Navy mess for a much needed cup of hot coffee. A couple of Merchant Marine guys passed by and asked me if I was up for playing double deck pinochle." Joe Gorga always loved a good game of pinochle so there was not much convincing him to go over to the Marine mess.

"We had barely sat down and to this day I do not even remember the first card even being dealt when the jolted impact of the torpedo was felt."

Brad Pruitt presents his own experience.

"Around half an hour beforehand at approximately 7.30 I was in what we would now call today the sick bay. It was a small room, located amidships on the port side set aside to accommodate anyone who was either injured or ill. All it had in it was just a hospital type bed. Earlier on in the Galley, I had developed this severe abdominal pain on my right side. I went to see one of the officers who indicated that he thought that it could be, of all things, an attack of appendicitis! He told me to go to the sick bay and to sit down and relax. After stripping off everything down to my shorts I laid on the bed. I remember looking out through the door, there was no reason to close the door as there were no lights burning that could be seen from the outside, we were still travelling under blackout. By this stage outside it was dusk. The sun was already down and the light was receding fast, but it was not quite fully dark yet.

When that torpedo hit, through the doorway I saw a sheet of flame pass by. The impact jarred me so severely it dislodged me from that bed directly to the ceiling above which was metal deck. I hit my head, bounced from there to the wall, where it hit me on the left side at the hip and then I slammed directly back down to the metal floor. I was out cold for how long, I don't remember."

John W. Duffy was a 23 old Able Merchant Marine Seaman from Fall River, Massachusetts. He was a graduate of the historical Fort Trumbull Merchant Marine School in Connecticut. Between 1939 and 1946 Fort Trumbull in Connecticut served as the main training facility for Merchant Marine officers during the war. Originally constructed in 1775 it was captured by the British during the American Revolution. During the Civil War it was used to train Union troops before sending them off to the battlefields. Today Fort Trumbull overlooking Long Island Sound serves the more peaceful purpose as a State Park and tourist attraction. Afterwards Duffy gave his own account of events.

"Joe Hamilton [a 20 year old Chief Pumpman from Glidden, Iowa] and I were in the bos'n foc'sle, the first room on the well deck aft on starboard side. Joe was sitting at the desk working out a navigational problem and I was standing behind him looking over his shoulder. All of a sudden there was this terrific explosion that jarred the ship violently throwing the stern out of the water and causing my head to make contact with the overhead above."

Tragically, below decks in the engine room two merchant seamen, 19 year old Thomas F. Vain a Wiper from Baltimore and 21 year old Frank Lucien Yohe a Fireman from Harrisburg, Illinois were instantly killed. They had both been standing the regular Oiler's watch, cleaning and conducting routine maintenance when the portside boiler exploded. It filled the after part of the ship with super heated steam at 440 lbs per square inch at around 710 degrees Fahrenheit temperature.

A loud grinding noise could be heard coming from the engines, then silence. They had now had now stopped. The fire room was rapidly flooding. Despite travelling under a blackout, all internal lights went off. All the power was now completely gone. The ship began to lose way and she came to an abrupt halt. It was like the whole vessel was suddenly stunned, reacting from the force of severe concussion.

In the confusion men came running out on deck with torches and flashlights, but were quickly ordered to extinguish them immediately. Michael 'Pop' Sherry was in the galley when the torpedo collided. Plates, glasses and other kitchen utensils shuddered, rattled and fell on the floor. The dull thud and impact instantly gave away that something serious was amiss.

Chief Cook Brad Pruitt points out that the impact in the boiler room was only about 25 feet away from where he was laid up. "When I came to I staggered to the door and stood there and I heard the Captain hollering through a megaphone *'does anyone know what has happened? Someone report back to me immediately'* then I blacked out again."

Able Seaman Duffy recalled, "After the engines stopped, there came the hissing of the escaping steam which filled the passageways. Hamilton attempted to get aft to get the emergency light hanging on the bulkhead, but the steam was too hot and stifling."

Initially at this stage it may have mistakenly been thought that the explosion had occurred internally and originated from somewhere on board ship. Soon a report was made. It confirmed his worse fears. Captain Andersen now knew that his ship had been torpedoed. This was aided by the *Fort Lee* being equipped with a torpedo sound warning device which activated loudly soon after it had struck.

Back in the mess hall the lock on the door aft was faulty and had not been working for some time. For some reason nothing had been done to repair it either. To escape from here a number of men had no choice but to squeeze through port holes. This is what Jim Wilson had to contend with.

"I tried to exit the mess room but was stopped from using the door by the heat created by the steam from the engines. So I had no other choice but to exit through a porthole."

So too did Joe Gorga.

"I grabbed a lifejacket but needed to climb through a porthole to get out. I was not able to entirely fit through and became stuck, so the other guys had to pull and push me until I was free. I was grateful to the guy behind me who handed me my lifejacket once I was able to get through."

Some were not so lucky. Another who found himself in this situation was 19 year old U.S. Navy Seaman First Class Lyle James Atkinson from Buffalo, Wisconsin. With several others he had been attempting to escape from the crew mess. Others managed to get out through the Galley, however Atkinson tried to go through the gunner's mess hall. As he did so his escape was cut short when the door to the fire room suddenly burst open and he was scalded by high temperature steam. He later said he could not see it for at this heat it was almost invisible steam. He managed to cover his eyes, which probably saved his eyesight, but suffered serious burns to both his face and hands. With his sense of humour intact, his only complaint afterwards was that his tattoo on his arm was now ruined.

Zeb Page Jr, a 26 year old 3rd Engineer Junior Grade from Durham, North Carolina was lucky. He had been with the 3rd Engineer John Frels from Austen, Texas. They were both standing by the log desk in the main turbine room when the first torpedo struck. Page later remarked that about two or three seconds before the explosion he heard a metallic like noise, as if someone had struck the outside of the ship's hull with a sledgehammer.

He was blasted into a corner and then inexplicably found himself floating against the over head, 30 feet above the turbine room deck. Wondering how to get out of this without being drowned, the water for some reason suddenly receded where he was then able to swim over to the engine room ladder and escape.

Similarly Frels too became the recipient of another lucky escape. He had become lodged high up in the ventilator shaft directly above the log desk. He could not get through due to the heavy wire screen cover. It was the Third Mate 35 year old Salem Stine who instinctively grabbed a fire axe and successfully managed to chop him out. Once free, Frels said that he was fine and then went off immediately to his boat station which was Lifeboat #3.

Up until the first strike, 19 year old Midshipman Cadet Second Class James Thomas Chaffin had been on bridge watch since 16.00 hours [4.00 p.m.]. He had been taking dead reckoning positions and then passing them onto Radio Operator Bill [Sparks] Hart. When out of sight of land with the absence of sun, moon or stars visible, the 'Dead Reckoning' position is calculated from the course and speed from the last 'Observed Position'. Some 54 years later in 1998 he was able to recall and confirm the exact time of the attack.

"It was two minutes after eight. Usually I would have been off by then but I hadn't finished [my work]. I was in the chart room, which is right off the bridge. You could walk right out to the bridge from the chart room. The first explosion knocked out all the main power and also the emergency power, so we had no lights or anything. So Captain Andersen came up and told me to go back out with a flashlight and see if there was any water on the deck."

This exactly matches the account given by Otto Giese and the crew of the *U-181* as they observed men with flashlights out on the bridge and deck.

"Water was already coming over the deck, so I went back in and told him [the Captain], 'ain't no deck back there-you can't even see back there!"

After the torpedo hit, Chaffin quickly reported down to his assigned station at Lifeboat #1 and secured the plug. All lifeboats are fitted with a bung or plug in the bottom which is left out, or rather un-plugged, while it [the lifeboat] is still secured to the davits. This is so that rain water can drain out. He then hurried back off to the now black out chart room and procured two sextants, a chronometer, a compass and the publication for that latitude and a chart that had been added by the Skipper.

"Everybody is assigned to a job in case of an emergency" he explained.

Normally there are two cadets for each ship, one engine cadet and one deck cadet. However there had not been enough cadets to go around and the Merchant Marine were unable to supply two for the *Fort Lee*. As it was James Chaffin was the only deck cadet on board.

"My job in the event of an attack was to secure navigational equipment and any charts handy and put them in the lifeboat, which I did. Also the chronometer which is essential in plotting your position after you get your sights and all." He then raced back over and placed all of these, and what else he could carry into Lifeboat #1.

At this stage no known fires had broken out but one crewman reported, "That a large hole was made in the port side aft, as also another large hole of equal proportions now appeared in the deck of the fireman's quarters on the main deck port side".

Another survivor later testified that he saw lockers falling into this hole and when he peered down noticed red hot pipes. The mess room began quickly filling up with smoke accompanied with the acrid stench of ammonia gas fumes which were beginning to become overpowering.

"I left Hamilton and hurried forward to the bridge" recounts Duffy. "Then I remembered that my boat station had been changed just a few days beforehand from #2 to #5, so I hurried over the Lifeboat #5 where the crew were assembling. We all had to get cork life jackets from an emergency box as no one had time to get their own in the confusion."

Now noticed for the first time was the seemingly deathlike silence that had gripped the ship since the engines had stopped. This was in complete contrast to many months of the familiar steady and constant humming that everybody had become accustomed to.

The radio antenna was broken and grounded. The antenna cable ran from between the foremast and aft mast. The violent impact shook the vessel that much that the cable snapped and a hurried attempt to rig up a new emergency one remained incomplete due to simply running out of time.

The general alarm system was dead and a command was passed by Andersen for the men to 'stand by their stations'. Though the order to abandon ship itself at this stage had not been issued, she did begin to commence settling by the stern without any noticeable list. This is despite both Duffy and Hamilton later saying that they had noticed that from the well deck, sea was pouring across from the starboard side indicating to them that the ship was listing to one side. Duffy noted that it curiously sounded very much like the seashore as each succeeding wave broke across the deck and poured straight into the pump room door that had been left open.

On board throughout the vessel there were raised voices, shouts of command, men racing through bulkheads, up ladders, down ladders, on deck. Amongst orderly confusion there were still moments of disorderly confusion. From seemingly everywhere came the command to "put out those God Damn lights!" Still not everybody was sure what was going on. Men who had been off duty now found themselves facing shipmates racing about.

"What is it? What's going on?"

"We've been hit. I think we have been torpedoed. Better grab your life jacket and get topside."

"A few were panicky" said John Duffy later on. "I came across Arthur [20 year old Able Seaman James Arthur] who seemed to be losing his grip. He was crying and holding his back and said it was broken. I told him to brace up. All hands realised by now that it was a torpedo and not a boiler explosion."

Meanwhile back on the *U-181* it was noted that the torpedo had indeed impacted the engine room. The submarine now stopped her own engines mainly to see if the crew aboard the tanker would man their guns. They observed what was purported to be the watch officer walking up and down the bridge. The black silhouette of the U-boat then slowly circled around waiting for her to start sinking. It soon appeared evident that she wasn't in a hurry.

Seemingly the one torpedo had not been sufficient.

Oberleutnant Otto Giese frowned. He turned to his commander.

"Why do we not puncture her with our anti-aircraft guns? We may need our other torpedo for something else. We have a long way to go," he added.

"No" replied Freiwald thoughtfully. "If we do that we would certainly bring the crew to her guns and therefore place ourselves at risk, thus delaying our mission."

Freiwald, like every U-boat commander was cautious and always mindful of protecting his boat and crew first.

"We stand no chance with our artillery against theirs. We'll deploy our last torpedo on her," he ordered with finality. Once again the alarm sounded for action.

Freiwald was not to know this, but on board the tanker no counter offensive was made possible or undertaken although the 5 inch gun was loaded and made ready a few minutes after the first torpedo had struck. However the forward 3 inch gun was out of commission on account of a jammed roller track. By now the main deck aft was awash with water.

Again from Able Seaman John Duffy. "I went up on stack deck and looked down through the escape hatch to see if anyone was trapped below. Choking hot steam was pouring out. I saw a flashlight moving about in the upper fire room which I later found out was the Captain and the Second Pumpsman," [35 year old Hugh Johnston from Parkersburg, Pennsylvania].

Duffy describes how at this point there were many false and confusing orders given to abandon ship, but most were ignored. However two lifeboats were indeed launched before the official word.

"Number 4 boat was lowered into the water empty. The First Engineer, Roy Shaffer was concerned that it would drift directly under Lifeboat #6 so he advised the Bosun, Jessie Marcum to lower it away as well. All hands laid in." Navy Armed Guard Lyle Atkinson who had been badly burned whilst attempting to escape from the mess room was carefully laid out in Lifeboat #6.

It is around this time that the first in a series of curious incidents commenced to manifest itself. They seem to implicate the conduct concerning the U.S. Navy officer in charge of the Armed Guards, Lieutenant James W. Milne.

Duffy later wrote:

"All the while the Navy gunnery officer was conspicuous by his absence. He came aft once for about half a minute then disappeared hurriedly back to his boat station forward immediately, without once telling his boys [the U.S. Navy Armed Guards] what to do. Neither did he command or advise what action to take regarding the submarine."

Duffy went down to the poop deck and saw that water was now creeping under the taffrail - the rail that goes round the stern of the ship.

"We grabbed woollen blankets and cigarettes and threw them in our boat."

At 20.24 hours [twenty four minutes past eight] Master Andersen now gave the critical order to officially abandon ship. Midshipman Cadet Chaffin quickly noticed that one able bodied seaman was missing from his post when the order to abandon ship was given. However another fellow filled in and took his place and both managed to lower the lifeboat down.

Four minutes later, at precisely 20.28 hours, the second torpedo impacted the *Fort Lee*. It was just under half an hour after the first torpedo had struck home. This time it smashed into the starboard side aft [rear] between the engine room and Number 9 holding tank amidships. It is this second torpedo that would increase the death toll and do more fatal damage on top of what had already been inflicted.

It was just as the forward fall of Lifeboat #1 was only a few feet from the water when this second torpedo impacted. The falls are the ropes or wires that lower the boat into the water. One is located forward and one aft. They are cast off once afloat. Up until this moment, for Tom Chaffin, lowering his lifeboat down into the water was an orderly affair.

On impact, the explosion created a sheet of flame that rose almost 200 feet in the air. At the same time it produced a blinding flash that lasted several seconds. The Skipper Ottar Andersen and Chief Steward Buric who were both descending into Lifeboat #2 located on the port side forward of the bridge, saw it and claimed that it certainly created a column of fire and smoke that rose higher than the 90 foot mainmast. It then quickly developed into a thick black mushroom type cloud.

George A. McCoy an African American Ordinary Seaman from Baltimore, Maryland was killed instantly from the blast whilst in his cabin. Up on deck at the last inconvenient minute, he suddenly realised that he did not have his papers on him and that they were still back in his locker. Unsure, he deliberated, then fatally made his mind up by deciding to race back to retrieve them just as the second torpedo slammed into the side of the hull directly below his cabin.

"He was standing by when he remembered his papers" recalled Duffy. "He went below to get them and although we tried to stop him, he was never seen again."

This second impact yielded further tragic results for it also struck directly beneath where both number 3 and number 5 lifeboats were still in the process of being lowered. From the explosion Lifeboat #3 was completely destroyed. It was smashed to pieces killing six men who had only just embarked into it.

Three of them were Armed Guards. One was 19 year old Gunner's Mate Third Class Bernard Gustav Storm from Owatonna, Minnesota. The other two were Seaman First Class Leon LeRoy Carrington from Sayre, Pennsylvania and 21 year old Seaman First Class Herman C. Dumas from Spencer, Louisiana. The other three were Merchant Mariners. One was 18 year old Ordinary Seaman Jimmy McLamore from Baltimore, Maryland. The other was James Arthur also from Baltimore that John Duffy had encountered only just minutes before on deck. The last casualty was 31 year old Third Engineer John F. Frels, who also only moments before had had his own lucky escape from the turbine room.

It was unfortunate for Herman Dumas. He was already wounded with a shattered arm. At some stage he had made his way over to Lifeboat #3. Originally he had been standing by Lifeboat #6 and had been ordered into it by Shaffer. Dumas refused to do so, on account that he was afraid to abandon ship without official orders fearing a court martial. Had he done so he could have possibly saved his own life.

Jim McLamore too had been a good friend of Brad Pruitt who by now had managed to come to again. Still suffering from concussion and attempting take in what was happening around him, he blinked and rubbed his eyes to focus.

"When I struggled to the door again and looked out onto the deck, I saw no-one – there was not a living soul to be seen. Then I looked back toward the stern, and over to the right and I saw the gun crew portside at their stations, still there, and also the gun crew on the starboard side of the ship. And then I saw the explosion."

Lifeboat #5 was split in two. The force of the impact was so powerful and intense that it dislodged the seven men who were waiting to board it and blew them sky high off the ship's deck straight in to the now murky oil caked water below. One was Joe Gorga who had been assigned to Lifeboat #5. Another was 21 year old Andrew Albert Lemanski also an Armed Guard from Yale, Michigan.

"Later when I was told that bodies were flying through the air, well, I was one of those flying bodies. I managed to regain consciousness whilst under water. It felt like I swam forever to reach the surface which was covered inches thick with oil," Lemanski recalled in 2002.

This is a notable remark that would be echoed by many of the survivors afterwards who were plunged into the water. Besides the oil, a profound sense of disorientation occurred where it was simply hard to tell which way was up towards the surface and which way was down towards disaster. Luckily for Andrew Lemanski he was soon picked out of the oily mess and lifted up over into Lifeboat #2. Also providential, for had he and Gorga already boarded the lifeboat then they too like those in the unfortunate Lifeboat #3 would have most likely been killed as well.

By now oil was leaking out everywhere from the bowels of the tanker. In the explosion adding to the human projectiles was deadly shrapnel in the form of pieces of wood, metal, broken oars and other debris that can become suddenly lethal objects. The situation exasperated that there was now a sizable quantity of men overboard in the sea.

Twenty year old Navy gunner Orville Adams from Cannelton, Indiana was waiting on the boat deck near Lifeboat #3 for orders. The following is a verbatim transcript of his own eyewitness account that he presented afterwards when interviewed by U.S. Naval Intelligence.

"The Second Mate and an able bodied seaman were making the lifeboat ready for launch. It was then that the second torpedo struck. I don't recall exactly what happened, but there was an explosion and I suddenly found myself in the ocean about 100 feet from the ship. When I regained my senses I realised I was not wearing my life jacket anymore – it had been blown off by the explosion. Luckily I saw an oil drum floating nearby and started to swim toward it. At this time I heard someone hollering that he was hurt. Upon reaching the drum, I swam and pushed it towards him. It was the 2nd Mate that was hurt and attempting to stay afloat."

The Second Mate was 29 year old Leslie Asher from Baltimore, Maryland. He had suffered a broken rib and numerous abrasions and cuts about his body.

"We both grabbed the drum and hung on. It was then that Hennessy started yelling asking how we were. I replied back that the Second Mate was hurt!"

Hennessy is 22 year old merchant seaman John (Jack) Leo Hennessy, from Minneapolis, Minnesota. He was nearby, contending with his own struggle in the water hanging on to another oil drum.

"I don't know how bad he is hurt and I don't have my life-jacket anymore," Adams managed to shout back.

Hennessy told Adams to hang on and that he would bring help. Leaving the drum he was holding on to, he then swam over towards the now sinking ship. By doing so Hennessy actually placed himself in grave danger by deliberately exposing himself to being pulled under by the suction of the ship as she was now starting to sink rapidly.

"We were both hanging on to our drum for some time when I heard Hennessy call out again" writes Adams.

"He told us to make straight towards him as he had managed to get hold of a donut raft. The Mate and I then pushed forward the drum and began swimming in that direction. Not being able to make headway against the current, we both let go of the drum. Getting closer we could see Hennessy. He had both hands over the side of the small raft paddling desperately. He had not even taken time to get out the small oars. Upon reaching us, he and I placed Asher [the Mate] into the raft and headed toward a lifeboat that we saw in the distance."

The three of them, with Adams and Hennessy pushing the small raft and the injured Asher aboard made off through the dark, blackened oily water. Suddenly somewhere off to the right they heard another cry for help and observed a small light swinging back and forth.

"Let's go get him" Hennessy yelled.

The little raft that was housing Asher was already taking on water. With great effort they still nevertheless managed to swim over. Here they found navy gunner George F. Kasper.

"His leg was broken," wrote Adams.

"But we pulled him aboard and continued on our way. Finally we came alongside the lifeboat that we had started for. It was the Chief Mate's boat – *Lifeboat #1*."

The men in this boat, which included James Chaffin, Joe Gorga and 20 year old Max Tarnowski, pulled the two wounded men on board over the bow. Both Hennessy and Adams drifted towards the stern before climbing in after them. The Chief Mate was 46 year old Charles Shenberg also from Baltimore. In this boat as well was the Armed Guard officer Lieutenant James W. Milne. With seven Guards all up and 13

Merchant Mariners there were 20 men in total. Only moments before Joe Gorga had been pulled over into this boat. By his reckoning he was saved owing to the little light attached on the lifejacket, enabling him to be seen in the dark surface of the water.

Due to overcrowding, both Hennessy and Adams and a third man, 19 year old Robert C. Brookins, a Galleyman from Sioux City, Iowa, would later transfer at around 9.45 pm from this lifeboat over in to another - Lifeboat #6.

Afterwards John Hennessy submitted his own following testimony of events.

"After having secured all available blankets and clothing that I could find from the gunner's foc'sle we were standing by the falls of Number 5 lifeboat. The order to abandon ship came."

John Duffy, Armed Guard William King along with Earl Smith a 19 year old Galleyman from Washington and another Navy gunner all got into the boat. This left Brookins and 21 year old Augustus Hoffler a Galleyman from Brooklyn, New York City and Hennessey on deck to lower away the boat. Hennessey went on to write:

"The falls were all slack when Brookins and myself went to the edge of the boat deck to wait for the monkey line to be thrown to us. Just as Brookins left the deck in a leap to catch a line the second torpedo hit. I remember seeing a flash and smelling gun powder."

Hoffler, tending the after fall, was blown back onto the 5 inch gun platform. Hennessy, like Orville Adams was thrown clear into the water from the force of the blast. After that he remembers little until waking up in the water about 100 feet away from the ship.

"There was an object ahead of me which I swam toward. It turned out to be an empty oil drum. About his time Adams came swimming by and managed to catch hold of another drum. We heard cries coming from the direction of the ship and started out for them. It turned out to be the Second Mate Asher who seemed to have been hurt by the concussion of the blast."

Hennessy had swum a distance of 75 feet to find something suitable to work as a support. This was when he returned with the donut raft.

John Duffy felt the immediate force of the second impact as well. "As the Chief Engineer [Roy Shaffer] had gone over to Lifeboat #6 being second in charge I took command of Lifeboat #5. Navy gunners Kirwin and Lemanski, Messmen Hoffler and Smith and Cecil 'Tex' Knauth a 30 year old Oiler from Vernon, Texas were the crew so far in it. As we started lowering, Peterson, a Navy gunner asked if this was his proper assigned boat. I shouted back to him to jump in! Hoffler and Hennessy continued to lower us away with Brookins standing by."

The lifeboat had become waterborne and Duffy was now busy attempting to hold her into the side of the ship with the metal escape ladder before releasing the falls. Number 3 lifeboat had already reached the water about a minute before with seven men in it.

"I was shouting up to Hoffler to hurry up and climb down the ladder when suddenly there was a terrific deafening and blinding explosion. I felt myself being hurled through the air about as high as the boat deck maybe 15 or 20 feet above the water. Our boat split in half and everybody else who was in it were flown through the air like rag dolls as well. On hitting the water I found myself going down very fast, as if being drawn in by suction...perhaps by the water now rushing into the gaping hole made in the side of the ship. I then had to contend with rope which had become entangled around my thigh, fearing that it might hold me under. I managed to work free of it by slipping it down past off my ankle...with immense relief!

Aided by the cork life jacket I swam as hard as I could to the surface. I thought I would never make it!"

The cool fresh air never tasted better and Duffy thankfully gulped in his want along with several unwanted mouthfuls of heavy bunker fuel oil. All told he reckoned later that he was underwater for almost a complete minute.

Still on board the sinking *Fort Lee* Brad Pruitt had by now recovered consciousness sufficiently enough to make his way over to the port side where the last boat had been launched. It was the Captain's lifeboat - Lifeboat #2.

"I looked over the side and it was already in the water. I could make out the Captain, some merchant men and five or so of the naval gun crew. They were about to cast off their ropes when I yelled out down to them. They all looked back up toward me, the Captain urging me to hurry up and abandon ship, less they get caught in the suction. So I grabbed hold of a heavy centre rope that had knots in it to prevent you from sliding too fast."

This is a knotted rope or a group of knotted ropes attached to a cross rope linked between the two davits where the lifeboats are secured. Pruitt describes how the intense pain in the right side of his body that he had experienced earlier now returned.

"As I was making my way down I released my hold on the rope and fell about 8 feet, landing in the water between the hull and the lifeboat. Luckily I was not crushed between the two. The men in the lifeboat then hauled me over into it. All I still had on during this time was a pair of shorts and I was completely soaked and covered in oil." As it turned out Brad Pruitt was one of the last known to abandon ship, holding perhaps the distinction of being the very last man to touch and feel the cold grey metal of the SS *Fort Lee*.

After gathering his bearings Able Seaman John Duffy swam as far as he could from the now rapidly sinking ship. He was aware of men in the water around him, some of whom he knew could not swim at all. His own lifejacket was in tatters and was split in two, and despite himself being a strong swimmer, decided it was better than having none at all so he allowed it to trail behind him.

"Just then I noticed a green tropical Navy helmet floating in the water. I swam over to it fearing that there may still be a body attached to it underneath. Fortunately not, it was just the helmet. Thinking that it might come in handy later in the sun, especially if I ever got myself into a lifeboat, I put it on my head and kept on swimming."

Four lifeboats were launched successfully. But there were still a lot of men in the water, some badly wounded. In another sense they were lucky as well for steel lifeboats had the potential to become 'frying pans' in the blazing oil fires that can commonly erupt from oil tankers. Wooden lifeboats smouldered but usually pulled free from the flames. Fortunately this was not the case here. On board nine men had lost their lives from the two torpedo attacks – six merchant crew and three Armed Guards.

"I heard voices," recalls Duffy. "Swimming over to their direction I saw three or four heads. I ask them if they were okay. They complained of being shaken up, one or two had gashes and one a broken arm. After a quick head count there was seven of us. I suggested that we should stick together. One of the boys noticed the wooden mast from our lifeboat floating in the water so we swam over to it and clung on. We were all covered in thick, heavy black oil."

It was here that Duffy also noticed that a fire had broken out on the side of the sinking ship from bunker oil, but the waves hitting against her was extinguishing it.

"I turned to the oil coated head next to me and asked if he was Hoffler [an African American who worked in the Galley]. In reply I received a very sharp, 'no fucking way, I'm Kirwin!' [a U.S. Navy Armed Guard]. They all had a laugh at me as all I had on was a pair of dungarees and the helmet on my head. My shoes and shirt had been torn off in the blast."

Overall from reports throughout the whole abandon ship process there was a general absence of panic and rather little chaos. Observing from a distance even those on the U-boat noted that all the remaining lifeboats went into the water in an orderly fashion.

The typical detritus that comes from a shipwreck littered much of the surface of the sea all around. Thick oil had also now laid down quite a sizable slick, as drums, wooden crates, and anything else that could float, bobbed away. Amid the darkness, lights from the lifeboats moving up and down could be seen in the moderate sea. The *Fort Lee* was now in her death throes. By 20.40 hours she was rapidly sinking by the stern. Her bow was showing approximately 15 to 20 feet out of the water.

"About a 100 yards off we could see the ship down to her stack. Debris was floating all about along with a couple of lights which we felt were life jackets. After about 10 minutes we saw a shape approaching very slowly. Some thought it was the sub, others a lifeboat. We remained silent and dared not yell until we were sure. Brookins began swimming towards it, saying he felt like the exercise. The rest of us started following, with the non swimmers still holding onto the wooden mast. In no time it was within 30 feet of us and to our relief it turned out to be Lifeboat #2."

Curiously not every Merchant Marine or member of the Navy actually knew how to swim, with only about two thirds of those on the *Fort Lee* knowing how to do so. The wounded Lyle Atkinson was one, who disliked the water and never learnt. Back then it seemingly was not a pre-requisite.

By this stage Duffy and the other six had been in the water for nearly half an hour. The cold was really starting to have effect.

"We all swam over to the boat and were pulled in one by one," writes Duffy. "I waited to see if there were any stragglers when one, Lemanski started drifting astern of the boat. He became hysterical, yelling that he was going down despite the fact that he had on a life jacket which would not let him sink. I swam over to him and told him to shut up or I'd belt him one. This seemed to quieten him down. By then the boat had backed alongside and I threw him in. I then threw over my helmet and climbed in after."

There were about 20 men in it now. Several would be later transferred over into other lifeboats. Most still were dry, except for Pruitt. Nevertheless they gave over what dry clothes they could. Duffy ended up with a Third Mates coat which he described as feeling like wearing a fur coat.

The convoy and routing instructions known as Mersigs, [Merchant Signals Manual - used by ships when sailing in convoy] and the Notices to Mariners and all other codes and papers were thrown overboard in a weighted bag. Mersigs is an acronym for 'Merchant Signals'. International code flags were used to pass messages from ship to ship, as were hooters, morse light signals and semaphore. If a convoy needed to turn quickly to port or starboard the leading vessel would hoist the 'I' flag for port or 'E' for starboard and each ship, would hoist the same flag indicating that they had seen it. All flags would then be lowered and a turn of 45 degrees made by all ships. Together the entire convoy would be moving in unison on a new course. All these manual code books were jettisoned overboard as a safeguard to prevent the possibility of them ever falling into enemy hands.

C.A.M.S.I. – or Confidential American Merchant Shipping Instructions and other restricted manuals were housed in a steel box located in the radio room. They too were never retrieved or saved and went down with the ship.

At approximately 20.45 hours the *U-181* resurfaced like some prehistoric monster from the deep. It emerged into view about 100 yards away from Lifeboat #6. From out of the darkness it slowly passed by Lifeboat #1 which was about 30 yards away and manoeuvred over to approach within approximately 30 feet of Lifeboat #4.

There is no doubt that all those in the lifeboats were apprehensive and fell silent when they saw the large black cigar shape of the submarine loom towards them. At this stage they possessed no idea who it was. Men silently prayed, fearful that it was Japanese. Men began to cram themselves as tightly as they could into the bottom of the lifeboats, and stopped breathing. Tales of them shooting survivors was a bitter reputation that preceded them. Then again if it was a German no one was certain what they would do either. The big MAN diesels idled. Like everyone in Lifeboat #2, John Duffy was apprehensive.

"I inched toward the side away from the sub, first removing what was left of my lifejacket. Should they start strafing us, as we all aware that Japanese submarines usually did, I was prepared to dive over the side and swim underwater as far away from the lifeboat as I could. I remember right next to me was Groves [18 year old Earl A. Groves, an Ordinary Seaman from Chanute, Kansas]. He was the ships bully, only just 18, rugged, tough and now whimpering and saying that our time was up and we might as well throw in the towel. This did not make us feel any better. Johnston on my other side said he thought that it looked pretty bad."

No one was prepared to lift their heads higher than the gunwale. They were hoping that they would be mistaken for driftwood or floating debris. Over in Lifeboat #6 Chief Engineer Paul Stauffer later affirmed that he thought the submarine initially attempted to establish contact by blinker signal.

Chief Cook Brad Pruitt supports this recalling that, "They turned on a light, not to blind us, but faced it down away from us."

In Lifeboat #2, "All we could see was very large shadow riding through the water with a riding light."

Emerging from the conning tower down onto the deck was Oberleutnant Otto Giese who had been ordered by Freiwald to question those in the lifeboats. In the enveloping darkness he noted all the lights on the life jackets coming from the lifeboats now bobbing up and down with the motion of the water. Off to the west the very last faint smattering of light was etched out like a thin line across the far horizon.

In the lifeboats some thought that they could make out others on the deck that appeared to be standing astride armed with sub machine guns. As the U-boat drew alongside to a position close enough to be heard, in his accented but clear cut and well mannered English, Giese cupped his hands around his mouth and called out:

"If you have transmitters do not use them immediately" he instructed.

"What is the name of your ship?"

Giese later described the castaways as being very well disciplined. Most questions were answered very matter of factly, but not all, especially at first.

"Where is your captain?"

Silence.

"Where is your Chief Engineer?"

Again silence.

"What is your tonnage and cargo?"

Still no reply. This response, or initial lack thereof, may have briefly confused Giese, for the Germans had originally thought the ship to be British.

"What nationality are you?"

Holding the most senior rank in Lifeboat #4 was 35 year old Third Mate Salem H. Stine from Baltimore. Staring back, straining his eyes trying to make out the silhouetted figure in the darkness standing astride the submarine's deck, he replied:

"We are American" was the hesitant reply.

Some distance away was the Skipper's lifeboat. Sound carries across water and those in Lifeboat #2 in the moderately calm conditions could just make out the conversation to both overhear and make out what was going on. Situated a little further off was Lifeboat #6.

"Where have you sailed from?"

"The Arabian Sea" replied Stine with some hesitation, now beginning to sense that the sub is not Japanese at least. Certain doubts ran quickly through his mind as to whether he should be answering anything back at all to what is in effect the enemy. At this stage he had no idea where the Captain was, and even if he did he was not going to give it away.

In Lifeboat #2 Skipper Ottar Andersen fearing that they could be questioned by the U-boat, threw his cap into the bottom of the boat and declared that if anybody asks; he had been the Bosun on board ship. Andersen then sat back quietly watching and listening to proceedings in the bad light. In the darkness hidden from the Germans view he was hanging onto his briefcase. In one hand with his arm outstretched over the side of the boat he was ready to let it go at the moment he felt any threat. Inside it contained a pistol and some papers that he managed to quickly salvage.

Giese again, "What was your destination?"

This time he received no answer.

"What year was your ship constructed?"

"It is only a couple of years old" was the only vague reply offered up. This may have been near enough to the exact answer as Chief Engineer Paul Stauffer later wrote that from Lifeboat #6 they overheard the words *'two years'* being exchanged. Stauffer also writes that they thought they heard a voice call out something that sounded like *'this makes twenty two Americanoes* [sic]' which gave those in the lifeboat the first inkling that it was German. Whatever that meant it could not have been in reference to the number of ships, because the *U-181* only ever sunk 4 American vessels. Most of her previous victims had been either British or Greek.

Giese then went on to inform them that they were approximately 1,900 nautical miles from land.

"Do you have enough provisions and water in the boats?" he enquired. He also apparently asked if anyone needed medical attention. It is not known what anybody may have exactly said in reply to this, but indicated to Giese was, that everything was all okay and that everyone was in seemingly good shape...considering. This is despite knowing that in the life-boats there probably really wasn't enough water or emergency rations to go round sufficiently.

There once had been made an obscure claim purporting that they were offered blankets, medicine, extra food and wa-ter along with a flare gun with several spare flares by the Germans. Perhaps it is true that most on the U-boat were not so much Nazis but rather sailors who adhered to the first law of the sea and that is to assist fellow sailors who are in dis-tress. Otto Giese himself was certainly no war criminal, just a sailor with a love of the sea who was serving his country.

However the claim is entirely false. There is no evidence to suggest anywhere whatsoever that this ever occurred. There is not one single shred and tangible piece of proof that the crew of the U-boat gave the lifeboats any provisions. No-where does Giese indicate this in any of his post war memoirs. In declassified documents and handwritten logs, there is no mention at all of this taking place and survivors from the *Fort Lee* make no assertion that it occurred either.

"It is a load of baloney" confirms Brad Pruitt. "I have read and been informed of this and it is lie. I was there and I wit-nessed it personally and I can tell you that the claim that the crew of the U-boat gave us provisions and supplies is utterly false and incorrect. The [German] officer spoke to us in clear English, and asked questions about us and about our ship. He was very polite as I recall, but they did not give us a thing."

Even today there are still several references that carry this false affirmation on various websites and suchlike. By who, why and where it originated from is unknown. But that does not really matter. What is important here is that an historical point in question, here in this text, has been finally corrected.

What is established and known is that Giese asked the lifeboats a series of questions. Confirmed by both sides is that a verbal exchange did in fact take place that lasted for no more than perhaps 5 or 6 minutes. With an assurance of satisfaction the last and only thing that Giese offered them was a 'Bon Voyage'. Conversely Giese offered no confirmation to his own nationality or that of the submarine. As it revved up its engines and began to move off, the men from the *Fort Lee* were still unsure who had exactly been the cause of this dilemma that they now found themselves in. Only much later would they find that out.

Everyone knew that this was a war zone where operations were actively carried out by *both* Axis belligerents, namely Germany and Japan. Until then the only description known was that it [the submarine] was big and the officer who spoke to them seemed European, suggesting that it was perhaps German.

Like a predatory hunter inspecting its victim the U-boat passed by the now dying tanker at 21.03 hours, exactly 35 minutes after the second torpedo had struck. Before recommencing once again her course down to the Cape of Good Hope it stayed on the surface and purposely took off in a northerly direction as a deceptive ruse. Her big MAN diesel engines could still be heard echoing across the water as she vanished into the night. The sound stayed within earshot of the lifeboats for up to more than half an hour until they faded away.

At approximately 21.15 hours or a quarter past nine on the evening of November 2 1944 the SS *Fort Lee* took her final plunge down into the abyss of the Indian Ocean. Sinking by the stern first she hung onto the surface by her forecastle head until the last waves finally lapped over leaving behind a swirling, bubbling effect of thick gooey oil contaminated water. Scattered with bits of flotsam much of the slick had now covered the immediate area offering the only tell tale sign of her existence. The groans and unholy noises that emanate from a dying ship raced across water.

"We watched the *Fort Lee* go through her dying pains" recalled Duffy. "We all sat around wet, cold and depressed with most just realising what had happened. We dared not talk above a whisper or light a cigarette. First, only the foremast and bridge was above water, then she slipped further and her bow end for about 50 feet was pointing to the heavens. She looked like a bread knife sticking out of the water. Then there was this deafening roar that lasted about ten seconds. It was everything in the fore-peak crashing through the hull...the anchor, chain, windlass, a hundred cans of paint, tools..."

Then there was silence.

The SS *Fort Lee* sunk and disappeared forever at the position of 83°11'E-27°35'S.

The location itself is due west of Perth and east from the island of Mauritius, meeting at a point almost exactly half way between the two. The survivors in the lifeboats gazed over to where she had once been. For many it had been their home for nearly these past 18 months. Now there was nothing. Eerie metallic sounds of her descent emanated back up towards the surface.

Into the dark void where no light penetrates she commenced her long descent down to the bottom. Trailing behind her was a thick oil slick. All the while her superstructure contracted, dented and began crushing in from the immense pressure. Some five kilometres below, what remained of the ship that was once the tanker *Fort Lee* settled on the seafloor, the violent impact no doubt breaking her back.

Back up on the surface the men were left with an ineluctable myriad of mixed feelings, a combination of shock, loss, lament, tragedy and anger. An attempt at making some sense of order and stability into the current set of circumstances was put in place and a quick roll call and head count now commenced.

"Is Carrington there?"

A moment's pause, "No-he's gone" someone replies.

"Malec?"

"Yeah – he's here."

"Frels?"....*Silence*...

"Davis?"

"Yeah – I'm over here!"

"McCoy?"

"Never saw McCoy again since he went for his papers."

And on and on it went until it soon started to become clearly evident as to who was lost and who by the grace of God had made it.

Nine men were either dead or missing. McCoy, Yohe, Vain, Arthur, Frels, McLamore along with the three Naval Guards...Dumas, Carrington and Storm. They all went down with the ship. They were shipmates. To others, friends. Only just over an hour before, somebody somewhere on board had been talking to them, working alongside them, sharing a joke or a cup of coffee with them in the mess. Now they were gone. Their bodies were never recovered. Their eulogy would be that constant that no family wants to hear – Killed in Action - Lost at Sea.

But for the survivors the real ordeal was just about to begin. They were now castaways. Their ship was gone and most of all their possessions that they owned went down with it.

"I lost everything, including $300.00 I had in a suitcase" laments former Armed Guard Jim Wilson who would eventually find himself in Lifeboat #6 along with 16 other weary and tired men. "All I had was the clothes on my back!"

With this remark alone he could be speaking on behalf of every survivor from the *Fort Lee* for that is all what they had. But the assembly of human misery now bobbing away with the motion of the moderate waves, they all possessed one simple common denominator– they were alive.

And with that, hope survives.

The only known image of the SS *Fort Lee* taken not long after her launch in 1943. She was impacted by two torpedoes the first one port side into the engine room directly underneath the boilers. The second on the starboard. She sunk at the position of 83°11'E - 27°35'S.

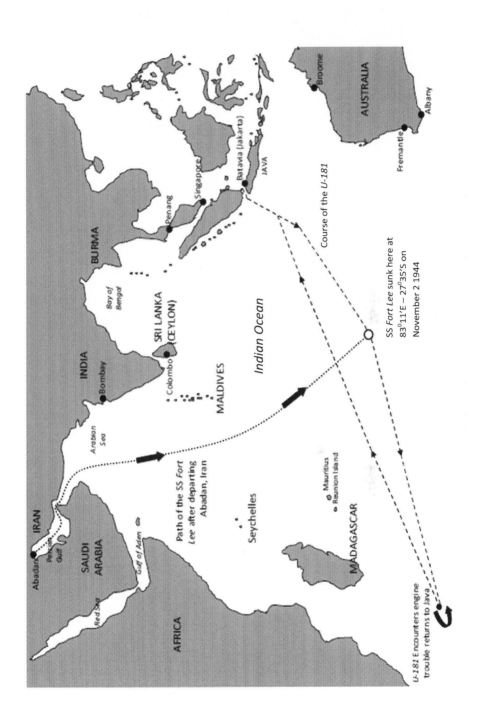

An aerial view of an American oil tanker listing heavily at the stern and sinking following an attack by a German U-boat off the coast of Florida in 1942. The scene depicted here would be almost identical to what befell the *Fort Lee*.

The Skipper of the *Fort Lee* Ottar Marius Andersen. An experienced and respected mariner he may have been at first unsure if the vessel had blown a boiler under its own steam. His suspicions were soon confirmed that the source was in fact that his ship had been torpedoed. This photograph here was later taken at the port of Fremantle in Perth.

Herman Claudell Dumas the 21 year old U.S. Navy Armed Guard and Seaman
1st Class from Spencer, Louisiana. Already sporting a broken arm he was
killed in Lifeboat #3 just as it was being launched from the impact of the second torpedo.

19 year old U.S. Navy Armed Guard Leon LeRoy Carrington from Sayre, Pennsylvania who also lost his life in Lifeboat #3 as it was being launched.

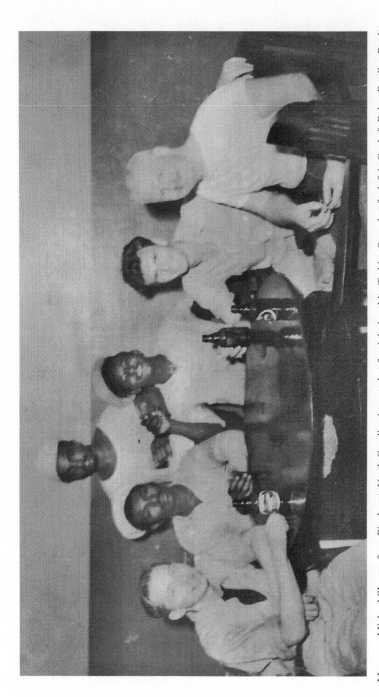

Messman Michael **Sherry** from Pinehurst, North Carolina is seated at far right in white T-shirt. Seated at far left is Cook & Baker Bradley **Pruitt** from Mt. Rainier, Maryland. Unfortunately the remainder cannot be positively identified, although two at least are thought to be possibly Earl Smith from Washington and Augustus Hoffler from Brooklyn, NY. It is figured that most if not all are fellow messmen or stewards enjoying a social occasion ashore maybe in Panama circa May 1944.

A group photograph of 12 of the U.S. Navy Armed Guards on board the *Fort Lee* taken before her fateful voyage. Those identified are: **Back row at far left:** George F. **Kasper**, Lyle J. **Atkinson**, Rowland R. **Crowe** (with eyes closed). Then possibly, but unconfirmed is Leon LeRoy **Carrington** killed in first torpedo strike. Next to him second from right is Warren S. **Finch**. Lastly on his immediate right is Orville D. **Adams. Front Row:** Seated at far left possibly Andrew **Lemanski**, second from left is James (Jim) M. **Wilson**, next **unknown**, Lee Roy **Prewitt** (third from right seated in the centre), then Harold J. **Holden** and lastly Herbert A. **Eaton** who were in Lifeboat #4.

Two separate images taken probably within several minutes of each other of unidentified crew on board the *Fort Lee* sometime in either late 1943 or early '44.

On board the *Fort Lee*. U.S. Navy Seaman 1st Class Lyle J. Atkinson from
Wisconsin is in the middle – the other two are unidentified.

James Marvin Wilson at graduation
prior to joining the Navy and the
Fort Lee in 1943.

Lyle Atkinson seen here ashore with what is thought to be possibly a Merchant Marine crewmate from the *Fort Lee* circa early 1944.

Ominous

The following evening of November 3, less than 24 hours after the *Fort Lee* took her final plunge into the depths, the *U-181* sighted another unidentified ship of about 7,000 gross tons steaming eastbound towards Australia. They commenced to give chase and attempted to close in on her. However now only armed with the deck mounted anti-aircraft gun after having used up the last two torpedoes it was decided that an attack on her was not worth the risk. Freiwald chose to

abort the pursuit and the submarine resumed her original south westerly course towards South Africa.

The U-boat never got close enough to the vessel itself to positively identify her. For all those aboard that unknown ship probably remained blissfully unaware and oblivious to this day that they were ever noticed or even much rather seen by the *U-181*.

Despite being a busy shipping lane and due to the suddenness of the attack that left the *Fort Lee's* aerial inoperable, no emergency message was emitted. Therefore at this particular stage most other shipping would have been apparently unaware that an enemy submarine was confirmed to be in the area. All the same, those in that eastbound steamer are no doubt very lucky for Otto Giese indicates that had they been better equipped, or at least had a supply of more torpedoes on board, they certainly would have indeed carried out an attack on her.

Lifeboat #6

All the while looking down on the events being played out below was the Milky Way which had commenced to put on her spectacular nightly show. Overhead was a generally clear sky as a kaleidoscope of stars illuminated themselves against a black backdrop. Some cloud, though not too much to blanket out the Southern Cross, that definitive constellation which embellishes the southern hemisphere, the four lifeboats numbered 1, 2, 4, and 6 would now spend their first night adrift out on the open sea. Already the temperature was plummeting towards zero. At least some were able to salvage the provisions and water that were in the five abandoned life rafts over into the lifeboats.

For the survivors, the rapid lowering of temperature at night and the uncomfortable privations of being a ship-wrecked sailor in a lifeboat would be something that all would have no choice but to accept. They were now at the mercy of the gods in the seemingly endless waters of the Indian Ocean. Many had suffered wounds, especially burns, particularly to the hands, wrists, arms and face. Besides Kasper who was nursing a suspected broken leg and the 2nd Mate Asher, there was also 35 year old Hughie Johnston in Lifeboat #2 the Pumpman from Parkersburg, Pennsylvania who had injuries to his ankle and right leg.

As they were scattered around it took about two hours or so to muster the four lifeboats together in the dark. Captain Andersen ordered that all four be secured together informing those around him that he would decide on what would be the best probable course of action to take during the night. As the diesel engines of the U-boat receded into the night everyone started to feel slightly safer and began to talk and light ciga-rettes again. Land, the nearest of which with the exception of some barren uninhabited islands well over 1,000 miles to the south was as Giese had indicated, over 1,900 miles away. Further to the west lay the islands of Mauritius then Madagascar and beyond that the east coast of Africa. To the north was Ceylon, India and South East Asia, half of which was under Japanese occupation. The rational choice was to try for the west coast of Australia.

They had company. Before long other uninvited guests had now arrived. Sharks, some measuring up to an estimated 15 feet in length began to menacingly circle the lifeboats. Attracted by the commotion and coupled with some odd in built sixth sense, they always seem to interpret peril at sea. The Captain motioned everybody not to make any undue noise or disturbance that would attract further the unwanted attention of these man eaters. The sharks stayed with them all through the night, continuously circling the four lifeboats until sunrise the next day.

First light arrived, where a true indicator of what the real situation was could now be properly assessed. It had been an uncomfortable night. Here the first opportunity arose to conduct a quick inventory of the emergency rations and exchange or top up and allot out equally the already existing bare rations held in each individual boat.

The four lifeboats sailed in company together until around 9.00 a.m. in the morning of the 3rd. Andersen had decided it best that they separate, figuring that between them, they each held a better chance of reaching land by going their own way. Notwithstanding that by remaining tied together was not a good option on the rough open seas as the waves presented the additional hazard of the boats crashing violently into each other. Thankfully at least the sharks were now evidently gone. They had mysteriously disappeared an hour or so after daylight on the first morning and were never seen again.

After severing their bounds they wished each other well. Some good humouredly as best could befit the situation, some with lament and uncertainty. Throughout the remainder of the day and into their second night out in the open sea, all four boats managed to keep within sight of each other until around 11.00 a.m. Saturday, November 4. Here the weather commenced to change. Strong currents coupled with likewise strong south westerly winds blew up which proceeded to disperse and carry them off. Those in Lifeboat #1 last saw their crewmates in Lifeboat #4 shortly before sunset that very same day.

Lifeboat #6 was the first to be launched. Paul Stauffer the Chief Engineer from Houston, Texas was at 51 years the eldest and most senior ranking. He automatically was placed in charge of the boat. The next oldest was 42 year old Francis [Frank] Joseph Smith, an Able Bodied seaman from Methuen, Massachusetts followed by three Messmen, 38 year old John Davis from Baltimore, 19 year old Earl Smith from Washington and Michael 'Pop' Sherry. With them also was 29 year old Roy Shaffer the First Engineer from Seattle, Washington.

This was followed by Zeb Page, who had his own tale of survival to tell from below decks, and 22 year old Bosun Jess C. Marcum from Big Stone Gap in West Virginia. In it too was 21 year old Augustus Hoffler, a Galleyman from New York City followed by 18 year old John L. Malec, a Wiper and second youngest in the boat who was from Baltimore. Lifeboat #6 had also taken on Jack Hennessy, Orville Adams and Bob Brookins the evening before at 9.45 pm. All three had transferred over from Lifeboat #1 due to overcrowding.

At 8.00 am the following morning on November 3, Armed Guards Jim Wilson and 23 year old William (Bill) Marion King from Bluefield, West Virginia, along with 18 year Gilbert Charles Share, a cook from Norfolk, Virginia, also transferred over into Lifeboat #6 from the Master's lifeboat. At the same time the badly injured Lyle Atkinson was exchanged from Lifeboat #6 over into Lifeboat #2 on account of his burnt hands and face.

And lastly there was young Messman Billy Mootz who at just 16 years of age was not only the youngest in the boat but also the youngest to have been serving on board the ship. It had only been just barely two weeks since he had first joined the *Fort Lee* back in Abadan. He had abandoned ship after the second torpedo impacted, diving straight overboard into the water. With no choice but to swim through thick oil, he began to make good progress but started to panic when he realised the distance he had quickly gained between himself and the sinking ship. He started to panic. Here the young adventurous sailor from Kansas was lucky. His cries of help alerted those in the already launched Lifeboat #6 which was some distance off circling the sinking tanker attempting to pick up stray survivors that had become stranded in the water. They made their way over to where he was.

Inadvertently Billy Mootz's screams for help saved the men in Lifeboat #6. Still on board the sinking tanker Armed Guards on the after boat deck mistakenly sighted what they thought was the shadowy outline of the submarine's conning tower coming into view, less than a 100 yards away. Instead it was the approaching lifeboat. The 5 inch gun was prepared and the breech slammed shut and they took aim, when suddenly they heard Billy's screams. A near disaster was averted.

Hauled in over the side, he was completely covered in thick brownish black gooey oil. Billy never thought he would ever get it out of his skin. When Stauffer was later informed of this near miss in the water he remarked that it was an act of God which made Billy scream.

The lifeboat now contained 17 men. Since separating from the rest they had decided to head north east. They believed that they were in the north-east current above Australia and at first figured that they could reach the coast in a little over 30 days or so –*if they could last that long.*

Given the little supplies of emergency food and water that was with them, the daily allowance in the boat was 12 ounces of fresh water. It was housed in a 5 gallon container and drawn out by a type of dipper at two ounces at a time. With the possibility of spending quite a time in a lifeboat at sea after being torpedoed, the fresh drinking water had to be strictly rationed and a dipper, shaped like a spoon, was used to dish out the same amount for everyone.

Included in this daily ration, known as *sea rations* were six malted milk tablets, which were basically useless due to the limited fresh water. Allotted to each man per day was one dried cracker biscuit, one small piece of chocolate about an inch square and a one third ounce of pemmican. Pemmican is a type of lean fresh meat that has been dried out and pounded. Its origins are North American Indian and can be mixed with fat and other ingredients like nuts, shredded coconut and raisins to make an ideal emergency ration.

The nights grew extremely cold where the temperature lowered dramatically, often down to sub zero. The men had to group close together to stay warm. Sleep, if any, was a broken affair where only 'nodding off' could be achieved unless out of simple pure exhaustion one could find some semblance of slumber. Soon the weather changed and in no time the wind began to constantly blow and the waves became higher, sometimes almost swamping the boat. So much so that on several occasions they could not bail water out fast enough just to keep afloat. The toilet needed no imagination.

Chief Engineer Paul Stauffer kept a daily log book. In clear handwritten text with a lead pencil, he commenced by marking down all those who were in it, their age, rank and providing full residential addresses from where they all originated. Then for each subsequent day that they were marooned at sea he entered important details recording the weather and sea conditions and the times of sunrise and sunset. Every day the remaining amount of provisions were all carefully measured with Stauffer making note of the times when the precious water and food were rationed out. He provides an invaluable and first hand window into the privations that they daily endured. It also reflects how the other lifeboats would have similarly fared as well.

It is more than appropriate that Paul Stauffer directly relates the story here first hand. From his logbook in Lifeboat #6 that has survived all these years, the following has been re-written verbatim - word for word.

We pick it up from Friday, November 3 1944 the very next day after the sinking.

Midnight–27°S lat. 83°E long. Drifting north wind, light calm sea.

Sunrise 5.35 am. Drifting, light north wind, calm sea.

Noon- South x East course, light N x W wind, calm sea.

Sunset 6.20 pm. South x East course, light N x W wind, calm sea.

On checking over survivors at dawn we found that of the six boats only three [other than our own] were to be seen and none of the five life rafts were sighted. After the exchange of men with the Captain's boat the Third Mates boat was sighted and joined with us. Now we had four boats and after a head count found we had a total of 66 men.

Set a course south x east and headed for the nearest land which was Australia 2,000 miles away. Sighted four of the ships liferafts but no survivors. Took out all provisions from the rafts, the water and all other equipment which we could use. Each boat [that is lifeboat] *stripped one raft each.*

We set four hour watch tillers in charge of 1st Assistant Engineer, Bosun, A.B. Smith and Oiler Hennessy, who was later temporarily relieved by Jr 3rd Page because of inflamed eyes from swimming in the oil. Treated Hennessy, Brookins, E. Smith, King and Adams for their eyes, account of swimming in the water. Also treated Hennessy's foot with sulfonamide powder, taped up King's ankle and Adams' knee.
Also Chief's ankle.

Issued quarter can pemmican per man, two 'C' ration biscuits and 2 ounces of water at 6.00 pm. Attempting to keep other boats in sight through the night. Insufficient clothing, used boat cover to blanket sleeping men. Poor headway. North east current.

Stauffer makes the point in brackets that he did not find out the true number of survivors until later and seemingly may have added it afterwards to the page. A common affliction as we have seen here and for many shipwrecked sailors is the awful condition of one's eyes being inflamed caused by being exposed to the oil in the water. The misery is amplified by having very little to treat it with.

Saturday, November 4 1944
Sunrise 5.35 am. Light northwest wind. Calm sea. East x South course.
Sunset 6.25 pm. Northerly wind. Sea choppy. East x North course.

Checked provisions and found that we had on board 2864.2 ounces of food and 278 quarts of water. Nice sunny day. Sighted 3 lifeboats dead ahead about 1.5 miles off. Broke out the oars for exercise. All hands in good spirits. Issued rations at 8.45 am. 2 oz Logan bar and 2 oz water per man. Later increasing wind made sea choppy with a long swell so the watch was doubled in case of an emergency. Sighted lifeboats off port bow. Issued rations then bedded down for the night. Sighted flares on Hennessy's watch who estimated them to be about 3 miles ahead of us. This we decided that it could not be the other boats so it must have been the sub tailing us and waiting for a rescue vessel.

Making very little headway into north east swells. Night chilly. All hands shivering visibly from cold. Men were solemnly informed that a 36-50 day voyage lay ahead of them unless we were rescued. Hoisted our large distress flag on a boat hook over the main mast during the day and struck same at night. Treated men for cuts, bruises and burns especially 1st Assistant [Roy Shaffer] *whose face and hands were burnt results of ruptured steam lines.*

They weren't to know at the time, but on the point that the submarine was still in the vicinity they could be wrong. Apart from tailing the unknown east bound steamer the day before the *U-181* was long gone and had left the area. By the 4th she had swung right around, heading well away to the south west.

Freiwald was keen to leave the area as soon as possible, should his own safety be compromised. The *Fort Lee* survivors thought that it was remaining in the vicinity to launch an attack on a possible rescue vessel. However the U-boat had no torpedoes left, so therefore could not really launch another strike, hence their abandonment of chasing the other east bound freighter that they had sighted. Apart from pursuing this freighter there is no evidence to suggest that the *U-181* indeed stayed in the area for several days after sinking the *Fort Lee*. Therefore the origin of these flares remains unknown and inconclusive. For the record a Logan bar was a D ration, a U.S. Army ration staple made by Hershey's Chocolate.

Sunday, November 5 1944

Midnight - course east x north. Fair north wind with a choppy sea.

Sunrise 5.30 am. Fair north wind, choppy sea, long swells.

Noon - same course, fair north east wind, moderate swells.

Sunset 6.35 pm. East x north course, north east wind, moderate swells.

2753.7 ounces of provisions, 276 quarts of water

Day partly cloudy, sea choppy and swells throwing boat off course. Lost sight of the other lifeboats during the night. Broke out two small oars at 6.45 am and began rowing on starboard side to keep into the sea and on a fair course. Issued rations and water at 7.00 am. Rechecked all provisions in boat. Issued rations and water at 5.30 pm.

Morning ration is usually 1 to 2 ounces chocolate and 2 ounces of water. Evening rations were quarter can of pemmican and one 'C' ration biscuit and 2oz of water. Malted milk tablets were distributed whenever anyone wanted them. Very few of the men will eat them at all. Still treating men for cuts and bruises. Night chilly. Men cold.

Monday, November 6 1944
Midnight – course east x north. East wind with light swell.
Sunrise 5.25 am. East wind with light swell.
Noon - East wind with light swell.
Sunset 6.40 pm. Course east x south. East wind with light swell.

Sunny and partly cloudy with a light chilly breeze. Issued rations at 7.30 am. Lookout Adams reported dark puff of smoke on horizon. Threw a daylight signal overboard. No other evidence of smoke of ship was sighted. Issued rations at 6.00 pm.

About 10.45 pm flare sighted off port bow. At 11.30 another flare in same direction. We did not answer signal for to our opinion it is the sub again. We decided that the smoke sighted earlier in the day was from the subs diesels.

Still bucking N.E. swells. F.J. Smith A.B. right elbow inflamed and infected after effects of torpedoing. Night chilly – as usual.

After this date the weather began to turn for the worse. Their plight over the next 48 hours was to be tested. Again they were mistaken that the smoke came from the U-boat. It could have been possibly from vessels that were seen in the distance but too far away for them to be noticed as reported much later by Lifeboat #1. Again it is unknown where the flares may have originated from, possibly one of these ships.

Tuesday, November 7 1944

Midnight – south x east course. Light east wind with light swells.

Sunrise 5.22 am. Light east wind with light.

Noon - north east course. Light south west gale. Very heavy seas & swell.

Sunset 6.45 pm. North-east course, light south west gale. Very heavy seas & swell.

2672.1 ounces provisions, 270 quarts water

Still bucking swells from N.E. Wind began to shift at 8.00 am. With current north east direction. Much rejoicing for our charts showed a cold stream about where we were and we thought this was it. At 9.45 am swells increasing and sea becoming very rough. Light gale blowing up. Wind, sea and swells increasing until finally at 2.30 am next morning the storm abated, leaving the lifeboat tossing around in the cross swells and leaving the 1st Assistant and Hennessy exhausted for they handled the tiller and the sheet continuously through the storm.

Issued rations at 9.30 am. Rained and men took water from the sails and all hands had their fill. Secured the lookout and rode out the storm as previously described. Night extremely cold as rain had left blankets wet and everyone damp. Men in good spirits account of forward progress. Boat shipped water several times during night, very close shaves. Boat was threatened to be swamped time & time again. Luck and Providence were with us!

Smithy's elbow still infected. Used salt water compress and heat bag on same.

A salt water compress involves treating a wound by soaking a square cotton cloth or cotton ball or any cloth material at hand in usually heated salt water and placing on the area to be treated and firmly attaching or holding it place until the compress is cold. Curiously salt water itself can be a curative and possesses many healing properties.

Wednesday, November 8 1944

Midnight – N course, SW wind. Heavy seas and swells.

Sunrise 5.20 am. N course, SW wind. moderate swells.

Noon – ESE course, SW wind. Medium swells.

Sunset 6.50 ESE course, SW x W very light wind. Medium swells.

2631 ounces provisions, 268 quarts water

Holding a due east course. Boat taking swells broadside but making favourable progress. Sky overcast and very chilly. Issued rations at 7.30 am. Been fishing constantly but having no luck. Wind shifting periodically all afternoon and evening causing very slow headway. Issued rations at 5.45 pm.

Bedded down for the evening which is a laugh for it is impossible to get much sleep. All hands are satisfied if they can keep warm. Night cold and chilly again, sky overcast. Wind dying, sails buffing, unable to get steerage way. Taking swells broadside, rolling and pitching bad and shipping water.

Very discouraging to say the least as a long voyage seems inevitable, but all hands seem to be in good spirits. All still can laugh at our predicament. We all laugh at Hennessy, who is still oil soaked from head to toe. He's afraid of becoming bald on account of the fuel oil in his hair.

Hope however was the one thing that everyone still clung to. It gripped every man when weighed against the uncertainty if they would be rescued. Despite that they were seemingly in good spirits, even managing to still find humour in the reference to Hennessy's hair. Stauffer, who was no doubt one of those instrumental in keeping up morale makes several notes on the men's state of mind. All felt that they were in this together, they had no choice. Nevertheless all co-operated, all were shipmates and all were now bounded by that peculiar and extraordinary camaraderie only found in times of extreme and adverse situations.

Would they ever see and be re-united with loved ones again? Home, would they ever see home again? People like Michael Sherry who had a wife and three sons all under nine years of age. Isolated in the middle of the Indian Ocean, home might as well be billions of light years away. A week had now passed since the attack on the *Fort Lee*. If any of the men had ever silently or even openly prayed throughout their ordeal, somebody must have been listening, for their prayers were about to be answered.

Survivor! 38 year old Galleyman Michael Joseph Sherry, one of the 17 men from Lifeboat #6 that arrived in Albany on board the *Tumacacori* in a photograph taken just after having been transferred to Perth.

John (Jack) Leo Hennessy a 22 year old from Minneapolis seen here in a photograph also taken in Fremantle, Perth. He was thrown into the water by the force of the blast. Like many he was completely covered in oil.

Jack Hennessy at age 20 just
after joining the Merchant
Marine in 1942.

James (Jim) Marvin Wilson, one of three U.S. Navy Armed Guards in the lifeboat.
70 years later in the year 2014 he is the last known living survivor from Lifeboat #6.

Seaman 1st class Orville D. Adams *(left)* who along with Hennessy assisted in helping the wounded 2nd Mate for which both were afterwards commended.

Seaman 1st Class William Marion King *(below)* the third Armed Guard in Lifeboat #6. It was he who first sighted the *Tumacacori* on the morning of November 9.

Billy Mootz seen here after being transferred from Albany to Perth. At just 16 years of age he was the youngest on board and had only signed onto the *Fort Lee* just a couple of weeks before in Abadan. He dived into the water and ended up becoming completely coated with oil. His cries for help saved Lifeboat #6 from friendly fire.

November 9 1944 – a photograph taken from on
board the *Tumacacori* as Lifeboat #6 comes in
to view after being sighted.

Rescue! A rare photograph taken by an unknown U.S. Navy Armed Guard from the *Tumacacori* captures the exact moment Lifeboat #6 comes alongside. 14 men can evidently be counted, the other three must be under the makeshift cover. Oars are stacked up as one fellow can be seen reaching out to a line that has been thrown to them. Looking directly down judging by the hair colour it is thought perhaps that the man in centre near the bow may possibly be Michael Sherry. This photo was given to Jim Wilson.

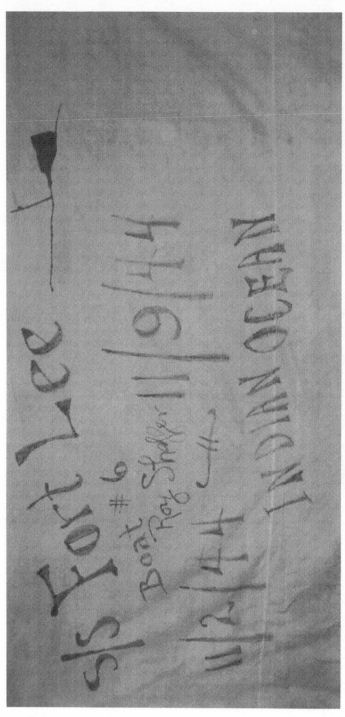

The distress flag from the *Fort Lee* that was hoisted and flown from Lifeboat #6. Bright orange in colour, after their rescue all 17 men signed it not only as a symbol of their comradeship and unity as shipmates, but also that they had been rescued. Here First Asst. Engineer Roy Shaffer's signature can be clearly seen as can Zeb B. Page just be made out (*lower left*). It is marked in black pencil with the dates of her sinking and their final rescue at sea. A caricature picture of a ship sinking has also been drawn on the top right hand corner. It survives today in the proud safe care of the Hennessy family.

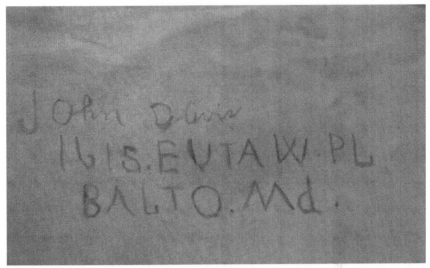

John Davis a 38 year old Messman clearly leaves his signature on the flag
from Lifeboat #6 along with his Baltimore address...

...as also Jesse Marcum from West Virginia.

SS Tumacacori

The morning of Thursday, November 9 1944 dawned. The first rays of sunlight offered the bleak prospect of being another day blurring into another. From horizon to horizon the seemingly endless waters of the Indian Ocean were relentless at denying no sanctuary or comfort for the 17 men in Lifeboat #6. The small amount of emergency supplies, though carefully measured, were now starting to run perilously low. Surprisingly morale was still high, despite the uncertainty of whether they would be rescued or not.

Sunrise 5.15 a.m.

Moderate sea, westerly wind.

No change in the weather. Broke out oars to get further S.E. to get in a westerly current. Issued rations at 7.40 a.m.

Suddenly smoke was sighted!

Vessel sighted by King at 7.50 a.m. on our port quarter. Hennessy tossed over a smoke pot and the vessel apparently sighted us for she changed course and headed straight for us.

From over the horizon the solid outline of a ship emerged into view. It was Armed Guard Bill King that had first sighted it. Jack Hennessy wasted no time in attempting to get the ships attention. At the very risk of capsizing in the ensuing excitement, every possible means at their disposal was employed to gain the attention of this very possible saviour.

The SS *Tumacacori* was another T2-A1-SE tanker just like the *Fort Lee*. She was relatively new having only been launched back on May 16 1944 following construction by the Kaiser Swan Island Shipyard [Yard #68] at Portland, Oregon. At 10,448 tons her official number was 245862. The keel was laid down on March 31 1944 taking only 40 days to construct followed by a further 30 days to be fitted out – some 77 days in all. The vessel was named after a small settlement in Arizona that was originally founded by Franciscan monks in the late 1700's. During the 1870's the site became a target for repeated raids by Apache Indians. Today the Tumacacori Historical National Park which borders on the edge of the present day town of Carmen, is a popular tourist and holiday destination.

Costing of $2,686,140.00 [U.S.] she was delivered to Pacific Tankers as the operating agents for the U.S. War Shipping Administration on June 14 1944.

For her maiden voyage, the *Tumacacori* left the port of Martinez, California in August. Since 1915 Martinez has been the site of several major oil refineries. The first one was constructed by the Shell Oil Company that quickly grew where today it is still a significant petroleum processing centre. It took seventeen days to sail across the Pacific Ocean and arrive at Sydney, Australia. Her cargo consisted of high octane aviation fuel which was intended for P-38 fighter planes of which a supply were boxed up in wooden crates lining her decks. The Lockheed P-38 Lightning was a revolutionary twin engine strike fighter. They were destined to be unloaded at Calcutta in India for the U.S. Air Force. Like other tankers the

Tumacacori carried almost the identical complement of 45 Merchant Navy crewmembers and 25 U.S. Navy Guards. One of those crew members was 18 year old Elmer Charles Fought.

Born on July 13 1927 in Oakland, California he had only enlisted in the Merchant Marines five months before on August 8 1944. Attending Santa Cruz High School he took on a trade and industrial course. He was also vice-president of his junior class, played football and became captain of the basketball team. A month prior to enlisting, Elmer married his high school sweetheart Euna on July 7 1944. Now he was half a world away working as a Galleyman and steward with the rank of 2nd Cook and Baker on board an oil tanker in the middle of the Indian Ocean.

The Master of the *Tumacacori* was 53 year old English born Sidney Fargo. He is described by Fought as a competent and experienced seaman who was fair and strict when he needed to be but at the same time a sympathetic and generous character. The son of a grocer, rumour has it that he ran away from home to sea as a young boy to escape the dominance of his two older sisters. After originally migrating to Australia he later left for the United States just as the first conscription plebiscite commenced in 1916 at the height of the First World

War. As it turned out, despite two referendums, Australia on both occasions rejected conscription. America at this time was still neutral and it was here that he first joined her Merchant Marine. Later on a voyage to South America, a young Fargo was locked up in Valparaiso, Chile when he and others jumped ship. By the time of America's entry into World War Two 25 years later, he had become a merchant ship's captain.

During the voyage across the Pacific there was one crewman who had been sick the entire time since leaving Martinez. His illness had rendered him so weak that he was unable to leave his bunk, let alone perform any work duties. Fargo perhaps not quite understanding the situation, decided to look into the matter personally and pay him a visit. He discovered a young able bodied seaman, his first time away at sea, seriously ill in his cabin. It was clear and evident what the ailment was and Fargo diagnosed it immediately.

Making his way up to the galley he found young Elmer Fought at work there. He was slightly surprised when the Captain enquired, "Do we have oranges on board?"

"Yes sir, of course we do" replied Fought.

"Will you gather a bunch together, we have a sick man on board and I know just the cure." Fargo selected a knife and commenced slicing up enough to make a supply of fresh orange juice. The ill crewman was suffering from an apparent case of scurvy. As every mariner knows when not on duty or watch, anything to keep occupied and stave off long hours of boredom was always welcomed. Arriving off Sydney Harbour the crew joked how strange it was pulling into Sydney as the captain's first name was also Sidney.

The *Tumacacori* spent the next 10 days here in dry dock having the boilers repaired. During this time Captain Fargo permitted himself to go ashore and visit his two sisters Elizabeth Jane Morgan and Ada Whitfield both of whom had by now married and migrated out to Australia themselves some years earlier. Meantime the crew were able to sample the sights and sounds of a bustling wartime Sydney. On one particular day a lucky handful were invited to go sailing in a private yacht on the harbour. Elmer Fought was one. At just 18 he had never sailed in a yacht before and the trip, again organised by the Red Cross where lunch was served out on the water, left quite an impression on him.

Before departing, arranged to take on board were some 250 cases of beer. They were big bottles, what is in Australia colloquially known as 'king browns' which provided small curiosity for the crew. The *Tumacacori* made her way down the New South Wales coastline rounding into Bass Strait, the stretch of water that separates the mainland and Tasmania and sailed westbound across the Great Australian Bight to arrive at the port of Fremantle, Western Australia. From here it was on to Colombo, Ceylon then up to Madras, India where half of the aviation fuel was offloaded. Following a narrow course up off the east coast of India, in the Bay of Bengal she finally arrived at Calcutta today known as *Kolkata*.

Due to the water being too shallow up the Hooghly River they berthed near a refinery at the port of Budge Budge located some 19 miles south west of Calcutta. This area has always been a central hub for extensive oil refineries and jute factories. Jute being a fibre made from vegetable matter that can be spun into rope, cloth and bags. It was here at Budge Budge that the crates of P-38's Lightning's and the remainder of the high octane fuel were unloaded.

It was now early October and just on the cusp of the wet monsoonal season commencing. The next assignment for the tanker was over to Bahrain Island. Her cargo was to be the same Navy bunker C fuel oil that the *Fort Lee* had been carrying – all 7 million gallons of it. The *Tumacacori* departed the Budge Budge oil docks just before 10.00 a.m. on October 15 1944. She anchored that night in the mouth of the river for 'gas freeing'. This is a process for cleaning the cargo tanks on commercial oil tankers. Air from outside is blown into the tanks to purge and remove the remaining poisonous gases that develop and remain from the storage of crude oil, thus lifting the oxygen level to normal, usually to around 20 per cent, so crew can then enter.

She departed Calcutta at 5.30 a.m. the following morning. After crossing the Arabian Sea in ballast, with an average speed of 15 knots, she arrived at the entrance to the Persian Gulf on October 24 where she was ordered to stop by a shore signal station for identification. At 8.55 p.m. the vessel was cleared and able to proceed overnight to Bahrain arriving there at three o'clock the following afternoon on October 25. At five minutes past seven she tied up at the oil docks. Two days later after receiving her full load of oil the *Tumacacori* departed Bahrain at 10.17 a.m. on Tuesday, October 24.

The *Fort Lee* had only departed Abadan on Saturday, October 21. Both vessels were sailing through the Persian Gulf in opposite directions within days of each other. But by the time the *Tumacacori* arrived on the 24th, the *Fort Lee* was ahead of her and she was long gone to the south in the Indian Ocean so there was no chance the two may have sighted each other. However after making her way back through the Straits of Hormuz, the course for the unescorted *Tumacacori* would be almost identical to that of the *Fort Lee*. The only real difference being that the *Fort Lee's* first destination was Brisbane, whereas the *Tumacacori's* was Sydney.

So far the voyage had been uneventful. At 10.00 o'clock in the morning of Saturday, November 4 1944 target practice was held using all guns focusing on a surface objective. This was usually a daily event, along with signalling drill, that could last anywhere between 15 to 45 minutes. On this day during the exercise there were no casualties or misfires. However a few hours later the vessel would experience a new problem all of her own.

At ten minutes past one the same afternoon the *Tumacacori* was dead in the water. There was apparent engine trouble. The ship was placed on high alert. Every engineer, electrician, oiler and mechanic was assigned. The Armed Guards and lookouts were placed on alert. What the hell was it? Master Fargo was frustrated. Here was his ship, completely disabled and presenting herself as a perfect sitting duck for any enemy submarine. Not to mention the delay.

After wallowing helplessly for the next 14 hours the fault was discovered and finally repaired. At 4.08 in the morning she was mobile again. The break down had been caused by an apparent short circuit in the main electric panel board in the engine room. But the lost time had to be now made up. On November 5 at 20.20 hours Fargo sent a radio message received by Colombo explaining the delay. The date and time group was 051412Z.

On Wednesday, November 8 1944 at 2.00 o'clock in the afternoon a BAMS [British and Allied Merchant Ships] broadcast radio message was received by the *Tumacacori* giving instructions to be on the lookout for a lifeboat in their path. This was the confidential message sent out by Colombo after having earlier picked up the intercepted transmitter signal sent out initially by Lifeboat #2 (*see page 313*).

Later that same evening Galleyman Fought was off duty in the mess hall watching other men playing poker. With him was fellow Californian Howard Bradley, a deck hand from San Mateo. Among the group were 'Spider' another Galleyman and 'Tex' (there always seems to be somebody named Tex on board an American merchant ship) a big burly Bosuns Mate with a striking crop of red hair and a large handlebar moustache to match. However the following morning would bring an unexpected surprise for all.

Thursday, November 9 1944 dawned. The sea had started to calm itself to a relatively moderate swell. Even the wind had abated a little. Unlike the *Fort Lee* the *Tumacacori* was actually sailing a zigzag path. Suddenly at 7.58 a.m. the look-out saw Hennessy's smoke and lifeboat. There appeared to be men in it. On board news travelled fast by word of mouth. From the bridge Captain Fargo immediately ordered the ship to alter course. Crew began racing up on deck to watch the tanker manoeuvre closer to meet where the lone lifeboat was. It was now 8.30 a.m.

Then she came to a halt. The position was $27°30'$S-$86°42'$E.

From the aft deck looking down on to the well deck, waves could be seen breaking across. The well deck sides are 3 to 6 feet above the waterline. Traditionally well decks were decks placed lower than the aft and fore decks. However their modern application well decks between with the space that could be used for aircraft and many other uses.

Elmer Fought recalls standing at the stern. A rope ladder with wooden steps was hoisted over the side as the lifeboat came within distance to the ship. Steadily they began to climb up over the side of the hull to come aboard. In all 17 were counted. Most were just wearing dirty white T-shirts and blue denim jeans. They appeared to be very windblown, oil stained, some nursing small wounds. Obviously shaken and tired, but relieved.

Relief was probably an understatement. It ended a week of uncertainty for the men. In that time they had travelled about 205 miles. But it sure felt good to be finally saved and to be rescued by a fellow American ship no less. Who was ever going to argue with that? But it could have been anybody...so long as it was friendly and not a Jap or German. They were all seen to and given immediate treatment. Hennessy for one was raced off to be showered down. He, like so many had found that salt water does not wash off the thick, claggy and almost claustrophobic effect that oil has when one has been dipped in it from head to foot.

The now empty lifeboat was not saved. At 8.50 a.m. Lifeboat #6 was destroyed. Cast adrift it was sunk by gunfire aimed into the bottom of her by the *Tumacacori's* own Naval Guards. They fired 180 rounds of 20mm ammunition into it as they sailed away. But as Stauffer later wrote, *"only after being riddled innumerable times. She went down stubbornly just like her mother."*

He draws an irony to the disposal of the lifeboat and the *Fort Lee*. It had been their 'home' for the last week, holding them in good stead. It was sunk in a deluge of bullet holes, a lamentable but necessary goodbye.

The rescued men began to relate their story. One of them to do so was 'Pop' Sherry. By describing that they had been victims of a torpedo attack by a German U-boat caused great concern for the Captain. It emphasised not so much the surprise of an enemy submarine operating late in the war when reversals for Germany were being reported on a daily basis, but more so that it was on patrol in the Indian Ocean. An alert was immediately placed on board the vessel and the watch doubled. Fargo by witnessing the results firsthand with the 17 shipwrecked mariners he now had on board confirmed to him that these were still dangerous waters. His own ship could now be jeopardised and become perhaps the next target. Who knows where this U-boat was if it was still lurking out there somewhere?

Under instructions from Fargo at 1900 hours the radio operator sent on ahead a message that was received by the Australian Station advising that they had 17 survivors on board rescued from the fellow American tanker *Fort Lee*. An additional message with further information was sent at 0500 hours the very next morning November 10 – date and time 091537Z. Being en route to Sydney by sailing across the bottom part of Australia, Fargo was informed that his most convenient and best possible port to disembark them would be

Albany, a small port town located on the southern coast of Western Australia.

Meantime the rescued group of men were shown on board the *Tumacacori* to cabins and bunks where fresh water, hot beverages and food was offered. After nearly a week in an open lifeboat it was readily accepted with overwhelming thanks and gratitude. Armed Guard James Wilson remembers, "We were put in bunks and fed soup to stretch our stomachs. Later we were told that our stomachs had shrunk and were the size of an apple."

Eighteen year old Galleyman Elmer Fought assisted to their needs by escorting several of them down to the ships stores for new clean shirts and other basic essentials. There was a feeling of overall good will permeating throughout the ship that they had participated in rescuing fellow mariners from immediate jeopardy – a testimony to the first law of the sea and that is to lend assistance to fellow sailors.

With the ever clear and present danger that still lurked beneath the water, Fargo wasted no time in making for Albany. Even though she was fully laden with her cargo of oil, the turbo-electric engines spent the next five days at maximum speed to reach there. Galleyman Fought throughout this part of the journey often spoke to and visited each and every one of the survivors as they continued to recuperate from their ordeal.

On the morning of Tuesday, November 14 1944 five days after having been picked up, the *Tumacacori* arrived at Albany. It was exactly 7.09 a.m. She swung around to enter the impressive expanse of King George Sound, the outer harbour of Albany. With Limestone Head off to portside and Breaksea Island at her starboard, she made for the entrance to Princess Royal Harbour. However this is where it becomes interesting.

The *Tumacacori* did not enter Princess Royal Harbour. Nor did she dock or berth at either the now long gone Deep Water Jetty old Town Jetty. Instead the tanker actually pulled up to halt just short of Ataturk Entrance, the name today given to the narrow channel that leads in to Princess Royal Harbour. Here, still in King George Sound due to the draft (the depth of the tanker sitting in the water due to the load) she dropped anchor. The weather conditions were calm and the sea was moderate to mild.

Fargo, whilst equally sympathetic with the plight of his fellow seafaring countrymen, nevertheless was keen to dislodge them as quickly as possible and resume the journey to Sydney.

Through a coded radio message the *Tumacacori* had announced her arrival to the authorities on shore. At 9.00 o'clock a small auxiliary lighter called the *St. John* part of the small group of local Albany Naval Patrol boats had been prepared on standby and sailed out to rendezvous with the tanker to take off the 17 survivors from the *Fort Lee* and land them ashore.

"I was again standing on the stern watching the proceedings where the launch pulled up alongside of us on the portside. We watched them embark over the side down into the lighter using the rope ladder with wooden steps. The process was the same but in reverse as it had been when they came aboard. We watched them depart and that was it." The lighter then moved away and headed back in towards shore. Elmer Fought stresses the point "that it appeared to everyone that the Captain was in a hurry and keen to get going again."

Quite rightly Fargo did not want to 'hang around' especially after the earlier delay incurred from breaking down in the middle of the Indian Ocean. It was still wartime and the *Tumacacori's* precious cargo of oil was much needed. Despite honouring the importance of rescuing fellow sailors at sea and fellow countrymen for that matter, orders were orders and delays and or distractions were to be avoided. The entire process from arrival and to land the men ashore then depart again had taken less than an hour and a half.

At 9.30 a.m. it was all over. Without delay the *Tumacacori* fired up her engines and proceeded to manoeuvre back out to sea. Passing both Breaksea and Michaelmas Islands, two prominent features in King George Sound, she headed back out into the Southern Ocean before turning hard a port and setting a course eastbound in that unpredictable stretch of water also known as the Great Australian Bight.

And that concludes the *Tumacacori's* brief visit to Albany. She played her role and performed her duty. Despite censorship and the like, it is with assured confidence to surmise that no resident in Albany at the time was aware that this transition had ever taken place. Apart from a handful of local port officials and naval officials, history tells us that is the case. The Harbour Master entered in the Port of Albany Register of Inwards Movements ledger for the date November 14 1944 the name of the vessel, her ownership and its destination to and from. In the column under the heading titled remarks, he has simply stated, '*In distress. To land survivors.*'

In a little over a month's time the little *St John* would perform another similar task when she rescued the entire crew from the Greek freighter *Michael J. Goulandris* that had run aground and sunk off Windy Harbour, further along the rugged southern coast of Western Australia west of Albany.

The *Tumacacori* arrived back in Sydney on November 19 tying up at Bradleys Head at three o'clock. Bunkers were taken on and the vessel was shifted to berth number 5 Darling Harbour for engine repairs and to take on stores. The next stopover was Hollandia, New Guinea. Located on the northern side of New Guinea, since 1962 it is better known today as Jarapura. Departing Sydney on November 24 at an average speed of 14 knots she arrived at Hollandia at 7.15 in the evening of December 1 1944.

Here, so the related story goes, the Harbour Master refused to let the tanker enter due the submarine nets already being in place. Permission would be granted for her to enter port the following morning. Venting displeasure at this decision, Captain Fargo in no uncertain terms informed the Harbour Master that he had a full cargo of oil on board and he was not going allow his vessel to become a perfect sitting duck for any Japanese sub waiting outside of the entrance. He had already recently rescued one lifeboat of fellow mariners who were victims of a submarine attack. He duly informed the Harbour Master that he was entering port whether he liked it or not.

Afterwards the tanker then proceeded to the Philippines where it anchored about 12 miles (20 kilometres) off the coast of Luzon. This was just after the Battle of Leyte Gulf, still the largest naval battle in history and the beginning of the Allied invasion of the Philippines, wresting it from Japanese control. The *Tumacacori's* role was to act as floating petrol station refuelling all types of vessels. In fact on one occasion Elmer Fought recalls being woken in the middle of the night by "a hell of a din and commotion going on." Getting up to go and discover the cause he recalls,

"That there were three destroyers hooked up to us, and we were pumping bunker fuel into them all at the same time. It was an awesome sight to watch them when they got ready to take off and peel away from the ship."

The vessel then made its way across the Pacific through the Panama Canal to the island of Aruba off the coast of Venezuela. On the return journey back in Panama a group went ashore and missed the curfew of being back on board by 11.00 p.m. As it turned out they ended up in jail for having caused a ruckus at one of the local bars. The Master would no doubt have to now go and bail them out. The task however fell to the First Mate as it was the Captain himself along with the Purser and the Chief Engineer that was amongst the group locked up – apparently something that was not unfamiliar for Fargo. The *Tumacacori* made for the Pacific to Enewetak Island part of an atoll in the Marshall Islands. Fought describes:

"The island appeared to be just a couple of beat up palm trees sticking out above the water. Once we got closer it looked like to be no more than about 18 inches above sea level. All around about 100 ships were at anchor." From here the tanker proceeded to Guam and then on to Tinian Island.

"We arrived just a few days after our forces had taken it. We unloaded our fuel and pumped it out to other ships there. A group of us were permitted to go ashore on Tinian where I saw large craters, like big pot holes from all the exploding shells. Before long though we were all ordered back on board ship because they were still fighting on the other side of the island."

The *Tumacacori* survived the war and was sold to the Greek shipping line Petros J. Goulandris and Sons. In 1948 it was renamed the SS *Petros*. Ten years later in 1955 she was converted to a bulk carrier flying under the United Shipping & Trading Company flag of Greece. Five years later in 1960 she was sold yet once again to the Belmar Shipping Corporation based in Piraeus. Finally after 19 years at sea, she was taken to Osaka in Japan and scrapped in 1963.

A post war photograph of SS *Petros* formerly the SS *Tumacacori* that rescued the 17 men in lifeboat #6 and bought them to Albany.

Sidney Fargo the Master of the *Tumacacori* seen here in an undated post war photograph at his home near Felton, Santa Cruz, California.

Galleyman Elmer C. Fought taken in early 1944 at his high school graduation prior to joining the United States Merchant Marine at age 18.

A snapshot of some of the crew from the *Tumacacori* taken in Panama City after the *Fort Lee* incident. Elmer Fought is third from left.

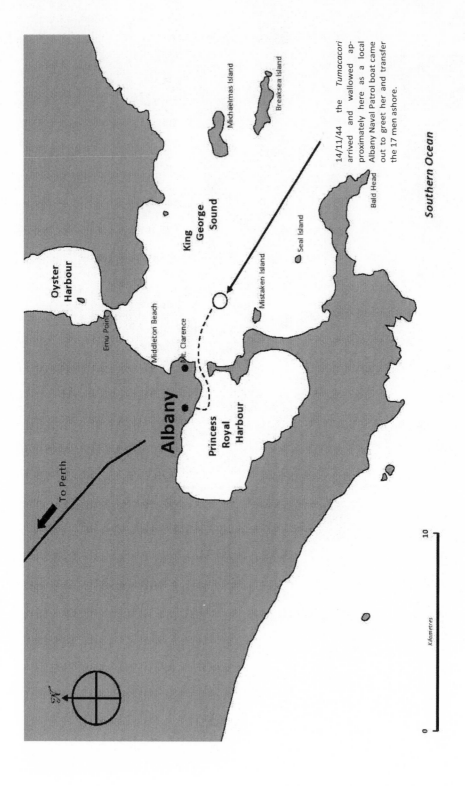

14/11/44 the *Tumacacori* arrived and wallowed approximately here as a local Albany Naval Patrol boat came out to greet her and transfer the 17 men ashore.

Southern Ocean

To Perth

Albany

Oyster Harbour

Emu Point

Middleton Beach

Mt. Clarence

Princess Royal Harbour

King George Sound

Michaelmas Island

Breaksea Island

Mistaken Island

Seal Island

Bald Head

0   10

Kilometres

A view of Albany circa early 1940's from Mount Melville showing both the Deep Water Jetty and Town Jetty (at right) in Princess Royal Harbour. Mount Clarence is to the left and King George Sound is in the background.

Picturesque Albany today in 2014. Both jetties have long disappeared and the wharf facilities have been altered. However the surrounding landscape remains the same.

1944

Date	N°	Vessel	From	Via	Registry	Net	H/S	C n B
Oct 15	23	Koomilya	Newcastle	Direct	Melb	1892	S	c
" 18	24	Margaret	I'tle		K.G.B.	500	M	
" 24	25	Loloma	Bunbury	✓	Melb.	1687	S	c.
Nov 14	26	Tumacacori	Bahrein	Direct	U.S.A	6301	M	oil
" 27	27	Santiago Oglesia	Fremantle	–	–	4378	–	Ballast
Dec 1	28	Port Fremantle	Fremantle	–	London	says	M	c
" 3	29	Mundalla	Brisbane	Melb	Melb	1757	–	✓
" 11	30	Empire Drives	Aden	Direct	W Hartlepool	4810	S	c
" 22	31	USL 704	Adelaide	–	Melb	100	M	Navy S
" 23	32	Port St John	Colombo		London	3306	–	c
" 26	33	Quenimba	Melbourne	✓	–	4772	S	c
" 27	34	Alpetia Nomikos	Colombo	–	Piraeus	2874	S	c
" 28	8	Bond Truck or Rail		cigarettes	USAS	USL 704		
" 29	35	Blackwood	I'tle		I'tle?	300	M	c

1945

Date	N°	Vessel	From	Via	Registry	Net	H/S	C n B
Jan 8	1	Kaikoura	N. Lincoln	Direct	Plymouth	5994	M	c
" 6	1	Bond Truck or Rail	Perth	Spirits		Ballot.		
" 9	2	"	"	Fremantle	Lub oil	ss "Aun"		
" 16	2	Aun	Sydney	Direct	Bergen	137	S	c
" 17	3	Bond Truck or Rail	Perth	Tobacco		SS "Aun"		
" 18	4	"	"			"Remo"		
" 21	3	Remo	Sydney	Direct	Oslo	1718	S	c
" 27	4	Vesse	Fremantle	✓	I'tle	300	M	c
Feb 5	5	Malika	Basra	I'tle	London	3012	S	c
" 28	6	Glen Mariner	Colombo	✓	Glasgow	2725	S	

Proof that she was here. Dated November 14 the arrival of the *Tumacacori* is entered (fourth from the top) into the Port of Albany Harbour Register of Inwards Movements 1944 (continued next page).

Remarks	Cargo Discharged Inward Wt/Meas Tons	O'seas Wt/Meas Tons	Passengers Num Cross	Light Dues Paid	From	To
Direct Load	18½			Melb	1.10.44	31.10.44
Stores transport supply		Exempt		8c Public Vessel		1.10.44
Fuel filled up				Melb	1.10.44	31.10.44
In distress, to land provisions			—	Exempt	8(d) Reg 48a	Nat Sea 85 Vessel underkeeper
In distress - landed sick Naval Gunner	Sick Naval Gunner			✓	8(d)	
				Fremantle	22.11.44	21.2.45
—	238	304		Pt Adel	1.10.44	31.10.44
Bunkers & Stores				Albany	11.44	10.3.45
Stores only Navy Supply by Vessel			Exempt	8c		
To land provisions only				Albany	23.12.44	22.1.45
Bunkers & Stores	—			Adel	27.11.44	26.1.45
	—	193		Albany	27.11.44	26.3.45
Army Transport Supply			Exempt	8c Public Vessel		
				Sydney	11.44	15.2.45
Bunkers & Stores – Pub Vessel – U.S. Army ASWSA			Exempt	Nat Sea Reg 48a		
Bunkers & Stores – Pub Vessel – U.S.W.S.A.			Exempt	Nat Sea Reg 48a		
Army Transport Supply			Exempt	8c Pub Sea Vessel		
Bunkers & Stores				Albany	5.2.45	7.5.45
Oil Bunkers & Stores			✓		28.2.45	2/5/45
		S.T.		Albany	16.3.45	15.4.45
Coal 3148		—		Albany	9.3.45	18.4.45

S/S TUMACACORI
NOVEMBER 13, 1944

TO CAPTAIN FARGO, CREW AND GUNNERS OF THE S/S TUMACACORI AND TO
WHOM ELSE IT MAY CONCERN :

THE EXCEPTIONAL KINDNESS, CARE AND ATTENTION SHOWN US
DURING OUR RECENT RESCUE BY CAPTAIN FARGO, CREW AND GUNNERS
OF THE S/S TUMACACORI, AND DURING OUR SUBSEQUENT STAY
ABOARD THE VESSEL DESERVES GREATER COMMENDATION AND PRAISE
THAN WE COULD POSSIBLY GIVE.
    ALTHOUGH WE ARE NATURALLY OVERJOYED BECAUSE OF RESCUE,
IT NEVER OCCURED TO US THAT THIS PARTICULAR FEELING WAS
MAGNIFIED MANY TIMES MORE BY OUR RESCUERS. NOT ONE MOMENT
WAS LOST IN ATTENDING TO OUR PARTICULAR NEEDS. COMFORT AND
GENERAL OVERALL FEELING OF WELCOME AND HOSPITALITY IMMEDIATELY
EXTENDED TO US LEFT ABSOLUTELY NOTHING TO BE DESIRED. SPECIAL
FAVORS AND PRIVILEDGES GRANTED US BY CAPTAIN FARGO AND CREW,
WE SHALL NEVER FORGET.
    INITIAL PROFFERINGS OF KINDNESS AND HOSPITALITY QUITE
NATURALLY WARMED US DEEPLY, HOWEVER, WHEN SUCH CORDIALITY
AND HOSPITALITY CONTINUED WITHOUT THE SLIGHTEST SIGN OF
DECREASING, WE ARE FIRMLY CONVINCED THAT A MORE SPLENDID
GROUP OF MEN COULD NOT HAVE RESCUED US.
    OUR EXPERIENCE ABOARD THE S/S TUMACACORI IS ONE LONG
TO BE REMEMBERED. WE WISH TO EXPRESS OUR DEEPEST APPRECIATION
AND GRATITUDE TO CAPTAIN FARGO AND HIS ENTIRE CREW FOR MAKING
OUR RECUPERATIVE STAY PLEASANT AND FOR AN EFFECIENT JOB, WELL
DONE.

RESCUED CREW MEMBERS OF THE S/S FORT
LEE

Typed letter written by the rescued survivors from Lifeboat #6 to the *Tumacacori* thank-
ing them for their rescue and kindness. As it is dated November 13 1944 a day before
they arrived at Albany, obviously suggests that it was drafted up and written before they
disembarked there.

NAVAL MESSAGE NAVY DEPARTMENT

DRAFTER   EXTENSION NUMBER   ADDRESSEES   PRECEDENCE

ASTERISK (*) MAILGRAM ADDRESSEE

FROM SS TUMACORI (VIA ... ...

RELEASED BY

FOR ACTION

DATE 1. NOVEMBER 1944

TOR CODEROOM 92

DECODED BY

TYPED O'NEILL/LA... (92)

BY ...

ROUTED BY

UNLESS OTHERWISE INDICATED THIS DISPATCH WILL BE TRANSMITTED WITH DEFERRED PRECEDENCE AND AS ADMINISTRATIVE.

PRIORITY
ROUTINE
DEFERRED

PRIORITY
ROUTINE
DEFERRED

IF OPERATIONAL
CHECK BELOW ☐

ORIGINATOR FILL IN DATE AND TIME: DATE   TIME

ON OUTGOING DISPATCHES PLEASE LEAVE ABOUT ONE INCH CLEAR SPACE BEFORE BEGINNING TEXT

(PASS TO ADMIRAL ... ... CEYLON) 23

1019

SF20E*. S.S. FORT LEE TORPEDOED 2ND NOVEMBER 2000
LATITUDE ... ... COURSE ... ... 99 DEG DISTANCE
275 MILES. SUBMARINE APPARENTLY GERMAN STAYED IN
VICINITY OF LIFE BOAT 2 DAYS. 3 BOATS WITH MASTER AND
46 MEN STILL ADRIFT BELIEVED TRYING TO INTERCEPT
SOUTHBOUND STEAMER. MASTER.

* CALL FOR SS TUMACORI

PASSED BY NAVCON TO ADMIRALTY

FX-3/...OFY...COG

PASSED BY NCR TO NCR FOR FURTHER DISTRIBUTION
TOR NCR 1245/10

COMINCH....16....30R....23....20G,...CNO....

NAVAIDE....39....AMPB....ATCC.

Make original only. Deliver to Code Room Watch Officer in person. (See Art. 76 (4) NAVREGS.)

OPNAV 19-60

U.S. Navy message received from the Master Sidney Fargo from the *Tumacacori* advising of the other lifeboats still at sea and unaccounted for, as well as surmising that the U-boat stayed in the area for two days.

A view showing just part of the expanse of King George Sound at Albany where the *Tumacacori* arrived. From left to right is Michaelmas Island, Breaksea Island then Limestone Head. The entrance to Princess Royal Harbour is at right of image.

Albany

Established in 1826 originally as a penal settlement, Albany is the oldest European township established on the west coast of Australia. Originally called Frederickstown, it possesses the title as the first permanent European settlement established on the west coast of Australia. Notwithstanding the shipwrecked survivors from the Dutch VOC sailing ship *Batavia* that foundered off the Abrolhos Islands in 1629.

With evidence indicating indigenous Aboriginal culture going back 12,000 years, the surrounding area was sighted by British Captain George Vancouver in 1791. Since 1788 when Australia became the tenure of the British Empire, to dissuade the French that had been showing interest in the area, it was agreed to establish a settlement at King George Sound.

Possessing one of finest natural harbours in the world, up until the turn of the 20th century it was in fact the chief port for Western Australia until Fremantle was dredged deep enough and made operational to become the fledgling states principal harbour.

However since its establishment Albany has been no stranger to the bustling comings and goings of ships and vessels manned by crews from a multitude of nationalities during both peacetime and war. It was from here that a significantly large proportion of Australian troops departed for the Transvaal to fight in the South African Boer War from 1899 to 1902. From their respective colonies they returned to their home states following Australia's federation in 1901.

One of the earliest relationships created with the United States Navy commenced as early as 1908 when the town received the visit of the Great White Fleet. A round the world goodwill cruise endorsed by President Theodore Roosevelt,

Albany was only one of three Australian ports that was visited by these sixteen gleaming white American battleships and their escorts, the other two being Sydney and Melbourne.

But it was her role as the initial staging and assembly point for the massive ANZAC troopship convoys throughout October and December 1914 that she is best noted. For many of the troops on board, Albany would provide for them the last glimpse of Australian soil. Before long they would find themselves facing the horrors of Turkey's Gallipoli peninsula and then the Western Front in Europe of which countless would never return.

A generation later during the Second World War again Albany played her role as an important naval hub. Following the surprise Japanese attack on Pearl Harbour, a large section of the United States Navy fleet of submarines became based in Western Australia. Throughout much of 1942 particularly after the fall of the Philippines over 30 submarines were stationed at Albany in an arrangement that she shared with Fremantle. Accompanying them were tender ships such as the USS *Pelias* and *Holland.*

The American crews arrived in their hundreds where most were housed at the former quarantine station overlooking the harbour on the opposite side. More familiar with warmer climates the Americans referred to Albany as 'Little Siberia'. But for the time that they were stationed here they created a favourable impression on the local populace. Submarines like the USS *Seawolf and Harder* conducted torpedo exercises in Frenchman Bay, the waters near the site of Australia's last whaling station that ceased operations in 1978. Though situated too far south geographically to come under any direct threat of an air attack by the Japanese, Albany was nevertheless scrutinised early in the war by German raiders.

On September 2 1940 the *Orion* laid small field of four makeshift floating mines off Eclipse Island located near the entrance to King George Sound. They were in fact old beer barrels inserted with a small detonating charge. During deployment one exploded on deck severely injuring a crewman and mortally wounding another. He was buried at sea the next day due south of Albany near the continental shelf, the first German sailor to be killed in action in Australian waters. Today a similarity with the construction of these types of bombs could perhaps be comparable to the IED's or Improvised Exploding Devices encountered by Allied troops in Iraq and Afghanistan.

A little over a year later on November 2 1941 a real German mine with its deadly protruding Hertz horns was discovered washed up on Goode Beach near Mistaken Island in Frenchman's Bay in King George Sound. Expected in port that very day was the flagship of the Royal Australian Navy the HMAS *Sydney*. The harbour was swept as best could be by the local Naval Patrol in case any others may have been lurking, until a shore party from the *Sydney* was despatched to ashore to destroy the mine. Two weeks later the Leander class cruiser and hero of the Mediterranean met her unfortunate end following a fierce gun battle with the German raider *Kormoran*.

In another incident the coastal steamer *Katoomba* in August 1942 came under attack by the Japanese submarine *I-32* at a position 300 kilometres offshore about halfway between Esperance, a coastal town further to the east and Albany. The *I-32* departed the New Hebrides for Surabaya, Java and had decided to take the long way around by way of the Southern Ocean of Australia. After a brief exchange, both escaped unharmed.

In 1944 the population of Albany barely stood at around 10,000. Today it is a small city of over 45,000 where despite other industries having become established it is still a busy and important port. Its strong links to its military past is exemplified in the ANZAC Day observations conducted every year on April 25. In fact Albany was the site of the very first ANZAC Day dawn service to be conducted in Australia in 1923. Australia and New Zealand Army Corps, or ANZAC Day, is the equivalent to the American Veterans Day, a date set aside to honour the nations fallen and all those who served.

In addition since 1980 a small ceremony is held every year honouring the crews of the U.S. Navy submarines that were stationed at Albany. In fact after the war several former U.S. Navy servicemen returned, married local girls and remained on in the town forging prosperous careers. Now once more it would play host to American servicemen. The only difference this time is that they were shipwrecked sailors.

From this point on, the only first hand evidence that we really have concerning the arrival of the men to Albany is the account from former Navy Armed Guard Jim Wilson. At the time of writing James Wilson is 88 years old and resides to-day in Troy, Missouri. Forgivably he is being interviewed by long distance correspondence and is attempting to describe and recall events that occurred 70 years ago concerning a particular small piece of this story that probably happened all so quickly and across the years now appear to be a blur. Remembering that there is nobody knowingly still alive who may have been there to witness this from a local perspective.

However according to Wilson when he and the other 16 men arrived aboard the Naval Patrol lighter they tied up at the dock, or wharf. It was not in his recollections that it was a jetty and was adamant that it was the wharf. This then rules out any one of Albany's iconic jetties that she once possessed, namely the Deep Water and Town Jetty as being the landing points where they arrived.

Nevertheless all 17 men were grateful to come ashore. It had been almost four weeks since they had last touched land which was back in Abadan and 12 days since their ship had sunk.

Greeting them ashore were a couple of elderly local Volunteer Defence Corps [VDC] guards and two newspaper reporters, one presumably from the local *Albany Advertiser*. The third party was a representative from the Navy. This could possibly be in fact the local NOIC, the Naval Officer in Charge which was a Lieutenant Ivan Bird. The reporters were forbidden to talk to any the men and Wilson recalls that they were ordered to keep away at a safe distance.

There is no doubt that this is the principal reason why there is absolutely no mention of the incident being recorded in any newspaper in Australia at all at the time. Curiously, despite censorship and wartime security there is no immediate press report, nor reference given at all to the sinking of the tanker, or the rescue of the men in any newspaper, anywhere. There is no reference of their landing in either Australia or in Ceylon. For the record, most headlines during the week of November 14 1944 were largely overshadowed by the daring raid carried out by R.A.F. aircraft to sink the German battleship *Tirpitz* in Tromso Fjord, Norway.

Almost immediately they were chaperoned over to a nearby waiting truck that had been organised for them. They were kept closely guarded together and were driven up to Albany's old hospital located in Vancouver Street. Named after the street that it is situated in, the distance from the wharf up to the site of the Vancouver Street Hospital is less than five kilometres or about two miles.

Named after the same British sea captain who had been reputedly the first European to sail into the harbour it was first constructed in 1897 and ran as the town's principal general and public hospital until its closure in 1962. Now a heritage listed building, today it serves a more passive role as an arts centre and gallery known aptly as the Vancouver Arts Centre.

Again unfortunately hospital records from this period and or from this facility seemed not to have survived. So there is no way of telling if there was actually any record kept of them being admitted or seen to. Similarly all Western Australian VDC records were destroyed shortly after the war much to frustration of many historians today. Here one can be thankful that just as well the Record of Inwards Movements has preserved the entry of the *Tumacacori*.

They were taken to the Vancouver Street Hospital for a check up and examination. As it turned out none of the men it seemed were in bad shape. No-one in this lifeboat had been seriously wounded and most had recovered sufficiently from the effects of their ordeal in the last few days since being aboard the *Tumacacori*.

Nevertheless, they were treated and examined by the local doctor and nurses for any suspected illness and or malady that they may have acquired or were thought to possess. They all underwent a thorough physical makeover. Whilst here, they also were fed a nutritious vegetable soup. The group was never split up and they stayed together at all times. Their check up comprised mainly of a general physical. They were then all informed that they were going to be transported up to Perth by train.

According to Jim Wilson after leaving hospital they were collected together and taken to wait in something that he describes as a type of 'fenced stockade'. He recalls it as being 'located above the town overlooking the harbour situated on a hill.' This where they waited until the train arrived. There are several facilities that could pass themselves off as a *'fenced stockade on a hill overlooking the harbour'* with several examples that still are in evidence today. Initially the first possibility was the headquarters of what is now the 11/28th Army Battalion parade ground on Brunswick Road. The other is the nearby Lawley Park tennis courts in existence since 1913. It is also possible that it was simply a fenced off area adjacent to the Albany train station itself, something perhaps near where the old Albany Ice Works once stood on the foreshore. Remembering that the Albany foreshore and much of the infrastructure surrounding the wharf facilities has undergone many changes and alterations in its landscape since the 1940's.

Another possibility is that they were accommodated somewhere still within the grounds of the Vancouver Street Hospital itself which overlooks the harbour.

To reiterate, with forgiveness one cannot stress enough the curse of memories dimly fading over 70 years especially where only barely six hours were spent altogether in one particular place. It would be comparable to stopping briefly for lunch or passing slowly by a town more than 70 years ago that is located on the other side of the world, where you have not been back to since, and at the time, owing to duress and hastily organised movements, it simply did not necessarily leave an everlasting impression.

Since 1940 Western Australian Government Railways [W.A.G.R.] who owned the Great Southern Line had operated a daily passenger service from Albany to Perth in both directions. It was a narrow gauge passenger night train that usually departed Albany mid afternoon. As explained to the author by the Western Australian Rail Heritage Society, passenger train records from this period unfortunately do not survive.

According to James Wilson's account he recollects that the entire group would have spent no more than six hours in total in the fair town of Albany. That is from the time that they landed in the morning to the time that they boarded the train in the afternoon.

Their wait however was not long before the train came. As it did so they were escorted over to the station where they proceeded to board. It is a journey that would have taken about eight hours or more. Arriving safely in Perth they were met by U.S. Navy officers and a representative from the consulate. From here they were boarded on to another train and taken down to Fremantle to the hospital.

To take the train from Albany to Perth today is impossible. The passenger rail service ceased service in 1978. The route was replaced by road bus and an air service. Prior to their departure there was seemingly *one* section of the local community that had been informed of their arrival. The Albany branch of the Red Cross were evidently permitted access to the American sailors during their brief stay, more likely while they were still at the hospital. There is a concise report and even then it only publicly appeared well after they had long gone under the title Red Cross Notes in the local newspaper *The Albany Advertiser.*

Dated Monday, 27 November 1944 it states that:

"Recently 17 shipwrecked men were provided by our members with cakes, fruit, chocolate and reading matter before leaving."

This oblique and vague report is the only clue that exists anywhere giving reference to those in Lifeboat #6 from the *Fort Lee* of their time in Albany. It was indeed a very quiet affair, with no publicity given to it at all. No further announcement from the press would appear again until the following February.

Albany earlier played host to the United States Great White Fleet during their visit in 1908. Here battle cruisers and colliers are at anchor in Princess Royal Harbour. In 1942 the harbour became a temporary home for U.S. Navy submarines.

The waterfront of Albany today looking back towards the township

The old Vancouver Street Hospital as it is today in Albany in 2014 where it is now an arts centre. Almost instantly after arriving ashore it was here that the 17 men from the *Fort Lee* were transported to for a physical check up before boarding the train for Perth.

Nurses from the hospital circa 1942. It could be that it was some of these that tended to the American sailors.

A fenced stockade? 70 years later a survivor who was brought to Albany describes that the group were accommodated in 'fenced stockade on a hill overlooking the harbour' until the train came. Another view of Albany harbour and town jetty just prior to the war.

The old railway station at Albany dated early 20th century. The harbour is to the left of picture and the township in the background. Although goods trains still shunt in and out delivering mostly grain for export out of the harbour, the regular passenger rail service ceased in 1978. Built in 1889 the station today serves as the local Tourist Information Centre.

Red Cross Notes.

ALBANY BRANCH.

On the 19th and 26th January, it is intended to launch a big appeal for prisoner-of-war funds. We hope all new members enrolled this year will help, as money is urgently needed.

During the year ended June 30, 1944, £1,569/13/2 was sent to Red Cross headquarters from our branch (this does not include cash value of goods received). Members are making toys for sale, also there are Red Cross Christmas cards. Call at the Lower Town Hall on Tuesday afternoons. A Red Cross box is still in the Town Hall porch to receive reading matter. A lot more is needed for servicemen.

Our Red Cross visitor attends the local hospital regularly, distributing cigarettes, face washers, soap, books, etc.; this all costs money.

Recently 17 shipwrecked men were provided by our members with cakes, fruit, chocolate, and reading matter when leaving.

Would be glad of some beads for milk jug and tray covers. Can buy net, but not beads. These are needed for hospitals.

The local *Albany Advertiser* dated Monday, November 27 1944 gives scant announcement virtually two weeks after they had departed.

Lifeboat #2

It contained 16 men most notably the Master Ottar Andersen. Joining him was the Purser, 28 year old Robert J. Banks from St. James Minnesota. The remainder in the boat were the Chief Steward I. Buric and the 2nd Pumpman Hugh Johnston 35, from Parkersburg, Pennsylvania and 20 year old Joe Hamilton, the Chief Pumpman from Glidden, Iowa. With them also were the two Radio Operators, 23 year old William [Bill] Hart from Hickory, North Carolina and the 2nd Radio

Operator John J. Lee Jr from Plymouth, New Hampshire, who always felt irony at serving on board a ship that bore the same surname as his. Then there was 18 year old Earl Groves an Ordinary Seaman from Chanute, Kansas and 20 year old Walter J. Searle another Ordinary Seaman from the nation's capital Washington DC and then Brad Pruitt. Rounding out the Merchant Marines was Able Seaman John Duffy.

Lastly there were five Navy Armed Guards. First was the badly burnt Lyle Atkinson, who had been transferred over from Lifeboat #6. He was in great pain and agony. Giving up his place for him was his friend and fellow Armed Guard Robert Lanning who transferred over into Lifeboat #4. Then James Kirwin, Andrew Lemanski, Tom Swank and Len Winn all with the rank of Seamen 1st Class. Like Lemanski and Atkinson, several were nursing nasty burns and wounds mainly on their hands and wrists. They had received shrapnel from the blast of the second torpedo. The last to join the lifeboat was Pruitt who was still in pain, not only from his fall into the water but also from concussion when the first torpedo impacted and had bounced him around like a rubber ball. The nagging abdominal pain wouldn't go away either.

"Everything I had went down with the ship, all my papers, personal effects as well as the Japanese souvenirs that I had been given back on the Marshall Islands in exchange for the sugar. I was given a .25 snipers rifle. That was the most accurate gun I have ever seen. We used that rifle on the ship to fire at cans and bottles. I also had a Japanese battle flag and sword that I was given. Everything that I had back on board in my locker, in my cabin – was all gone."

Lifeboat #2 certainly did not have to concern itself as to who was in charge as it contained the Skipper. However this did not provide them with any extra relief, nor any special exemption from the privations and unpredictable weather conditions that was about to confront them. After separating from the others, whilst they did not know it, they were on a direct collision course straight into a storm.

On their first night Duffy recorded the following.

"We all sat huddled against the gunwales, some trying to get a few winks of sleep, all shivering. Smith was talking incessantly to himself about nothing at all. Craig a 20 year old Fireman on the 4 to 8 shift sat opposite me and related how fortunate he was in that he had been relieved at 7.55 only minutes before the first torpedo struck."

Robert John Kelly Craig from Pennsylvania, whom everyone called Jack told how he had only reached the mess hall for a cup of coffee, and was about to place it to his mouth when the torpedo hit. The impact killed his friend and replacement Fireman, 21 year old Frank Yohe who had just commenced his shift along with Wiper Thomas Vain. Vain too had been filling in for 'Tex' Knauth who had been feeling ill all day. To make way for more wounded Craig later transferred over into Lifeboat #4 and Smith over to Lifeboat #6.

"At the first hint of light the following day after being sunk, we stretched out our cramped limbs," relates Duffy.

"We had all been cold and we shivered. The Captain got some of us to help rig up the radio antenna – a long pole lashed to the top of the wooden lifeboat mast with wires running down to the radio box."

These were the transmitters that Giese had told them at first not to use.

"Once we rigged it in place 'Sparks' [Radio Operator Bill Hart] crossed his fingers for good luck and started sending."

The small battery was good for 48 messages of two minutes each. Being a transmitter only it could not receive signals. Its range was no more than around 200 miles with the best emitting conditions being at sunset and dawn. They were well aware of what their exact position was. It so happened that the first message *KC2MV* was actually received by a fellow American tanker heading in the opposite direction. It relayed it on to Colombo, Ceylon, Joint Allied Naval Base.

Despite not being able to send a Mayday actually from the *Fort Lee* due to her damaged antenna when she was hit, at last an alert was now placed for all ships to be on the lookout.

Andersen then set course for Australia. Some were despondent saying that they would not make it. From the earlier empty life rafts, Lifeboat #2 managed to salvage a light, a flag, a mirror and some extra rations. Duffy, now stripped completely naked as his wet dungaree pants were drying out, managed to free a 25 gallon water tank and haul it over into their boat.

"Apart from me with my helmet, the only others which possessed a hat was the Captain, the Purser and 'Flags' [Signalman First Class Leonard Winn from Hempstead, New York]. The rest tried to make something out of pieces of cloth."

It was wearisome work stripping the abandoned life rafts apart as all they had to work with was some blunt rusty hatchets that had at one stage been left in the lifeboat. After this, the Captain issued out the first of the emergency rations. They fared no differently from the other lifeboats with the meagre provisions that they had. Carefully and equally measured out, allotted to each man were five malted milk tablets [to anyone who wanted any] one hard tack biscuit, pemmican, a square bit of Hershey chocolate bar followed by an allowance of three gulps of water.

"We spent the day dozing," Duffy later wrote. "Those that had been in the water tried to clean the oil off each other's faces with some special solutions, but for me, my three month old beard made this impossible. We had exchanged two boys who had been badly burned. One was Lyle Atkinson. He was a horrible sight. His face was all puffed up and his arms and fingers were twice the normal size. The ships Purser, Robert Banks, wrapped them daily with some ointment. Poor Atkinson was not capable of doing anything. We had to light his cigarettes and then give them to him."

Most of the injured, especially the worst cases were placed into Lifeboat #2 as it was figured they were better equipped to treat them. Even then all they had to administer to them was some tannic acid and ointment. Ottar Andersen too felt on his part that no matter what had happened, everybody, including the wounded were all still his responsibility and wanted to personally monitor their situation in his boat.

But sea conditions would get worse before they would get better. By the middle of the next day waves had reached between 10 to 15 feet high. They had put out a sea anchor, of which each lifeboat contained two. Sometimes also known as *drogue* it looks rather much like a wind sock attached by a rope. They assist particularly small boats in heavy weather to prevent roll by the action of the breaking waves. At the height of this awful storm the tiny lifeboat was a like a cork as waves soon reached as high as 30 feet.

"It was some of the worst weather I have ever been in and endured in any vessel big, little or small. It was bad. We did not know if we would survive it," recalls Brad Pruitt.

"We were all frantically bailing out water just with our shoes as fast as we could bail water, simply because that's all we had on us to do this."

For the next several days the weather hardly abated.

"Even though we were about 1900 miles from land, I don't recall ever seeing a bird. If we did we would have probably tried to catch him. We saw no more sharks, no whales, nothing but storm driven rough sea weather."

The men in Lifeboat #2 were actually the first to be discovered and rescued. On the morning of November 7 1944 at 10.44 a.m. a cargo vessel was sighted steaming northeast. It had intercepted the radio message sent out from Colombo. After five days since the *Fort Lee* was sunk, the weather was still foul. As best they could the lifeboat attempted to head in her direction sending up flares and lighting smoke floats as she did so. Finally, perseverance paid off and the ship altered course to their direction. Lifeboat #2 had indeed been sighted.

At 12.04 p.m. in the position of 28°34'S–85°30'E they were finally picked up.

It turned out to be the British cargo freighter MV *Ernebank*. Launched on November 17 1937 the *Ernebank* was constructed by that prodigious shipbuilder Harland and Wolff in Belfast, Northern Ireland. She commenced regular passenger and merchant freight services from the south and east coasts of Africa and Madagascar to Burma, Singapore, Hong Kong and other parts of Asia. Similarly like the *Garoet* and many other cargo ships plying the Indian Ocean, she was made up of a crew largely consisting of European officers and Indian and Bengal Lascars.

The *Ernebank* was part of the fleet of Bank Line ships which in turn was a subsidiary of the Andrew Weir Shipping Company. A majority of their ships were easily recognisable due to their names ending with the suffix '*bank*'. Established in 1885, Bank Line Shipping Ltd was founded by shipping magnate Andrew Weir in London U.K. in 1905. It operated a regular service throughout most corners of the globe from

Europe to the South Pacific. Since then the line has been sold to the China Navigation Company Ltd, which is under the umbrella of the massive Swire Group.

Andrew Weir Shipping operated several service lines including the India-Africa Line which originated following the 1932 takeover of the India Natal Line. The *Ernebank* served her time during the war as a DEMS [Defensively Equipped Merchant Ship] and went back to her peace time role afterwards until she was scrapped in Hong Kong on May 4 1963. Two noted sister ships were the *Araybank* and the *Shirrabank* both of which were constructed by the same shipyard in 1940.

The *Ernebank*, en route to Fremantle from Bombay, was off course as she had actually been attempting to outrun the storm herself and also the position given by Colombo was some 70 miles out of her way. At this time on board, one of her lifeboats had worked its way loose due to the rough weather. Her Captain turned her about and headed in to the seas so that they may be able to secure it. According to Brad Pruitt it was a lonely lookout stationed aloft in the ships crows nest that had first managed to spot them.

At first it was thought that it may have been the exhaust from a submarine, however on second look through the binoculars the lookout sighted the little lifeboats red flag sail.

Afterwards the American sailors wondered with complete amazement how the hell on earth could he have seen the tiny lifeboat off to starboard through the rolling and pitching of the ship, not to mention the bad visibility. The Skipper of the *Ernebank* too commented after that he hoped that they would not lower their sail as that was all he had to go on to steer towards them.

As she pulled over to the leeward side, hoisted over was a heavy cargo rope ladder where they were each helped up to climb aboard. This posed a further problem. The *Ernebank* was a diesel motor vessel and when at sea she carried no reserve air for reversing the engines. Therefore her Skipper could not stop, for if he did he would be unable to start them again. But it was achieved and every man was aboard. After the last had evacuated, the gunners on the *Ernebank* sunk Lifeboat #2 with a burst of 20mm machine gun fire, leaving no trace of it behind.

As many of the crew from the *Fort Lee* had already found out, seawater does not wash off oil. Five days after abandoning ship Brad Pruitt was just one of many unfortunates that was still caked in it. As soon as he was helped on board the *Ernebank* he was led away to be given a good wash and scrub down. The Armed Guards with their wounds were immediately seen to. All that there had been to treat their hands these last five days was tannic acid. Those that had the misfortune to swim in the oiled infested water saw that their eyelids were now given some relief and treatment as they had by now become openly red raw.

The British Master of the *Ernebank* informed Andersen that the destination was Fremantle, Western Australia. No one was going to argue with that as they were all grateful to have been seen and rescued in the first place.

"It was the most beautiful sight to see that English cargo ship come into sight," former Armed Guard Lyle Atkinson fondly remembered many afterwards.

A coded message was sent through advising Fremantle of the unexpected arrival. On board the *Ernebank* like the *Tumacacori* the 16 castaways were attended to with diligence and care. The British crew were friendly and provided the men with hot soup and dry clothes. Following his thorough scrub down, Pruitt was given a new pair of pants and shirt. Afterwards most preferred to stay down in the engine room where it was warm and dry. They slept anywhere from 12 to 16 hours.

For the remainder of the voyage the lookouts on the *Ernebank* were placed on heightened alert. The weather was still bad for another 12 hours before it showed any signs of clearing. Her captain was now more concerned for his own vessel as a potential target for any rogue U-boat still lurking about. It was still only five days ago that the *Fort Lee* was attacked. The *Ernebank* had already undergone several near misses herself throughout the war, none more so than back on September 27 1942 when she narrowly avoided being sunk by a U-boat west of Bombay.

For Able Seaman John Duffy his odyssey did not end exactly the way he maybe would have liked it to.

"I did a very foolish thing on the night we were picked up. I had learned that the Skipper was going to search for the other three lifeboats until 8.00 p.m. I volunteered for lookout from 6:30 in spite of the rain that set in. Johnston did also and he developed a very bad cold from it."

The *Ernebank* arrived in Fremantle Harbour on November 14 coincidentally the very same day that the *Tumacacori* arrived in Albany to disembark her thankful human cargo. Interestingly it took longer to be landed, some seven days, than it did for the entire time that they were stranded at sea in the lifeboat. Nevertheless it was good to be on land again.

Upon disembarking at Fremantle they were greeted by U.S. Navy officials. Brad Pruitt recalls one incident, that he has never forgotten where their initial welcome was marred with a mixture of disbelief and disappointment.

"After the ship arrived and tied up, right there on the dock were assembled tables full of tea and coffee pots, cakes and sweet rolls, more than enough to feed 150 people. As we came off the *Ernebank* we all wondered what was going on. We walked over to where they had gathered and some of us asked if we could have a cup and a cake? Those manning the tables turned around and retorted "*absolutely not!*"

We explained to them that our ship had been sunk and that we had only just arrived. It felt like weeks since we had a good cup of coffee. It made no difference. We found out that the spread had been exclusively laid on for 25 Australian troops who were about to embark overseas and this was a farewell gathering for them. We asked '*who laid this on?*' and they replied, '*the Red Cross*'. Since then from that day on I have never had use for the Red Cross."

Temporarily demoralised they were ushered away to a waiting vehicle. Not quite the usual friendly Australian welcome becoming for our American friends, especially ones that have just been rescued at sea. Despite the less than desired initial 'welcoming party' the 16 were taxied over to the Fremantle Hospital in Alma Street where they would undergo a complete physical and spend further time recuperating. At least here the reception was much better and they were soon seen to by a doctor and nurses. Here too a total freeze was placed on any news reports and no members of the press were permitted to come near them. During their brief stay here the mountainous paperwork and intense interviewing by Naval Intelligence would commence.

However a small celebration was waiting in store when it occurred that they would be soon reunited with their ship-mates from Lifeboat #6. Prior to their repatriation back to the United States a photograph of all 16 men who were in Life-boat #2 was taken in Fremantle. Seventy years later Brad Pruitt was able to confirm that the photograph was indeed taken in Fremantle, but is unable to recall exactly where. However it is thought that it was possibly taken in the grounds of what is today the Fremantle Arts Centre. Constructed in 1864 originally as an asylum, it has served many purposes over the years. Between 1942 and 1945 it was used by the U.S. Navy as an administration building and depot.

A further clue in support of this is the unmistakable lime-stone brick wall that they are standing in front of. Limestone is a common building material synonymous in the construc-tion for a lot of older landmarks throughout Fremantle. A feature is the unique wooden shutters on the windows behind that are hinged at the top and secured at the bottom when opened. Photographs of the other men who were in Lifeboat #6 were also taken by U.S. government authorities.

Here in Fremantle, Perth it would be the last time that the Armed Guards and the Merchant Mariners would be together. For many it would be the last time that they would all see each other for immediately after they were separated and split up for their passage back to the United States.

The MV *Ernebank* one of the Bank Line vessels that rescued those in lifeboat #2 and brought them to Fremantle.

In the Merchant Marine, Brad Pruitt in April 1943 on the steps out the front of number 2904 Bunker Hill Road, Mt Rainier, Maryland.

Bradley Royce Pruitt a year later in April 1944 just before the *Fort Lee* sailed for her fatal voyage. He was knocked out cold from the force of the blast from the first torpedo.

Able Seaman John W. Duffy from Fall River, Massachusetts. A capable sailor he played a pivotal role during the abandoning ship process.

Seaman 1st Class Lyle J. Atkinson from Wisconsin in 1943.

Lyle Atkinson in uniform circa 1944. He was wounded suffering badly burnt hands and arms and placed in Lifeboat #2 swapping places with his best friend and fellow Armed Guard Robert Lanning who went over into the ill fated Lifeboat #4.

Chief Radio Operator Bill 'Sparks' Hart from North Carolina was able to transmit a signal from the lifeboat indicating their position.

18 year old Earl Groves (*centre*) from Chanute, Kansas and 2nd Pumpman Hugh Johnston from Parkersburg, Pennsylvania also in Lifeboat #2.

Aerial view of Fremantle Harbour circa 1940's. It was here that the *Ernebank* arrived to disembark the men in Lifeboat #2. The harbour is itself actually the entrance to the Swan River that snakes its way past Perth, the capital city of Western Australia.

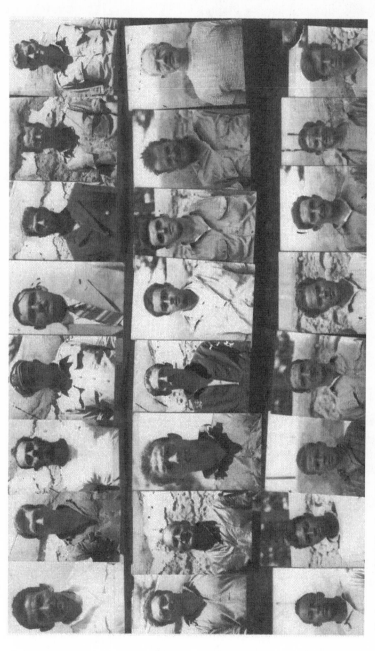

Composite images of 24 Merchant Marine crew from both Lifeboats #2 and #6 taken after rescue in Fremantle. Those identified are: **Top Row** from left, Hugh D. **Johnston**, Earl A. **Groves**, Walter J. **Searle**, Master Ottar **Andersen** fourth from left, fourth from right Purser Robert **Banks**, John **Duffy** third from right, William **Hart** second from right and John J. **Lee** far right. **Middle Row** second from left I. **Buric**, fourth from left Bradley **Pruitt**, third from right Jack **Hennessy** and then Michael **Sherry** at far right. **Bottom Row**: Most here are thought to be from Lifeboat #6. Bill **Mootz** is identified second from right.

The 16 men here are all of the survivors from lifeboat #2 rescued by the MV *Ernebank* and brought to Fremantle. **Top row left to right:** Hugh D. **Johnston** (with crutch), Earl A. **Groves**, Walter J. **Searle**, Captain Ottar M. **Andersen**, Robert J. **Banks** (Purser), John W. **Duffy**, William S. **Hart**, John J. **Lee** Jr. **Bottom row**, l. to r.: Joseph T. **Hamilton**, I. **Buric**, James J. **Kirwin**, Leonard **Winn**, Andrew A. **Lemanski**, Thomas C. **Swank**, Lyle J. **Atkinson**, and lastly Bradley R. **Pruitt**. The photograph here may have possibly been taken in the grounds of what is today the Fremantle Arts Centre, a clue being the limestone brick wall behind. During the war the facility was used by the U.S. Navy. Note the two sailors Lemanski and Atkinson in front row with bandaged hands.

DRAFTER	EXTENSION NUMBER	ADDRESSEES	PRECEDENCE
		ASTERISK (*) MAILGRAM ADDRESSEE	

FROM CNB FREMANTLE

RELEASED BY

DATE 15 NOV 1944

TOR CODEROOM 0856

DECODED BY BOWKER

TYPED BY LYON MacFarlane

ROUTED BY WHITTINGTON

FOR ACTION CNO

INFORMATION AMERICAN CONSUL PERTH
COMINCH
COMSERV7THFLT
COMSERVSUBCOM7THFLT
CTF 71

PRECEDENCE:
PPPP PRIORITY
ROUTINE
DEFERRED

PPPPP PRIORITY
ROUTINE
DEFERRED

UNLESS OTHERWISE INDICATED THIS DISPATCH WILL BE TRANSMITTED WITH DEFERRED PRECEDENCE AND AS ADMINISTRATIVE.

IF OPERATIONAL CHECK BELOW

150352   NCR 3219

ORIGINATOR FILL IN DATE AND TIME: DATE   TIME   GCT

ON OUTGOING DISPATCHES PLEASE LEAVE ABOUT ONE INCH CLEAR SPACE BEFORE BEGINNING TEXT

(CNB FREMANTLE SENDS CNO INFO COMINCH COMSERV7THFLT
COMSERVSUBCOM7THFLT CTF 71 AMERICAN CONSUL PERTH.)

10198

SUNK BY 2 TORPEDOES 1434Z 2 NOVEMBER SS FORT LEE

POSITION 27-35 SOUTH 83-11 EAST COURSE 129 DEGREES

TRUE. SUBMARINE BELIEVED TO BE GERMAN. CONFIDENTIAL

AND SECRET PUBLICATIONS IN BRIDGE SAFE SUNK. 33

SURVIVORS AT THIS PORT. REPORT FOLLOWS.

RL.
ECC.

COMINCH.. ACT

20G....FX37....39...16..19...200P...NAVAIDE...CNO.

20R... ADD 23...(PER 23)

ACTION:
F-0
F-00
F-01
F-02
F-06
F-07
F-1
F-2
F-20
F-3
F-30
F-31
F-32
F-33
F-34
F-4
FX01
FX37
FX40
10-00
VCY0

Make original only. Deliver to Code Room Watch Officer in person. (See Art. 76 (1) NAVREGS.)
OPNAV 19-68   150352

U.S. Navy message dated November 15 1944, the day after the men in both lifeboats arrived in Perth. Noted is the comment 'confidential and secret publications in bridge safe sunk'. Sent from Fremantle it says '33 survivors at this port'.

Lifeboat #1

Lifeboat #1 was the third to successfully get away. It contained a further 17 men. All up were eight Merchant Mariners and nine U.S. Navy Armed Guards, the most Armed Guards out of all four lifeboats that were despatched. Taking charge in senior rank was 46 year old Chief Mate Charles Shenberg from Baltimore, Maryland. With him also was the wounded and fellow native from 'Charm City', the Second Mate, Leslie Asher. Then there was 30 year old 'Tex' Knauth, an Oiler from Vernon, Texas, followed by Ernst Reeves a young Wiper, then Frankie Lopez, a 24 year old Able Seaman from Waysum in West Virginia then Ordinary Seaman Lawrence Cochrane. Here too of course was Midshipman Cadet James Chaffin.

In this lifeboat was 20 year old Maxwell John Tarnowski a Messman from Garfield, New Jersey. Tarnowski like many had been thrown into the cold water of the Indian Ocean where he felt it had an unfathomable depth. Years afterwards he would describe the difficulty of how confusing it was to tell which way was up to swim towards the surface and which way was down to certain doom. Like Atkinson, Tarnowski was also suffering from painfully burnt hands from contact with steam pipes, a condition that would long plague him after the war.

The lifeboat also contained the Naval Armed Guard senior officer Lieutenant James W. Milne. Accompanying him was 19 year old SM 3/c Bernard Levin from Pennsylvania, RM 2/c Jerome J. Bird and BM 2/c Gottfried Johnssen, followed by Seamen First Class Lee Roy Prewitt a 20 year old from Harrodsburg, Kentucky, Russell B. Peterson, George F. Kasper, Rowland R. Crowe from Indianapolis, Indiana and finally Joe Gorga.

Again whilst their conditions as shipwrecked survivors fared no better than the others, their fortunes however would take them in another direction – *literally*. When Gorga was pulled into Lifeboat #1, apart from his clothes the only personal possession he had on him was his wallet.

"It was empty. All it contained was a picture of my future wife which I managed to save. That same picture remains in my wallet today. Apart from the clothes on my back that was the only thing I saved."

Like Jim Wilson and no doubt a large section of all the other rest of the crew, Joe Gorga also laments the loss of hard earned financial gain.

"I had about nineteen hundred bucks still in my locker when the ship went down. They were the winnings mostly from various card games and other bets that I had won throughout my travels."

Some of those hard earned dollars had been won back in Curacao and Aruba where Joe had a brother stationed. Twice in the last twelve months he had been luckily enough to visit him since he had joined the *Fort Lee*.

For nearly two weeks Lifeboat #1 and her 17 castaways bobbed away in the middle of the Indian Ocean.

"For some reason we could not find the row locks. Instead we had to put our legs up to use in place of the missing row locks in order to row," James Chaffin later wrote.

"At first during the sinking, we had to row with urgency because if you don't the suction when the ship goes down will pull you back into it. My legs were afterwards skinned up for a long time."

For the first few days at least, especially with most being in their early twenties, the situation was greeted with good humoured optimism. However that optimism soon began to run out. Many were still nursing various small wounds. Joe Gorga had lacerations on both his sides. He had also injured his arm and shoulder. The most aggravating was that common scourge where he had gotten oil in his eyes from landing in the water.

They were all severely windblown, sunburnt and tired. If rescue did not arrive soon, it was only a matter of time before the first would succumb. All the signs of extreme exposure to the elements were now openly displaying themselves. The emergency rations were perilously low and only a few ounces – barely a couple more days supply of precious fresh water at most remained; unless of course it rained and fresh water could somehow be captured.

Their austere rations had been identical as the other three lifeboats had to contend with. Lifeboat #1 too had their daily allotment of a small piece of Hershey chocolate, a dry cracker biscuit, half a dozen or so malted milk tablets for what they were worth, and just over half an ounce of pemmican dried meat.

"We also had six blankets in the lifeboat, one for about each three of us" describes Chaffin.

"There was a little cover on the end of lifeboat. Because we had some of us who had been hurt, we had them laying in there. So you slept squatted down, in there, between the seats. It was hot as hell during the day and cold as hell at night. About the time you finally managed to get some sleep or get comfortable, a wave would suddenly come over swamping us. And then you'd be bailing out water for the rest of the night."

Adding torment to their plight was either the absence or lack of certain provisions. It was widely known that a lot of the guys would often pilfer and steal emergency supplies out of the lifeboats to sell on the black market in various foreign ports for extra cash. Highly illegal, that if caught, one would be on the receiving end of some severe disciplinary action, if not dismissal. Perhaps now some may be silently regretting to themselves that this was ever done, as that extra piece of ration could mean all the difference between salvation and death.

Out of the four lifeboats launched if there was ever a question of any building resentment or vexation to arise, then those in Lifeboat #1 were the unfortunate recipients. Notwithstanding that it would be them that would ultimately spend the longest at sea before final rescue.

There are puzzling reservations concerning the conduct of the Armed Guard officer Lieutenant James Milne. If he was the least bit unpopular before, he seemingly wasn't aspiring now to remedy his questionable popularity as a fellow castaway. The task to carefully measure out the daily twelve ounce ration of water was left to Milne. For days now it had become increasingly noticeable that he had acquired a nasty habit. After everyone had each drunk their allotted ration, Milne raised the ire of the others by indulging himself to drink any drops of water that may have remained behind in the dipper.

Whilst the meagre rations were keeping them alive, it was barely enough to keep them nourished and all had lost much valuable body weight. The fat reserves had already begun to reach the point of exhaustion. Some had cause at taking turns to hang out over the side in the water in an effort to rehydrate their bodies. Each day the men began to grow weaker. Sea conditions grew worse. Incessant was the thought of rescue racing through everyone's minds. But mostly their thoughts were on home and loved ones. Occasionally sometimes these thoughts turned to wondering how their fellow ship mates had faired. After separating and watching them drift away, where were they now? Had they found rescue yet? Were they even still alive?

After a week on the 8th of November more ominous storm clouds gathered and again severe winds blew up. For the next several days the sea conditions continued unabated. In fact they grew steadily worse as a storm blew up that refused to cease for the next three days. The nights were freezing. Expectations and morale were reaching the lowest ebb. The seas grew higher and the tiller became harder to control. The boat kept filling with water that needed constant bailing out.

On the tenth day marooned at sea Sunday, November 12, rescue nearly came when a ship was sighted. Several flares were sent up. James Chaffin said...

"We sighted one ship on the tenth day we were out in the lifeboat. But it didn't see us. We shot smoke flares, but it was real windy that day and the wind just blew the smoke back down on to the water. They didn't see us, but they [the ship] was headed toward Australia."

The vessel steamed on. The lifeboat remained unnoticed.

"This is what really got to us," remembers Joe Gorga. "Then to make matters worse another storm blew up!"

Chaffin again: "We were in this storm for about two days and two nights. It produced waves about 20 feet high. One time you look down and you're way down there, you can see the bottom of the wave..."

So far the experienced seamanship of the Chief Mate Charlie Shenberg had kept them afloat and on course, not-withstanding the valuable compass and other navigational equipment that Cadet Chaffin had put in the lifeboat prior to launching. Shenberg had improved on this by also salvaging an extra sextant on board.

Waves became mountains as the surface churned with white topped swells. More than ever, in order to remain afloat, all hands were needed to bail out the water that was now quickly filling. This endless and unremitting task was met with no more enthusiasm than before. They were exhausted.

Their strength was beginning to fail. In fact a sense of hopeless despair and despondency began to manifest itself. Trapped in this tiny lifeboat with a raging and angry sea all around them, with no immediate signs of rescue, weakened by the conditions, hope was fading. The men were about to give up. There was now four inches of water and rising in the boat. Suddenly the Chief Mate pulled out his pistol and ordered everyone to all start bailing otherwise he threatened to shoot the first man who refused to do so.

Weary heads turned and oil stained eyes attempted to focus on the 1911 model pistol, standard Coast Guard issue, that he held and was pointing, waving from side to side.

"Start bailing I say – *now!*"

For an instant no-one moved. Partly owing to the initial shock that one of their own deemed it necessary to point a gun at them. All eyes were fixed on Shenberg. No one spoke.

"Go on – start bailing. Its sink or swim, and we, all of us, are going to swim" he commanded in his southern Texan drawl.

"You, sailor," he looked at Crowe, "start bailing that water out now!" Crowe squinted and tried to blink looking directly down the barrel of the gun, unsure if it was really happening whilst attempting to fathom the surreal reality. Shenberg turned around to the rest, "we *are* all going to make it and we *are* all going to go home. I am not going to give up and nor are any of you. Start bailing!"

Needless to say basic order and discipline soon quickly returned. All hands, some reluctantly at first began bailing out the water with what they had – shoes, hands...anything. With respite Shenberg put away his firearm and breathed relief.

"It was this dramatic but necessary call to arms that was the exact motivation we needed to get our spirits up and find strength again" recalls Joe Gorga 70 years later.

"It really was through the efforts of the Chief Mate that truly saved us all."

The desire to help each other and stay afloat soon took hold again. Hope returned, largely through the efforts and encouragement of Chief Mate Shenberg.

"He would not let anybody give up," Gorga says of Shenberg. "He was one of the older Merchant Marines and it was clearly his experience that kept us going, urging and encouraging us on. All throughout the ordeal he made us keep our lifeboat afloat in the right direction, hopefully towards land. He kept us going. I would not be here today if not for that man."

Apparently this was not the first time that Shenberg was forced to threaten to use his firearm in the boat. In an earlier incident the man placed in charge of allotting rations was caught one night stealing water.

"The Chief Mate was armed with his pistol. It was the only firearm in the lifeboat." Chaffin later wrote.

"He simply put the gun to this fellow's head and said, 'if we just catch you doing it one more time...' immediately after another man was placed in charge of rations."

Shenberg informed everyone that in this instance he was permitting himself to act under the '*Color of Law*'. This is mainly an American terminology which refers to giving oneself the appearance of legal power to act, but which may operate in violation or contravene the law.

It was now the 14th day marooned at sea. Two weeks had passed since the *Fort Lee* was sunk. An attempt at a sort of makeshift sail, or much rather a flag from a sailor's jacket had been hoisted up and fluttered in the wind. But the emergency rations were just about depleted.

"We had no food at all by now," Gorga recalls. "We tried fishing but we never even got a nibble."

"In the lifeboat we had lines, hooks and artificial bait" Chaffin wrote. "We fished for fourteen days and fourteen nights and caught nothing."

Despondency and anguish began to creep back into the mindset again, their empty bellies crying for food. There is no doubt that morale at this time was nearing its lowest ebb. It was only a matter of time where possibly even the threats and or attempts at encouraging motivation from the Chief Mate would begin to fall on deaf ears.

Then unexpectedly at approximately 10.30 a.m. on the morning of Thursday, November 16 1944 smoke is sighted on the horizon. It is a lone wisp that could very well be their salvation. Chaffin, the 19 year old Midshipman Cadet raises his head in the attempt to squint through his eyes. Windswept, sunburn, along with a combination of salt water and the awful glare of the morning sun had made it difficult to open one's eyes. Slowly the blurred image of what appears to be a ship emerges.

Refocusing and blinking soon confirms that it is indeed a ship steaming about 6 miles [10 kilometres] away. Immediately, with great effort the men in the lifeboat arouse themselves into a desperate state of exhilaration. Certainly this had to be for real and not a mirage and certainly not another vessel that would pass by leaving them unnoticed. Moreover is the hope that it is not an enemy ship.

With what little physical strength remained smoke bombs are set off and flares are fired, shooting up into the sky. The passing vessel did not notice these as it was directly away from the sun. She sailed on. For the 17 men in lifeboat #1 rescue will initially show itself to be almost as hazardous, if not more so, than being actual shipwrecked sailors.

Eight kilometres away at approximately 11.15 a.m. the Armed Guard lookout stationed on the bow of the Liberty ship SS *Mary Ball* sighted an object in the water bearing in the sun at about 300 degrees. At first it appeared that it could have been a submarine or possibly the periscope of one. When news of the sighting was relayed back up to the bridge, the Master, P.T. Jensen immediately took evasive action ordering the ship to swing hard to starboard away from the unidentified object. Two minutes later at 11.17 a.m. the general alarm was sounded.

The manned 4 inch gun mounted aft was ordered to open fire. The gunners on the *Mary Ball* had now been alerted to a foreign object lying approximately some 4,000 yards off portside. Still unsure what it was, the chief gunner nevertheless gave the order to open fire.

Suddenly for those in lifeboat #1 geyser like plumes of water impacting as large fountains splashed and shot up both in front and behind them. Horrified, they could not believe that they were being fired upon. The first thought now of course was that it is indeed an enemy vessel. Damn if it is a

Jap. After four years of war cases of their atrocities were now widely known.

The shots were falling short, but for how long? Shouts and waving of shirt tops, arms, hands - anything that would represent a signal to show that this is a receptacle containing human cargo were deployed.

A parachute flare, the last, was fired off.

Rapid fire continued. 12 rounds had been let off, until those on board the *Mary Ball* realised their error. It became quickly evident that the object in the water was indeed a lifeboat filled with living human beings. The firing ceased immediately. The Liberty ship atoned for her blunder and swung back around to steer straight for them.

The *Mary Ball* came to a halt at the position of 27°26'S–93°06'E. Whilst a rope ladder was hoisted over the side, all were very weak and tired. Their feet and legs had become completely swollen as a result of the depravation and length of time in the lifeboat. Each one was pulled on board assisted by a rope that they had to tie around themselves. George Kasper the Armed Guard who had broken his leg needed assistance to do so and was helped by crew from the *Mary Ball*. It must have been a painful experience for him. As too for the wounded 2nd Mate Asher.

After 14 days in an open lifeboat enduring storms and high seas, as well as days under a glaring hot sun with no shelter, they were finally saved. And just as well, as James Chaffin would later attest to when interviewed by naval authorities afterwards. They had endured some of the worst elements that the Indian Ocean could throw at them. Any longer and they would have begun to perish. Like the *Tumacacori* the *Mary Ball* possessed no real medical officer as such, however some of the crew had been trained in basic first aid. They were provided with fresh drinking water, fed hot soup, somewhere to wash, given new clothes and later shown to cabins to rest. The experience when delivered on board the *Mary Ball* was one of elation and jubilation.

On October 9 1944 the SS *Mary Ball* departed Los Angeles. Carrying a cargo of planes and other war material her destination was Calcutta, India via Australia. Her first port of call was Melbourne arriving there on November 4 where she took on stores and received routing instructions. She departed at 11.00 a.m. the next day on November 5. A 7,176 ton Liberty ship she was built by J.A. Jones Construction Company at the Wainwright Shipbuilding Yard in Panama City, Florida. The keel was laid down on July 20 1943 and her design number was ZEC2-S-C2 labelled as hull number 16. Launched three months later on October 12, she was delivered to the United Fruit Company as the operating agents for the United States War Shipping Administration on November 23 1943.

The vessel was named after Mary Ball Washington the second wife of Augustine Washington and mother of George Washington, the first President of the United States of America. Born on November 30 1708 in Liveley, Virginia she lived for 81 years until her death from breast cancer on August 26 1789 at Fredericksburg, Virginia, living just long enough to see her eldest son George become inaugurated as President in the same year. Augustine died in 1743, and despite the four children he fathered with his first wife Jane, with his second wife Mary, they went on to produce six more together. She never remarried and lived out the rest of her years in the house that was purchased by her eldest son George, where in her will she left him the majority of her lands and estate of which he was also her executor.

Today there are several institutions named after her including both the University of Mary Washington and the Mary Washington Hospital in Fredericksburg, Virginia and also the Mary Ball Washington Museum and Library. A monument was erected in honour of her memory in 1833 which was dedicated by then President Andrew Jackson. Unfortunately it was left incomplete until 1894 when another statue was later issued by President Grover Cleveland. The house that was purchased by George where she lived from 1772 until her death has been restored and is now a historical museum open to the public harbouring some fine examples of 18th century American antiquities.

Curiously the shipyard where the *Mary Ball* was constructed had, prior to January 1943, no actual shipbuilding experience. A year earlier in January 1942 it was reasoned by the United States Maritime Commission that ample vessels were either in construction or were planned for and any excess would be contrary to the capacity of existing and available shipyards. Furthermore the Commission decided not to undertake any additional shipbuilding expansion unless ordered by decree from the President. Soon enough and without surprise President Roosevelt did, as shipping losses began running at a high, precipitating the need for urgent replacements as well as the mounting demands from military authorities for ever-increasing war material.

A new slipway shipyard was built at Brunswick in Georgia. However by January of 1943 the Commission concluded, even though the yard itself was incomplete, that the Brunswick Marine Construction Company had not made yet sufficient progress in actual shipbuilding. Hence it was decided to transfer the contracts over to the J.A. Jones Construction Company.

Having never built a ship before, they were nevertheless awarded the contract simply on the recommendation that they possessed good management. Senior personnel were primarily made up of construction engineers from wealthier families in North Carolina. This is in contrast to a lot of the employees who were from the poorer agricultural and small rural communities in the Deep South.

They involved an assorted array of workers including former boxing prize-fighters, professional golfers, bankers and jockeys through to ex-clergymen. Additionally in keeping with other new yards entering the domain of shipbuilding for the first time to assist the war effort, the Jones Company began to implement new and untried methods in the art of constructing ships. At the yards in both Brunswick, Georgia and Panama City, Florida, the Jones Company experienced some difficulty in meeting all demands, but being a large concern they were able to bolster the strength of their workforce by new management and transferring labour from other projects.

Despite shipbuilding remaining a rather minor part of their overall operations, nevertheless for the next two years until war's end they still managed to successfully construct some 85 Liberty ships.

Founded in the early 1890's by James Addison Jones the company become one of the biggest construction firms in the United States until it merged with the Holzmann group of companies in 1979. However it experienced bankruptcy in 2003 and her subsidiaries were subsequently sold off. One of Jones's most recent and ambitious projects before their decline was the construction of the two well known 452 metre high twin Petronas Towers in Kuala Lumpur, Malaysia.

Back to November 1944 as the *Mary Ball* was heading for the nearest safe port, that being Colombo, the weather became warmer.

"We were not really interested in sleeping below deck at this stage, so most of us remained above" relates Gorga. "However for our whole time on board the *Mary Ball* we were treated very well and soon began to recover. I recall one guy giving me a pair of shoes. We were all just so glad to have been saved."

On Friday, November 24 1944 eight days after having been rescued the 17 survivors were landed on the dock at Colombo, Ceylon. In all it had now been just over three weeks since the *Fort Lee* had gone down. The crew aboard the *Mary*

Ball had done as much as they could for them and had seen them back to reasonable state of health. Waiting to receive them on the wharf were members of the Red Cross and U.S. Naval and government representatives.

Upon arrival in Colombo they were transport by truck and admitted to the noted Durdans Hospital. Sometimes known as the 'White House' it was a British military hospital where they spent four days. Here they all were given a thorough physical examination and had time to recuperate on land. Most were suffering immersion foot. Sometimes better known as Trench foot it is an awful condition caused when the feet are exposed to damp, wet, unsanitary and or cold conditions. It was a condition experienced with much frequency with troops during the First World War, hence the term 'Trench'.

All had lost weight. Max Tarnowski had lost approximately 27 pounds when rescued. James Chaffin weighed about 140 lbs at the time of the sinking and had lost about 26 pounds. Adding to this a couple of men apparently ran the gauntlet of attempting to drink seawater. One of these was Radioman Second Class Jerome Bird. A native Indian American, Bird apparently began to steadily become disturbed. "We had to stop him from drinking the sea water" said Chaffin.

"He was a big fellow. He weighed 200 pounds but during our ordeal at sea he lost about 70 pounds."

Although drinking small amounts of seawater is actually harmless, consuming concentrated amounts without fresh water to dilute and supplement it will eventually poison the kidneys and potentially leading to death.

"The last time I saw him he was still in bad shape."

Bird had already once been earlier wounded a year before in June 1943 when serving on the transport ship SS *Lewis Morris*.

Four days later on November 28 they boarded an R.A.F DC3 Dakota, also known as a C-47 Skytrain and were flown to Bombay [today Mumbai] in India. For Chaffin and undoubtedly many others in the group, it was the first plane he had ever been on. On November 30 1944 they were all placed aboard the U.S. Navy troop transport USS *General H.W. Butner* for repatriation back to the United States. There were about 5,000 on board consisting of a multitude of nationalities and seemingly well catered for and entertained. On board was the 'This is the Army' band led by no other than Irving Berlin.

The *Butner* sailed for Sydney, via Fremantle then up to Brisbane before making its way back to the United States. En route it also called in at New Caledonia to take on wounded amputees and troops suffering from mental breakdowns, what we would today call Post Traumatic Syndrome.

Lifeboat #1 as it eventuated spent more time stranded at sea than the other two lifeboats that had already been rescued. Lifeboat #2 was rescued only after five days and landed in Fremantle after a further seven. Those in Lifeboat #6 were saved after seven days at sea and landed in Albany after five. Number 1 endured exactly two weeks marooned in the open sea and a further eight days on board the *Mary Ball* before they were landed in Colombo.

The testimony to their survival battling through storms, mountainous seas, enduring thirst, lack of nourishment and coping with near despair can be attributed to not only the valiant efforts and encouragement from the Chief Mate but also to each individual mans own resilience at overcoming great odds in the spirit of comradeship, courage, support and hope.

Three lifeboats had now been rescued. Apart from remembering the nine crewmates who went down with the ship, so far all had made it alive. However there was still one more lifeboat at sea, still unaccounted for, out there with 16 men on board, somewhere in the vast expanse of the Indian Ocean.

The SS *Mary Ball*. She nearly decided the fate of the men in lifeboat #1. Nevertheless the Liberty ship rescued the 17 men and successfully took them to Colombo, Ceylon.

19 year old Midshipman Cadet James Chaffin from Monticello, Georgia. He was on the bridge when the first torpedo struck. Afterwards he wrote his own account of the attack. It is possible this photo was taken on board the *Fort Lee*.

20 year old Galleyman Max Tarnowski from Garfield, New Jersey. He suffered severe burns to his hands that affected him for the rest of his life.

Some of the Armed Guard from the *Fort Lee* enjoy a dinner gathering in Panama circa mid 1944. Those identified are, at far left at back and almost partly obscured is Andrew **Lemanski**, Second from left Russell B. **Peterson**, next him is unknown. Seated second from right is Joe **Gorga**. Seated at far right is Robert **Lanning** who later lost his life in Lifeboat #4 on Sumba Island. The two seated nearest at the forefront half turning to face the camera are unknown, although the one at left with the partially receding hairline had the nickname 'Curly'.

S 1/c Rowland R. Crowe

S 1/c George F. Kasper   S 1/c Russell B. Peterson

Three of the nine U.S. Navy Armed Guard survivors that were in Lifeboat #1.
Kaspar was injured with a broken leg and placed in Lifeboat #1 by Adams
and Hennessy.

Seaman 1st Class Joseph Gorga from Paterson, New Jersey had just come in off his shift and was preparing to settle down to play a game of cards when the first torpedo struck. From the mess room he had to climb through a port hole to escape.

Apart from himself and the clothes on his back, the only thing that Joe Gorga managed to save from the sinking *Fort Lee* was his wallet containing a picture of his future wife Margaret both seen here in Paterson, New Jersey just before he joined the Navy. They married not long after his return to the United States.

19 year old Signalman 3rd Class Bernard Levin from Philadelphia, Pennsylvania was also one of nine U.S. Navy Armed Guards that was in Lifeboat #1.

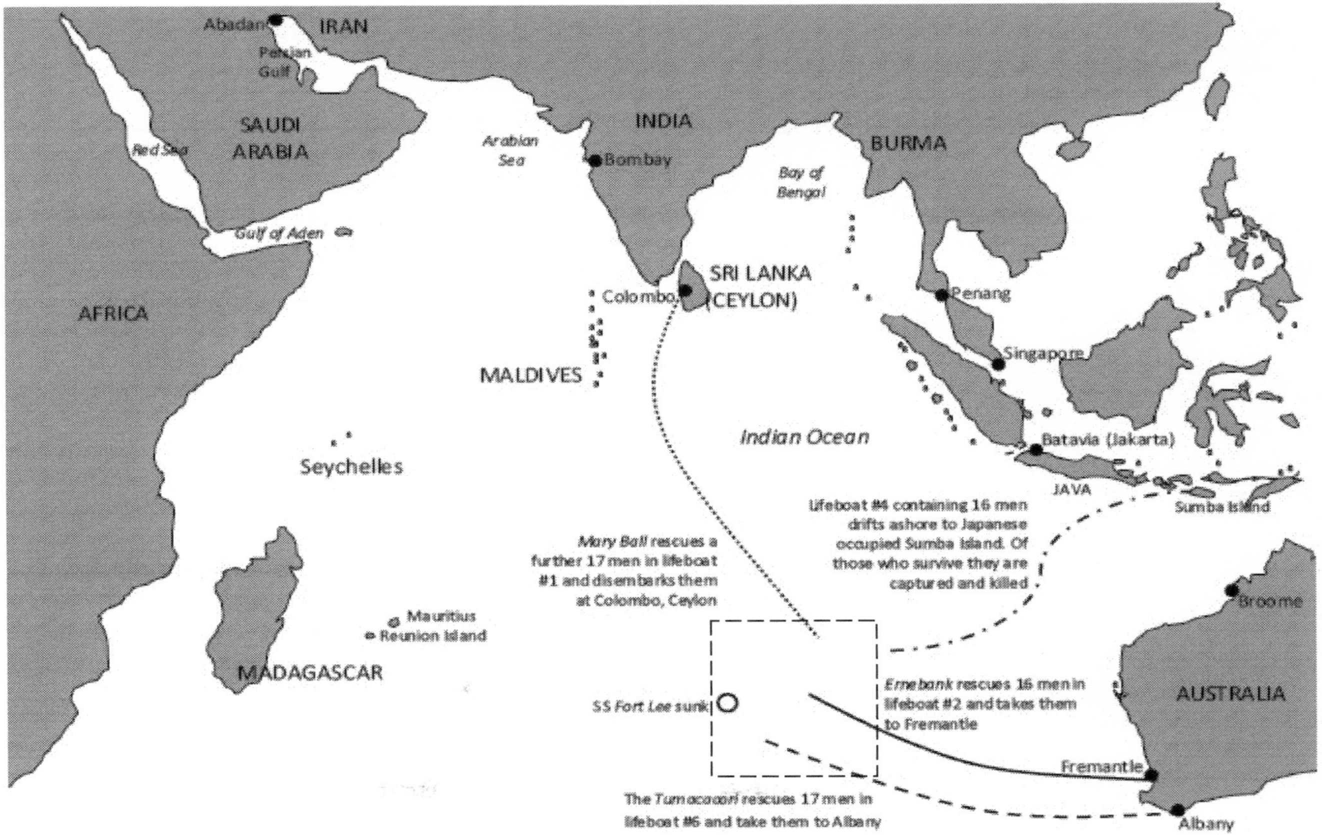
Abadan
IRAN
Persian Gulf
SAUDI ARABIA
Red Sea
Gulf of Aden
AFRICA
Arabian Sea
INDIA
Bombay
Bay of Bengal
BURMA
SRI LANKA (CEYLON)
Colombo
MALDIVES
Penang
Singapore
Batavia (Jakarta)
JAVA
Sumba Island
Indian Ocean
Seychelles
Mauritius
Reunion Island
MADAGASCAR
Lifeboat #4 containing 16 men drifts ashore to Japanese occupied Sumba Island. Of those who survive they are captured and killed
Mary Ball rescues a further 17 men in lifeboat #1 and disembarks them at Colombo, Ceylon
SS *Fort Lee* sunk
Ernebank rescues 16 men in lifeboat #2 and takes them to Fremantle
The *Tumacacori* rescues 17 men in lifeboat #6 and take them to Albany
Broome
AUSTRALIA
Fremantle
Albany

Aerial view of Colombo port and harbour, Sri Lanka (Ceylon) as it is today

The USS *General H. Butner* (AP 113) the troop transport that the men from Lifeboat #1 were placed aboard in Bombay, India. En route she called in to Sydney where the remainder of the Armed Guards from both Lifeboats #2 and #6 were picked up to sail back to the United States together, minus the Merchant Mariners from these two lifeboats who returned on the SS *Tjibadak*.

Fremantle

It is the principal port of Western Australia. Situated about 20 kilometres from the centre of Perth, the state capital, the port of Fremantle was established around what is effectively the estuary of the Swan River. Named after Captain Charles Fremantle who as commander of the Royal Navy frigate HMS *Challenger* raised the Union Jack flag there on May 2 1829. A month later Captain James Stirling arrived to establish a settlement further upstream known as the Swan River Colony, which would later become the city of Perth.

During World War II it served as the biggest submarine and U.S. Navy base in the Southern Hemisphere. Following the attack on Pearl Harbour the United States Navy relocated much of its submarine fleet and tender vessels to here. Although earlier the port had been busy with sending troop ships full of Aussie diggers to the Middle East, one of the first acts of war in Australia was triggered in Fremantle Harbour when the Italian liner *Remo* was captured in June 1940 as it was still berthed alongside Victoria Quay. From 1942 until 1945 more than 170 Allied submarines were based out of Fremantle. Working in co-operation with Albany, of these up to 125 alone were American, followed by more than 30 British Royal Navy and 11 free Dutch submarines.

The 16 men in Lifeboat #2 were taken to the Fremantle Hospital for their physical examination and check up. Although there was a modest casualty ward established as early as 1885, Fremantle Hospital was opened for in patients in 1897. Situated in Alma Street, Fremantle over the years has undergone a myriad of extensions including a major redevelopment in the late 1970's.

It was evacuated for a brief period during 1942 at the height of the threat of Japanese invasion.

On the same day that the 16 men in Lifeboat #2 were dropped off by the *Ernebank* in Fremantle, their 17 ship mates in Lifeboat #6 arrived up from Albany by train. They too were taken to Fremantle Hospital for further examination. Here 33 men from the *Fort Lee* were re-united.

They were all interviewed by an officer from the Office of U.S. Navy intelligence. Many questions were asked and statements made regarding the actual attack, the lead up to it, the U-boat, identification of the U-boat and its description. At this stage the positive identity of the U-boat was still unknown. Survivor Chaffin in a signed declaration simply stated that the submarine was large and possibly German in origin.

In the summary of statements filed to the Navy Department for the Office of the Chief of Naval Operations document number Op-16-B-5 states that, they were under the impression *"that the submarine was German."*

It also confirmed that a reply was made to Giese's questions where *"the interrogator spoke English with a German accent."* It further confirmed that a reply was given by those in Lifeboat #4 to Giese's questions regarding nationality, name of the ship, year built and destination. Years later Otto Giese confirmed that they initially mistook the name of the vessel to be British, only finding out much later that it was in fact American.

Other statements were taken regarding the conduct of the Armed Guard Officer Lt. James Milne and the Master Ottar

Andersen. This was in regard to the overall management and handling of the abandon ship procedure. Testimonies were signed by both members of the Merchant Marines and Naval Armed Guard crews.

It transpired that there was one incident that was brought into question. It involved the conduct of Lieutenant Milne. Whilst carefully aware to refrain from engendering any unnecessary sensationalism, something however did occur that was not quite right and perhaps an attempt was made afterwards to cover it. To this day there are certain elements concerning this that are still unclear and perhaps clouded in a veil of obscurity of which it will probably always remain so.

In a later report made out in December 1944 and also again in early January 1945 that was submitted to the Office of Naval Intelligence [O.N.I] several points were raised that though considered minor, were nevertheless deemed serious enough and could have been tantamount to being breaches of discipline raised against Lt. Milne.

Milne of course was the senior officer commanding the 26 Navy Armed Guards on board. One breach was the absence of a lookout stationed at the bow. The reason explained [by Milne] that the weather was such to make this position extremely uncomfortable and that the forward gun could not be trained due to a jammed roller track.

However the real serious disregard of discipline by Milne was the fact that he may have ostensibly initiated the motion to abandon ship before the official order was given by the Master. Milne endorsed the lowering of Lifeboat #6 along with five life rafts at supposedly 20.20. Master Ottar Andersen did not officially give the order to abandon ship until 20.25 just minutes before the second torpedo impacted at 20.28 hours.

Years after the war Jim Wilson visited Orville Adams who was now residing in Henryville, Indiana. He also visited another ex-Navy Armed Guard Rowland Crowe, who had been in Lifeboat #1 and was living in Indianapolis.

Wilson had read Adams' report after acquiring declassified records concerning the sinking from the archives in Washington. He felt that something was not quite right.

Adams told him that he had lied. He admitted to Wilson that a lifeboat filled with men, including the officer [Lt. Milne] that was with him, had left the ship before the word to abandon ship was officially given. He thought because of this action, they would all be court-marshalled so he changed his story.

As it was Lt. Milne ended up in Lifeboat #1 whilst Adams [along with Hennessey and Brookins] later transferred over into Lifeboat #6.

Afterwards further information and recommendations were received and drawn up by the Office of Naval Intelligence [O.N.I.] on December 27 1944 that was forwarded to the Department of the Navy, Chief of Naval Operations - document Op-23L-js referenced from document Op16-E-5. Verbatim it read:

"Enclosure (A) is forwarded with the request that arrangements be made for the commanding Officer of the Armed Guard Center (Atlantic) to determine if directives and instructions concerning the Armed Guard Service were disregarded by Lieutenant James W. Milne, USNR 211503 during the period preceding the torpedoing and loss of the vessel and if disciplinary action is warranted in the premises."

It went on to recommend and add:

"It was shown that condition #1 had not been held during morning and evening twilight as required by Article 3102 of General Instructions to Armed Guard Officers, 4th edition. Reason given for this by the Armed Guard Officer (Milne) was to relieve daily monotony for a short period. Although he

had no authority for this action, it is not construed to be a serious breach of discipline."

Addressing the custom for lookouts to relieve immediately after having come from brightly lit quarters directly, it was determined that this practice was *"against the requirements of Article 3202 (1) of General Instructions to Armed Guard Officers 4th edition."* A recommendation was made *"to make this matter the subject of a directive, since this laxity may exist generally."*

Concerning the absence of a lookout stationed at the bow at the time of the attack, of which Milne later admitted in his report, contravened Article 3202 (c) of the General Instructions to Armed Guard Officers.

"It is felt as it is believed that the weather conditions at the time of the attack were not such to make this position dangerous to personnel." It further recommended that *"a forward lookout should have been kept (there) in spite of the immobilised gun."*

Lastly the document espouses, *"That it was stated by the Armed Guard officer (Lt. Milne) that it was not customary to man the 20mm guns in case of surface attack. While there was no target visible in this instance, it is believed that if one should have appeared it would have become visible at short range in the darkness, and all guns could not have been brought to bear to comply with Article 3307 of the aforementioned publication."* [General Instructions to Armed Guard Officers 4th edition].

Furthermore it was noted by the rescued men from the lifeboat that Milne all of a sudden had become noticeably friendly. It was though he was attempting to 'make up' or buy his friendship with the survivors. After the rescue and during the journey home Milne would give chocolate, share extra rations and divide anything that he could get his hands on to the survivors. Several of those from Lifeboat #1 later remarked that there was a sense of ill-feeling towards Milne due to his actions.

Perhaps Milne lacked sufficient experience and found his leadership skills challenged when hit with the realisation that the vessel he was on was sunk and lives were lost. Perhaps he was unable to fully grasp the situation that led to making a hasty decision in failing to observe correct protocol. However one must remember, popular or unpopular, in defence of Milne he was a survivor just, like the rest and *like* the rest endured the same privations of being a castaway at sea. Nevertheless despite what perhaps the United States Navy officially thought of it, it is probably best in this instance, here in this particular book especially after 70 years, to quietly observe that what happened at sea remains at sea.

As it turned out, any case that could have resulted in the court martialling of Milne and or any other person was dropped and no further action was taken.

Just prior to being discharged from Fremantle Hospital all the Navy Armed Guards were each issued their survivor cards. These cards are *confidential* and carry a thumbprint and signature of the recipient. Upon receiving a survivor's card the receiver is required to keep it on them at all times and show it *only* to Naval Officers and or other qualified officials of the United States Government. They were not permitted to present it to members of the press or public nor were they given consent to discuss their experience with anyone other than Naval and or Governmental representatives. These directives were in the interests of contributing to the war effort.

Survivors also made some interesting comments regarding lifeboat equipment. These were officially noted and recorded and may directly led to a future overhauling of lifeboat provisions in the U.S. Navy, Merchant Marine and Coast Guard. One was the observation advising that the ordinary type blanket be replaced by a blanket that is waterproof on one side. This could be used to catch rain water as well as for its usual use.

Another was that the emergency equipment contains a rubber hose to use with a funnel for refuelling water tanks or to suck out water when the dipping measure is lost. Also suggested was that at least four points of the boat compass be self illuminated and that a frictional device be installed on the fall drums to prevent falls running out too fast.

After their short stay and check up in Fremantle Hospital the U.S. Navy Armed Guards and the Merchant Marines were separated. Michael Sherry and all the other mariners were accommodated at the British Sailors Society branch located at 28 Marine Terrace in Fremantle. Here he wrote several letters back home to Nancy in New Jersey on paper adorned at the top with the *British Sailor Society* letterhead.

To read through these private letters provides a personal insight into the thoughts and observations experienced by a foreign sailor in a foreign port, a long way from home. Some have been evidently censored with the occasional deletion of a word or phrase that has obviously stated a date or place name. There is suggestion in Sherry's letters that wartime America did not perhaps undergo the same restraints as Australia did, with rationing and ration stamps and the availability of basic items. However they also provide a small insight into everyday life in wartime Fremantle. In a letter dated Sunday, November 19 1944 he writes:

"Dear Sweetheart

Well dear we are still here at the same place and all is going along well and some of my old gang is here with me. We are only two blocks from town which is very small in itself you can walk all over town in fifteen minutes [in reference to Fremantle].

I never did so much walking in all my life since I have been here. That is about all one can do. There are two movies [picture houses or cinemas] *here and I have seen the pictures that are playing for the next week.*

Two other fellows and myself went to the larger city [Perth] *today and had a nice time at the zoo. I saw some of my long lost brothers in a cage. It was something like the Bronx zoo but not as big.*

[The reference here is the well known Perth Zoo located in Labouchere Road South Perth. Since opening in 1898 it celebrated its 115th anniversary in 2013]

I weighed myself the other day – 165 [pounds, about 74 kilograms]. *That is not so bad. I think I will put on some more before I leave here as there are a lot of milk bars and we all go for milk shakes every time we go up town. The place where I am staying is not too bad and the food is fair but nothing to write about so we go into town and have fish & chips. Now I am getting sick of that so will have to try something else. Sure will be glad to get back to the States and home to get a square meal.*

Everything is rationed here, socks and hankies, there's nothing you can buy without stamps and the stores are only open a few hours each day and only a half day on Saturday. Everything is closed on Sunday and only a few trolley's [trams] and buses running and there is no-one on the streets after dark it is just like a ghost town.

I went to the Flying Angel it is a mission house for seamen and read some books and listened to a girl band until 8.30 tonight then had fish and chips again. The time is going by fairly well as long as I have my health. The days are nice and cool, also the evenings. We may leave in a few days. Will try and write you before we leave. Please excuse pencil, lost pen and can't buy one anywhere for love or money. Will close with all my love to you sweetheart. Don't worry all is fine."

There is a small indicator that perhaps a sense of boredom has begun to develop whilst the men are waiting further instructions to be shipped out. Or rather it is probably mixed feelings of homesickness. There also seems to have been a severe shortage of ink in wartime Australia. Two days later on Tuesday November 21, Michael Sherry purchased what appear to be mostly handkerchiefs from A.J. Noble & Company, clothiers, drapers and house furnishers store located at 99 High Street in Fremantle of which the total amount came to £1, 8-8 or one pound, eight shillings and eight pence. The building is still there, however since the war Noble's have long disappeared. Residing in its place today the premises now has the ironic honour of being the site of an adult sex shop.

In another letter he attended St Josephs Church, being there for the rosary and also going to confession. Afterwards he visited the rectory where he says that he spent over an hour talking with Father Conway. Apparently he had a brother who was a priest in Brooklyn and asked Sherry to contact him when he returned to the United States. Unfortunately Father Conway later lost his life in a fire in the Philippines in 1949.

It was also on this date that he sent a telegram to his sister Marcy addressed to the department store where she worked located on Springfield Avenue in Summit, New Jersey. The last letter from Fremantle is written on American Red Cross paper dated November 21 1944. He begins with that well versed requisite wartime title "Somewhere in Australia."

"Dear Sweetheart

Well we just received the good news that we might leave sometime [censored, it may say 'tomorrow'] *so just thought I would drop you a line and let you know. I only hope it is true. We were told to get all the things we needed and be* [censored] *as they* [censored] *for us. If so this may be the last letter you will get from me until I get to the States. I suspect I would like to be home for New Years Eve. I am just hoping and praying.*

I just brought a new outfit as I know it will be cold when I get back there and I will have to have something warm to travel to New Jersey. They have their summer weather here now and it sure is nice. We have a dance here three times a week and after the dance the ladies serve tea and cakes."

Michael Sherry concludes to say that he misses the mail from home and expresses that he cannot wait to see Nancy and boys again, hoping that they are all well and safe.

For the others, their short stay in Perth manifested experiences of their own. Twenty three year old Able Seaman John Duffy from Fall River, Massachusetts discovered firsthand the meaning of the term 'small world'. Whilst in Fremantle attending a local dance he met close friend Gerry Holloran from his church parish back in Fall River. Young Bill Mootz was issued with his temporary Seaman's Certificate in Fremantle.

Brad Pruitt recalls his own memories of Perth.

"After being checked over and discharged from hospital we were given a small advance of pay and taken to a specialist clothing store in Perth to purchase new clothes. Here I bought new pants, shoes, socks, a shirt, underwear for the journey home. I remember one evening, the night before we were due to sail back to the United States, of going to an ice skating rink. I remember meeting two nice young girls here who kept on following me around."

On Friday November 24 1944 the 14 Merchant Mariners that had been in Lifeboat #6 and the 11 that had been in Lifeboat #2...all 25 of them, boarded the Dutch registered passenger and cargo ship SS *Tjibadak* in Fremantle. After stopping in at Sydney the vessel headed over to briefly call in at Suva, Fiji for supplies before carrying onto the United States. It crossed the Equator on December 8. Finally on Christmas Eve December 24 1944, the *Tjibadak* docked at San Pedro, California. It was an uneventful journey without incident, but they were finally home. After staying in a base camp for Merchant Marines, most who resided on the eastern seaboard left San Pedro by train on January 9 and arrived in New York on January 13 1945.

In Australia, apart from the short train journey from Albany to Perth for the 17 who had been in Lifeboat #6, the Merchant Mariners and the Armed Guards did not travel together. Those in the Merchant Marine were officially considered civilians, whereas the Armed Guards were U.S. Navy – and the Navy like to look after their own.

Back in Fremantle, Perth, the eight remaining Armed Guards namely Wilson, Adams, King, Atkinson, Kirwin, Lemanski, Swank and Winn all received their *Survivors Card*. They then boarded a twin engine DC-3 Dakota also known also as a C-47 Skytrain at Guildford Airfield, better known today as Perth International Airport. They were flown first to Adelaide where they were billeted overnight in a hotel.

The following day they were then flown across to Melbourne where they stayed at the Ritz Hotel, which had been commandeered for use as accommodation by the U.S. Navy. During much of the war Melbourne had been the headquarters for General Douglas MacArthur and the Allied command of the Pacific theatre. In Melbourne wounded Navy men like Atkinson and Lemanski received ongoing treatment for their wounds. Departing Melbourne they boarded the train up to Sydney where they were billeted at the Hotel Grand Central, again used for U.S. Navy personnel. The very next day they embarked on the USS *General Butner* which had arrived all the way from Bombay via Colombo and Fremantle. It was here that this group were reunited with their ship mates from Lifeboat #1. All of the survivors from Lifeboat #1 and the eight Armed Guards from both Lifeboats #6 and #2 finally arrived at San Pedro, California on board the SS *General Butner* on January 7 1945.

Fifty survivors from the SS *Fort Lee* were now all safely home back in the United States.

But there was still one lifeboat missing. Out there, somewhere in the vast lonely reaches of the Indian Ocean, there was still Lifeboat #4 with 16 men unaccounted for.

YOUR GUIDE TO
WESTERN AUSTRALIA
and
A Memento of Your
Visit to Fremantle

With Compliments of the
MERCHANT SEAMEN'S COMFORTS FUND
of the
MISSIONS TO SEAMEN
Cliff & High Sts. Fremantle

Souvenir –the cover of a tourist guide of Western Australia dated 1944 that Michael Sherry acquired whilst in Fremantle.

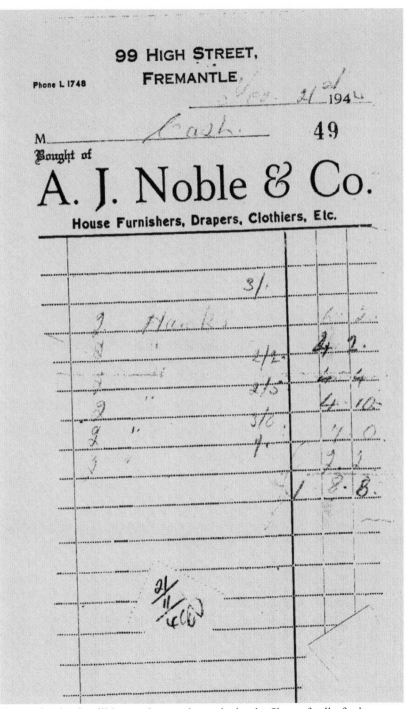

The receipt that is still kept today as a keepsake by the Sherry family for items purchased by Michael Sherry at A.J. Noble & Co in Fremantle on November 21 1944, a Tuesday. The total amount comes to one pound 8 shillings and 8 pence. Australia converted to dollars and cents in 1966.

High Street Fremantle with the Town Hall in background circa the 1930's. A.J. Noble's shop of Drapers, Clothiers at number 99 High Street is the premises in the middle at right of picture.

99 High Street today, second from left. Where once A.J. Noble & Co was is now an adult shop.

Marine Terrace Fremantle circa early 20th century. The white Edwardian building in the centre background is the British Sailors Society. At right in foreground is the old State Savings Bank.

The old Mission to Seamen 'Flying Angel Club' building in Fremantle on the corner of High and Cliff Streets facing west. It was here that the men stayed and were accommodated. In the background is the Old Roundhouse one of the oldest buildings in Western Australia. In 1966 the mission relocated to new premises in Victoria Street.

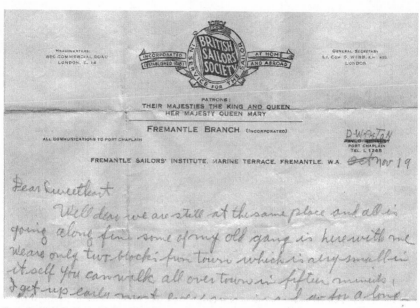

On a British Sailors Society letterhead a letter written by Michael Sherry to those back home and similarly a telegram (*below*) dated November 20 1944.

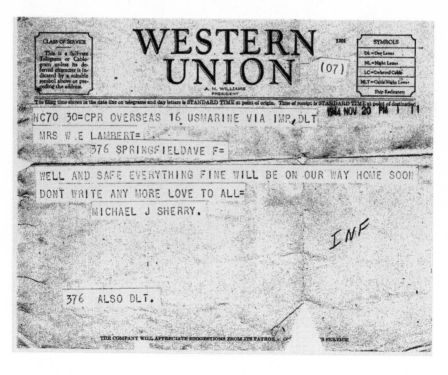

A snapshot of Perth city circa 1944 as depicted in the travel brochure collected by Galleyman Michael Sherry from the Seaman's Mission in Fremantle in November 1944. He kept it with him where it survives today as a family souvenir in North Carolina. The Perth skyline has undergone many changes since this photograph was taken.

Showing at the Princess Theatre, Fremantle for the week of November 20 to the 28 1944. In Perth during the war there were less than ten cinemas.

Two views of Fremantle Hospital from circa the late 1940's.

MEMORANDUM :

American Seamen .. Survivors from s.s."Fort Lee".

For the information of the Secretary it is reported that the persons whose particulars are shown hereunder and who debarked at Western Australian ports are survivors from U.S.Tanker s.s."Fort Lee" :-

Debarked at Fremantle from s.s."Bruebank", 14.11.'44 :

Anderson,	O.M.	Master.
Banks,	R.J.	Purser
Hart,	V.S.	Chief Radio Officer.
Lee,	J.J.	2nd "
Duffy,	J.	A.B.
Hamilton,	J.	Chief Pumpman.
Johnston,	H.D.	2nd "
Searle,	W.J.	A.B.
Burie,	J.	Chief Steward.
Groves,	E.A.	O.S.
Farrington,	B.	Chief Cook.
Swank,	T.C.	U.S.Navy.
Winn,	L.	"
Lemanski,	A.A.	"
Atkinson,	L.	"
Kirwan,	J.J.	"

Debarked at Albany from "Tumacacori", 14.11.'44 :

Stauffer,	P.	Chief Engineer.
Shaffer,	R.	1st Asst.Engineer.
Marcum,	J.	Bosun.
Smith,	P.J.	A.B.
Hennessy,	J.	Oiler.
Heffler,	A.	Messman.
Share,	G.C.	3rd Cook.
Maloo,	J.	Wiper.
Smith,	K.	Messman.
Brookins,	R.	"
Sherry,	M.	"
Hoots,	B.	"
Page,	L.B.	Jnr.3rd Asst. Engineer.
Wilson,	J.	U.S.Navy.
King,	W.	"
Adams,	O.	"

2.   In view of the fact that the Agents of the torpedoed vessel have made adequate arrangements for the accommodation and maintenance of the members of the ship's crew, no action was taken in respect of the Immigration Act & Regulations.

3.   The United States Navy personnel are being cared for by the United States Naval Authorities at this port.

COLLECTOR OF CUSTOMS W.A:

The Secretary,
Dept. of the Interior,
CANBERRA.   A.C.T.   Copy for Passport Office

List of the survivors that landed at Albany and Fremantle as drawn up by the Collector of Customs of W.A.

The SS *Tjibadak* that took the Merchant Marine survivors from Lifeboats #2 and #6 back to the United States. It is depicted here in a painting by Willem Pieter van der Does – Scheepvaartmuseum 1935.

JW/GE.

44/H.864.

24 NOV 1944

Immigration Report s.s."Tjibadak", 18.11.44.

For the information of the Secretary it is reported that the s.s."Tjibadak" arrived at Fremantle from Overseas on 18.11.'44 and sailed again direct for the United States on 23.11.'44.

2.   Included among the persons on board were eighty-six coloured deck passengers as per attached sheet, who are proceeding to the United States as relief crew for a K.P.M. vessel. As these persons were unable to produce the required travel documents they were deemed to be prohibited immigrants vide Section 3(gf) of the Immigration Act and Form 9 was served on the Master accordingly.

3.   All these persons were on board when the vessel sailed for Overseas.

COLLECTOR OF CUSTOMS W.A.

The Secretary,
        Dept. of the Interior,
            CANBERRA.   A.C.T.

27. 11. 44

Another from the Collector of Customs W.A. announcing the arrival and departure of the *Tjibadak* and some of her human cargo on board.

BERNUTH, LEMBCKE CO., INC.

GRAYBAR BUILDING
420 LEXINGTON AVENUE

TELEPHONE MOHAWK 4-9414-5-6

NEW YORK 17, N. Y.

January 15, 1945

Mr. Michael Sherry
16 Passaic Avenue
Summit, New Jersey

Dear Sir:

This will certify that the MS TJIBDAK, on which

vessel you were an passenger, en route to the United

States, crossed the equator on December 8, 1944 at

180° longtitude.

Very truly yours,

O. M. ANDERSEN

Master - S/S FORT LEE

Letter confirming the crossing of the Equator to Michael Sherry signed by the master of the *Fort Lee* Ottar Andersen.

Op-23L-js
Serial No. 08123
(SC)L11-1/QS1

CONFIDENTIAL

4 January 1945

From: Chief of Naval Operations.
To : Chief of Naval Personnel.

SUBJ: SS FORT LEE, 10,198 G.T. - Sinking of.

Ref.: (a) O.N.I. Conf. Memo. Op16-B-6 of 27 December 1944 with
       attachment.

Encl: (A) Original of reference (a).

1. Enclosure (A) is forwarded with the request that arrangements be
made for the Commanding Officer of the Armed Guard Center (Atlantic) to
determine if directives and instructions concerning the Armed Guard
Service were disregarded by Lt. James W. Milne, USNR, 211503, during the
period preceding the torpedoing and loss of the vessel and if disciplinary action is warranted in the premises.

/s/ V. D. CHAPLINE
     By direction

Letter addressed to the Chief of Naval Personnel (U.S.) in pursuit of possible action against
Lieutenant James Milne USNR.

NAVY DEPARTMENT

IMMEDIATE RELEASE
PRESS AND RADIO

FEBRUARY 5, 1945

U. S. TANKER TORPEDOED, SUNK

The SS FORT LEE, a medium sized U. S. tanker, was torpedoed and sunk in the Indian Ocean early in November 1944.

Survivors have landed in the United States.

***

Not giving much away. A copy of the rather brief official press release from the Navy Department.

U.S. LOSES TANKER & SUB.

The U.S. Navy has announced the loss of the tanker Fort Lee, which was torpedoed in the Indian Ocean last November. Survivors were landed in the United States. It has also been announced that the submarine Tang failed to return from a patrol and is presumed lost. The Associated Press says the Tang is the 37th American submarine lost in this war.—(A.A.P.)

The announcement of the torpedoing of the *Fort Lee* is publicly revealed for the first time albeit three months after it had occurred. From the *Brisbane Courier Mail* dated Wednesday February 7 1945.

U.S. TANKER TORPEDOED

WASHINGTON, February 6.—The Navy has announced the loss of the tanker Fort Lee, which was torpedoed in the Indian Ocean last November. The survivors have been landed in the United States.

The *Townsville Daily Bulletin* February 8 1945.

Tanker Sunk in Indian Ocean.

WASHINGTON, Feb 6.—The Department of the Navy has announced the loss of the tanker Fort Lee, which was torpedoed in the Indian Ocean last November. The survivors have been landed in the United States.

The loss is also announced of the USN submarine Tang, which failed to return from patrol and is presumed lost.

Tang is the 37th American submarine lost in this war. Tang's normal complement is about 70.

The *West Australian* dated February 7 1945.

Two Washington Men Spend 8 Days Adrift After Torpedoing

William Searle and Earl Smith, both of Washington, spent eight tense days adrift in a lifeboat after their merchant vessel was torpedoed in the Indian Ocean last November. Their lifeboat was one of the three picked up. A fourth was lost.

In the log book, which was maintained while the men were adrift, the story of their anxiety and dramatic rescue was related.

The tanker was hit aft by a torpedo. The explosion caused the port boiler to explode, killing two men, shutting off all power and rupturing the main and emergency radio antennae, thus making all radio communication impossible.

Lifeboats Shattered.

One lifeboat was lowered within a few minutes. Just as two other lifeboats were lowered, a second torpedo hit the ship between the two boats, breaking one in two pieces and tossing its occupants clear, and completely demolishing the other. Seven men were killed in the latter boat.

The ship was sinking rapidly after the second torpedo, and all men were ordered to abandon it.

The three remaining lifeboats were lowered, along with five rafts. About 30 minutes after the vessel had been abandoned, the submarine surfaced in the vicinity of one of the boats. An officer with a heavy German accent asked the national-

Area Mariner Tells Saga of Tanker Crew

A Mount Rainier merchant marine officer yesterday told how 16 crew members of the torpedoed U. S. tanker Fort Lee were lost at sea

PRUITT

because they preferred to strike out alone rather than risk being used as decoys by a Nazi submarine.

Steward Bradley Pruitt, 2904 Bunker Hill rd. Mount Rainier, Md., one of three Washington area men who told also how officers of the raider escaped in three other lifeboats, who claimed to have sunk 21 other Allied ships questioned the survivors at sea, then wished them a "bon voyage" as they drifted alone in the Indian Ocean.

The tanker, Pruitt said, was first attacked on October 26 by a torpedo which barely missed. For a week the submarine stalked the Fort Lee and finally rammed home another torpedo on November 2 and followed it up with a third when the ship did not immediately sink.

Nine men were killed in the explosions and the remaining survivors had barely time to launch the four undamaged lifeboats before the ship went down.

However the American press was more explicit actually naming the ship and giving details. Both articles are from *The Washington Post* dated February 4 and 7 1945 respectively.

Lifeboat #4

But there is still one more lifeboat that has not yet been fully examined. Out of the four that were successfully launched, it is those in Lifeboat #4 that ended up facing the most tragic ordeal. Their ultimate fate remained a complete mystery for the next 45 years. That is until clues suggesting to what became of them were discovered largely by accident. The scant details were not revealed until 1990.

It contained 16 men. The most senior ranking was the Third Mate, 35 year old Salem Humbleson Stine from Baltimore, Maryland. It can be assumed that Stine was in charge of this lifeboat. The oldest was 45 year old Joseph John Sorace, the Second Engineer from New York City.

There were also six U.S. Navy Armed Guards. The first was 19 year old Warren Smith Finch from Saratoga, North Carolina. From a family of eight children [seven boys and one girl] he had been brought up on farm near Saratoga. Three of his brothers were also currently away fighting in the services. Warren had joined the Navy the year before in 1943. Then there was Harold John Holden from Rockford, Illinois, Herbert Anthony Eaton from Peoria, also in Illinois, Victor R. Delmonte from Rochester, New York and Robert Franklin Lanning from Chicago...all Seamen First Class. Lastly there was Gunners Mate Third Class William Mellert from Kingston, New York.

With them were a further eight Merchant Marines. They have been identified as Frank Bell Wood, a 39 year old Able Bodied Seaman from Edgefield, South Carolina, followed by Maxwell Savolsky a 31year old Electrician from New York City, 18 year old fellow New Yorker Harry Robert Fraleigh a Messman from the Bronx, 21 year old Jack Robert Hoffman another Able Seaman from Wauwatosa, Wisconsin followed by Edward Kenneth Simms a 21 year old Fireman from Lockwood, West Virginia and Fred R.C. Stokely a 39 year old Galleyman from Del Rio, Tennessee.

Here too was 20 year old Fireman Robert John Kelly Craig from Fredonia, Pennsylvania. Known as Jack, he had only just been relieved by fellow Fireman Frank Yohe five minutes before the first torpedo hit. Originally in the Masters lifeboat, Lifeboat #2, he had transferred over into this lifeboat to make way for the wounded men. The eldest of four boys Jack had joined the Merchant Marine in July 1943 serving at various stations in the U.S. until he signed on to the *Fort Lee* in May 1944.

The last man in the lifeboat was 26 year old Rudolph Edward Broedlin. Married with a young son he was from Bridgeport in Connecticut. Tall and thin at 6'1", green eyes, brown hair and weighing 165 pounds he had only just joined the *Fort Lee* as an Oiler in July following training at Sheepshead Bay. This was his first trip away in the Merchant Marine.

After it was decided that the four boats stood a better chance if they went their own separate ways, one of the first to disappear from view was lifeboat #4. The last to visually ever see them were the men in Lifeboat #1. This occurred just before sunset on the following day, Saturday, November 4 1944. In the far distance they became a speck until finally they slipped over the horizon in a northerly direction. The 16 men vanished and were never seen again.

They obviously drifted and found themselves at the mercy of the Indian Ocean undergoing the same privations just like those in the other lifeboats. In the end however, unlike their other crewmates their plight was not be so fortunate. Like so many similar cases before them, they went on to become one of those seemingly endless and enduring mysteries of the sea.

Unforgiving, jealous and protective is that mistress - the sea, whereupon she rarely, if at all ever reveals or gives up her secrets. She commands respect and admiration. But sometimes, every now and again she lets her guard down and a clue is uncovered. In this case it was not so much what she washed up or revealed, but rather what was discovered by chance amongst files relating to Japanese war crimes.

Maritime historian Arthur R. Moore is a former Captain with the United States Merchant Marine. In November 2000 he received a telephone call from a certain Emerson M. Wiles III a civilian working for the U.S. Army Central Identification Laboratory at Hickham Air Force Base in Hawaii. 'Tripp'

Wiles requested assistance in locating the crew list from the SS *Fort Lee*. Moore advised him to contact the National Archives at College Park, Maryland where the Naval Armed Guard records are stored.

Expressing further curiosity, Moore asked him the reason why he was interested in the crew list. Wiles replied that an Australian military history researcher Tom Hall had recently contacted him and explained that he had in his possession evidence suggesting the possible fate of 16 missing seamen in a lifeboat from a ship called the *Fort Lee*. Hall is a retired Australian Army Major and Vietnam veteran.

Wiles went on to further explain that he [Hall] had chanced upon a vague reference made to the tanker amongst some documents relating to Japanese war crimes. The findings of this information inspired Moore to compose the work *Never Seen or Heard From Again* which he published online in 2001. Moore also composed an abridged version which appeared in the *Anchor Light* the official U.S. Merchant Marine newsletter in 2002. Moore's own research and work is second to none.

After contacting and corresponding with Arthur Moore in the United States, myself [the author] attempted to track down both Major Hall and also Emerson Wiles. For me both proved to be equally elusive as each other and my efforts to contact them eventually proved to be in vain. Moore himself had duly informed me that he had not any contact with either of them himself since 2001 and knew not of their current whereabouts. After many months of trying without luck, I commenced to simply resign myself to the quest and placed it on the back burner; other more important areas of research were pending and needed attention.

However shortly after, I received contact details that led me to an unexpected but seemingly reliable source which subsequently produced not only results but also some sense of clarification.

Lynette Silver does not need any introduction in Australian military history circles. She is one of the most preeminent authors and investigators particularly in the field concerning the fate of Australian and Allied POW's at the hands of the Japanese during World War II. Awarded the OAM - the Order of Australia Medal in 2004 which was presented to her by no less than the Governor-General of Australia, she has dedicated herself over the last 30 years to this cause.

She is the author of some six books including the acclaimed *Blood Brothers – Sabah and Australia 1942-1945* and *Sandakan – A Conspiracy of Silence*. Amongst her many accolades is that on ANZAC Day each year, she assists in organising tour groups for visitors and relatives of POW's to Sabah and Sandakan on the island of Borneo.

It was Lynette Silver who first exposed in 2009 the bizarre case of 83 year old Queensland man Rex Crane. For 22 years Crane had been falsely passing himself off as a former Prisoner of War claiming that in 1942 as a 15 year old he was part of a guerrilla group fighting in Malaya. He openly declared that he was captured by the Japanese who then forced him to work on the infamous Burma Railway.

Inconsistencies in his story first came to the attention of Ms Silver when he permitted himself to be elected president of the National Ex-POW Association of Australia. Investigations by her soon revealed that in 1942 he was actually still a humble school student attending Adelaide High School in South Australia. By the time he was eventually exposed, Crane had collected over some $750,000 worth of pension payments that he was not entitled to via the public purse through the Department of Veterans Affairs. The judge sentenced him to four years in prison of which he served only six months after good behaviour. Lynette Silver's *bona fides* are held in high esteem and are beyond reproach.

However there may have been some apparent confusion or rather some misrepresentation as to who it actually was that originally discovered the information pertaining to the fate of the missing men in Lifeboat #4 as described in Moore's account.

According to Silver it was indeed Tom Hall who found the file. However she informs the author and explains that it was *she* who read and finely combed through it all only to discover and isolate the story back in 1989. Throughout several documents she discovered fragmented references referring to '*American mariners*' and the name '*Fort Lee*'.

At the time both she and Tom Hall were collaborating on a separate project documenting the *Rimau* operation. Silver was seeking information on William (Bill) Roy Reynolds, a captured Australian Merchant Navy seaman involved in the *Jaywick* operation and who went missing on the island of Java after being captured and held on Balikpapan. Operation *Rimau* was the doomed follow up mission after the better known and highly successful Operation *Jaywick*.

In September 1943 a commando group consisting of 11 Australians and four British led by Captain Ivan Lyon, sneaked into Singapore harbour and planted limpet mines on Japanese shipping. Using three two man collapsible folboats [a type of canoe] they either sunk or damaged seven enemy ships amounting to over 40,000 tons.

A little over twelve months later in October 1944 *Rimau* was an attempt to emulate *Jaywick* by again attacking Japanese shipping in Singapore harbour. This time the unit consisted of 23 men, again under the command of the now promoted Lieutenant Colonel Ivan Lyon. Out of these, 13 of the group including Lyon himself were all eventually killed whilst attempting to evade capture. However 10 of the commandos, including Australian Private Douglas Warne were captured. Ultimately none these men survived either. In one way or another they were all later executed by the Japanese, the last in July 1945. As it turned out Reynolds too suffered the same fate, being executed earlier on August 8 1944.

However Hall's role in the development of this book was apparently that of researcher only. Both he and Silver have not collaborated on any work together since 1992. It is understood that mention made concerning the fate of the men in Lifeboat #4 first appeared Lynette Silver's book '*The Heroes of Rimau*' published in 1990 some 45 years after it occurred and not 57 as in Captain Moore's account. So it seems that by her efforts alone the reference pertaining to the men from the *Fort Lee* pre-dates Moore's version by 13 years.

Whilst credit can fall to Silver rather than Hall and Wiles as to who discovered this information first, it is important however not to undermine or lay fault to the good work done by Captain Moore as he was just simply presented with the information in 2000 by Hall via Wiles and was probably at that time completely unaware of Silver's work.

However no party here needs to become embroiled in any particular controversy and I defend myself from doing so. Personally I adhere to the *lex non scripta* [the unwritten rule] that history belongs to everyone and no individual or corporate body owns it. Regardless of who originally discovered the clues as to the fate concerning the men in Lifeboat #4, the important factor is, that they are genuine and portrayed in the best interests for the betterment of history and everyone concerned.

Without surprise the file is apparently enormous. The original name was *'Java 3'*. It is labelled *War Crimes Java – The Disappearance of Lts Sachs and Perske at Sourabaya* now held in the National Archives of Australia in Melbourne. Lieutenants John Sachs and Clifford Perske were members of a combined U.S. and Australian mission called *Politician 7*. In March 1945 after being despatched by an American submarine, the USS *Bream*, they were both captured in their folboat after attempting to lay limpet mines on a Japanese convoy that had anchored in the Java Sea. Following capture they were both taken to Surabaya for interrogation and internment.

In this particular file there is a small but unique reference pertaining to some captured American sailors from an oil tanker torpedoed and sunk in the Indian Ocean. This information, relating specifically to the men from the *Fort Lee* is fragmented and is like a jigsaw. Some information is based on conjecture. But overall the data can be linked and pieced together to reveal the following.

It interprets that either on or about Saturday, January 13 1945 a lifeboat washed ashore onto a beach on Sumba Island. It further suggests that the lifeboat may have at first landed somewhere on the southern coastline of the island. Nevertheless, from the position where the *Fort Lee* went down to Sumba Island, the distance covered is over 4,600 kilometres or some 2,850 miles. Notwithstanding that for those in it, this meant enduring over two months, or in excess of 70 days in an open lifeboat in the Indian Ocean...a miraculous journey on its own.

Sumba or *Soemba* Island is of course just one of the many that make up present day Indonesia formerly the Dutch East Indies. Measuring over 11,000 square kilometres [4,300 square miles] it is situated about 650 kilometres or 450 miles south east of Java, nestled in between the two larger islands of Timor and Flores and is geographically one of the most southerly in the Indonesian archipelago. With human habitation going back as early as the Bronze Age, it was first discovered by Europeans in 1522. Once known as Sandalwood Island due to the prolific amount sandalwood trees that grow there, today Sumba Island is popular as an eco-tourist destination.

However between 1942 and 1945 it was under austere Japanese military occupation. There were in fact at one time about 8,000 Japanese troops stationed on the island and like most everywhere else the local native population suffered, being subjected to forced labour and or ordered to grow crops for the war effort. Any Dutch civilians had long been rounded up. In this time the Japanese built three airstrips on the island, the largest being Kawangu near Waingapu in the east.

Two days after Japan announced her surrender on August 15 1945 the modern state of Indonesia proclaimed independence. Australian troops briefly landed on Sumba Island on November 8 1945 ahead of the returning Dutch who were anxious to reclaim her colonial status.

Returning to Lifeboat #4 there were reputedly only *three* survivors still left alive in it. One can only imagine how terribly sunburnt, malnourished they would have been; not to mention suffering from severe dehydration. Their clothes were filthy dirty and they had matted beards and hair. On landing ashore one of them reportedly died very soon after from complete exhaustion.

This is stated in the Goslett report, named after Lt. Colonel D. L. B. Goslett, Second Australian War Crimes Section, Tokyo, Japan. Dated 2/12/1947 it is titled *War Crimes – Surabaya (or Soerabaya), Java.* Here he is named as being one 'R.F. Raining, U.S. Merchant Navy'. It states that he died near the small village of Memboro or *Mamboru* which is located on the north-west coast of Sumba Island.

If this then is the case, it means that the three men were transported either overland or by water from the south side of the island around to the north side. It is believed he was buried somewhere on Sumba Island by members of the local native population, ostensibly near the village of Memboro - the exact site is unknown. There is no mention made as to what possibly became of the lifeboat itself or any personal items belonging to the survivors that may still have been in it.

It is unsure of course exactly when they fell into Japanese captivity, however one would have to assume it was almost straight away. The local native population, whilst sympathetic, could not risk secretly hiding them from the Japanese in fear of reprisals. The story has it though that the two remaining unidentified sailors were then carried by natives under Japanese guard from Memboro overland to Waingapu, the principal village on the island. Here they were held at a naval depot before being transferred across to the city of Surabaya in eastern Java and straight into the hands of the Kempetai [the notorious Japanese Secret Police] for interrogation.

As for the sailor 'Raining' there is no one amongst the entire *Fort Lee* crew who possessed this particular name. But there is one certain U.S. Navy Armed Guard who bears the name Robert Franklin Lanning and *he* was known to have been one of the 16 men in Lifeboat #4. By inserting an 'L' thus taking away the 'R' and then adding an extra 'n' whilst deleting the 'i' spells the name *Lanning*. Liberal interpretation by both the local natives and the Japanese could easily confuse the spelling and pronunciation of the man's name.

Seaman First Class Robert Franklin Lanning was from Chicago, Illinois and was only 20 years old. He is the son of Mr and Mrs Robert Brewer Lanning of 4536 West End Avenue, Chicago. It is unsure if Lanning's death resulted from his already weakened physical condition or it was hastened by the maltreatment meted out by the Japanese. Probably a mixture of both. Lanning was best friends with the wounded Lyle Atkinson. Like Jack Craig he was originally in Lifeboat #2. Lanning had given up his spot for his wounded friend and transferred over into Lifeboat #4. Sadly, further tragedy was dealt to the Lanning family as Robert's older brother Harold, also in Navy, was killed not long after on April 7 1945 off Okinawa whilst serving aboard the USS *Maryland*.

Meanwhile the two other remaining sailors, now under Japanese guard, arrived at Surabaya. It has been said that they were taken to a place called the 102 Naval Hospital located in the suburb of Darmo [or *Darumo*]. This title, for what it is worth, does not appear to exist as a common reference. Nowhere does a '*102 Naval Hospital*' make itself out to be widely known. Curiously it seems to only pop up amongst the information from the file that Hall and Emerson submitted to Moore. But there is however, one particular facility in Surabaya that does match the description. It is actually the civilian Darmo Hospital [or *Darmo Ziekenhuis* in Dutch]. Located on Darmo Boulevard it was built between 1921 and 1922 and during the occupation was confiscated by the Japanese military forces. This of course included the Imperial Navy.

Here in another file, again fragmented, a vague description is provided by a former Japanese guard, giving a possible clue as to the identity of at least one of the sailors. He stated:

"That a POW, apparently a sailor bearing a tattoo of an anchor and a heart with some English characters round it came into the hospital [Darmo Hospital]. *He was not wounded in any way, but seemed to be suffering from malnutrition and exposure."*

So, a sailor *"bearing the tattoo of an anchor and a heart with some English characters around it..."*

Admittedly it is a vague and obscure clue but nonetheless is seemingly the only hint that so far has ever transpired to give any possible identification to one of the two seamen. From the testimony submitted by this former Japanese guard under interrogation, he does not indicate where it was on the body and surprise-surprise provides no further information.

But it is doubtful that it would be been something that he would or could have made up. Unlike today, despite being around for centuries, back in the 1940's tattoos were still a novelty....an uncustomary form of body artwork that conjured up less than salubrious connotations and interpretations. Basically they were not common, especially in post-feudalism Imperialistic Japan.

Was there one sailor in Lifeboat #4 from the *Fort Lee* that possessed a distinctive tattoo of this description on his upper arm, chest or leg? In the course of writing this book the specific question was presented to the handful of still living survivors. Keeping in mind nearly three quarters of a century has passed, unfortunately none were able to recall or identify if a fellow crewmember from the ship could have possibly had a tattoo of this design.

In early March 1945 a directive was issued by senior Japanese commanders that all prisoners held in Imperial Navy custody in Java were to be executed. This was to take effect immediately following interrogation and those deemed to be of no further use to intelligence. The Japanese began to step up and intensify needless wanton massacres as the war progressed unfavourably for them.

However news of this directive had reached a certain Doctor Hirosato Nakamura. He was a surgeon, a medical doctor with the rank of Captain in the Imperial Japanese Navy. He was with the 2nd South Seas Expeditionary Fleet attached to the staff of Vice Admiral Yaichiro Shibata, the naval commander in Surabaya. Nakamura was presented with information that all these prisoners were to be exterminated.

The 'good' doctor had for some time now been working on anti-tetanus experiments. A genuine serum so far seemed elusive for the Japanese. Nakamura had been seeking an alternative with which to inoculate troops. An alternative would be a tetanus vaccine, which uses inactivated toxin, or tetanus toxoid. Statistically the death rate among Japanese forces was extremely high... some ten in every 100,000 cases, compared to U.S. Army and Navy figures where only a total of 16 deaths in all had occurred to date.

In her book *Deadly Secrets – the Singapore Raids 1942-1945* Lynette Silver describes how the prisoners already in this hospital at Surabaya became guinea pigs for crude Japanese medical experiments. In addition Nakamura had also become aware of the work carried out by a certain Commander Natase Ide, a bacteriologist who had recently developed a possible substitute originating from the deadly tetanus bacteria itself. However its instability, due rather much to its origins, attested that its administration could be lethal. Even the slightest overdose possessed the potential to cause death. So far tests with the as yet untried formula had only been carried out on monkeys. But what Nakamura really wanted was human 'guinea pigs'. He was desperate to find an anti tetanus plasma.

All the prisoners were 'detailed' to take part in Dr Nakamura's draconian experiments in this hospital at Darmo...the *Darmo Ziekenhuis*. Already in the hospital was Private Douglas Warne, the captured Australian *Jaywick* survivor and our two survivors from the *Fort Lee*. Incarcerated over in the Naval Barracks located near Gubeng Station, both the aforementioned Sachs and Perske were handed over to the hospital staff for inoculation.

Also forced to take part in this experiment were some nineteen Indonesian and Chinese civilians along with two captured American airmen. The natives had been condemned to death for the machete murder of a Japanese national on Lombok Island. The two flyers, Flight Officer Mason Schow and Sergeant Donald Palmer USAAF were the sole survivors of a B-24 Liberator that had been forced down near Makassar whilst attempting to return to base following a bombing raid over Sandakan, Borneo on October 24 1944.

Not that it probably would have mattered, but apparently the Japanese interpreter mistakenly informed them all that they were being inoculated for typhoid, telling them that a high fever may result. Nevertheless they were all lined up to receive their vaccinations. At first all the prisoners seemingly tolerated the treatment well. However to test efficacy [effectiveness] Nakamura then injected them all with a pure tetanus toxin. Needless to say after a couple of days all the men became seriously ill.

Symptoms such as muscle paralysis began to take hold in their legs, synonymous with the first signs of tetanus. This was particularly noted in the case of Private Douglas Warne. So much so that that he was placed on a 'special ration' consisting of a 'watery rice gruel' as he could now not swallow. Seriously ill too were all the local Javanese and Chinese civilians as well as the American airmen and our two sailors from the *Fort Lee*.

Nakamura was apparently meant to make provisions for a placebo, an otherwise simulated or medically ineffectual treatment for a disease and or other medical condition intended to deceive the recipient.

"These prisoners of war are very important." He growled to the hospital guards. "They must not be permitted to die!"

This bombastic decree did not help nor alleviate the appalling condition that had now befallen one Douglas Warne. In constant pain and suffering terribly, he died an agonising death soon after. The Japanese during their war crime trials initially claimed that Warne was in good health before he became ill, expressing that he had 'died from the combined effects of complications involving unexplained stomach troubles'. As it turned out, they all died.

In 1947 a Captain Jack Sylvester was appointed to the Second Australia War Crimes Section [2 AWCS]. Based in Tokyo, Sylvester was assigned to investigate the disappearance of Lieutenants John Sachs and Clifford Perske both of whom were still officially classified as *'Missing – Believed Prisoner of War'*. Interned former Japanese officers indicted on war crimes proceeded to give up a lot of information whereupon Captain Sylvester managed to uncover many other horrific offences that were committed. Unfortunately however, countless would never be brought to trial.

Nonetheless he did manage to unearth enough evidence to make certain that those responsible for the deaths of Sachs, Perske and Warne be tried. This of course would have included the murderers of our two unidentified sailors from the *Fort Lee*.

As it apparently transpires both Perske and Sachs were executed on Good Friday, March 30 1945 somewhere in the vicinity of the old Surabaya Dutch Naval Base. In colonial times it was known as the *Marine Etablissement* or more popularly the *Oedjoeng* [or Headland, Ujung in present Bahasa Indonesia, hence 'Pelabuhan Ujung']. The base was used by the Japanese Imperial Navy during the occupation as an execution ground. Sometimes incorrectly called the 'Eastern Fort' or *Eastern Port* the reason for this could be derived from its location due east from the mouth of the River Brantas [or Kali Mas]. The much larger merchant harbour known in Dutch times as Tandjoegperak, now *Tanjung Perak* lies to the west of the estuary. Equally, Tandjoengperak-Tanjung Perak has never for that matter, ever been referred to as the 'Western Port' either.

From what can be determined it was around this same date that the last two survivors of Lifeboat #4 from the *Fort Lee* died as well in the Darmo Hospital or *Darmo Ziekenhuis*. The Japanese claimed in their testimonies that the two American Merchant Mariners had died in similar circumstances involving 'other undefined causes'. Basically they endured and suffered the same awful treatment as Private Warne and the others.

Afterwards they were unceremoniously buried, or more likely 'dumped' together in an unmarked grave somewhere in Surabaya's Kembang Kuning cemetery which is located not far from this hospital. To this day there is no knowledge that the area where the two bodies of the unidentified seamen were supposedly buried has ever been excavated.

Immediately after the end of hostilities joint Allied investigation teams arrived in Surabaya only to discover that not a single prisoner, either European, Indonesian or from any other Asian background was in custody. In 1949 one Japanese prisoner openly lied to Captain Sylvester stating that no Allied POW's had been held captive in Surabaya at all. Following persistent and unswerving questioning from Sylvester, this same guard relented and afterwards admitted that not only were prisoners held at the Naval Barracks near Gubeng Railway Station, but others also had indeed been executed.

A year before, Allied recovery teams commenced digging up an area that was known to have been used as an execution ground in the Marine Etablissement, the former Dutch Naval Base near the harbour. An arduous task, after much toil, unearthed was a lower jawbone and some small bone fragments. It was thought that they ostensibly belonged to Lieutenant Clifford Perske. However the destruction of evidence was so thorough that preliminary questioning elicited no information about any Australians, and no hint whatsoever that Allied prisoners had been executed without trial, some of them after

Japan surrendered. As it turned out the remains of both Perske and Sachs had been cremated on a piece of corrugated iron.

Captain Sylvester continued his investigations and uncovered many other war crimes, some previously unknown and unsolvable due to their complexity. He not only discovered the fate of Bill Reynolds and Doug Warne, but serendipitously our American sailors.

In 1951 captured former Japanese officers charged with War Crimes were presented before the Allied Military Court conducted at Los Negros on Manus Island off the north coast of New Guinea. Here the court was adamant that Doctor Hirosato Nakamura and his accomplice Ei Tatsuzaki along with two other medical officers named Yoshino and Konishi and a Captain Tamao Shinohara all face heavy punishment.

But globally at this time the political climate was once again altering. The dawn of the 1950's had spawned a new menace with the gloomy spectre of Communism. For the victorious Allied governments the Second World War was behind them and in the contemporary politics of the day, emerging was the omnipresent threat of the Soviet bloc. The *Cold War* was in full swing and bordering almost on the paranoia new enemies were being finger pointed everywhere, including *'under the bed'*.

Consequently new friends sympathetic to the west were now eagerly needed. Japan was one. Therefore lighter sentences were being handed down to those indicted. Nakamura for his part was convicted of unlawful killing and received only 4 years imprisonment. Tatsuzaki on the other hand received only 36 months, although Shinohara at least went to the gallows on June 10 1951.

The official U.S. Navy death certificates for young Robert Lanning and the other five Armed Guards reads *'Bodies non-recoverable.'* For the Merchant Mariners it is *'Lost at Sea'*.

Despite the detailed missing gaps as to what became of these two remaining men, one thing is established beyond doubt. It is remorseful and unfortunate that the three surviving sailors from Lifeboat #4 found no salvation either on Sumba Island or even Java after enduring not only the sinking of their ship, but also a harrowing nearly two and a half months at sea combating the elements in an open lifeboat.

One can only imagine that as the emergency rations began to dwindle - then run out, thirst then hunger became the enemy. There were 16 men in this lifeboat. How must have it been when one had succumbed to exposure that the others had no choice but to simply dispose of him overboard. The psychological impact of having to do this to a fellow crewmate and friend must have been profound. One cannot really know or understand how it must have been to do this until one is forcefully confronted with the experience themselves.

Following the sinking on November 2 these were the ones that spent the longest duration at sea.... over 76 days. 76 days of freezing cold nights, hot burning days, wild storms and mountainous waves. All this and the added anguish of waking up to a seemingly endless ocean day after day not knowing if rescue would come. Perhaps there were instances of being spotted by a passing friendly ship or plane but for one reason or another they were just simply not seen. We will never know.

Another tragic irony unbeknown to those who remained alive in Lifeboat #4 is that by the time they finally arrived ashore on Sumba Island, their ship mates in the other three lifeboats had all long been rescued. In fact most had already either arrived home or were now well on their way back to the United States.

We can assume that Lifeboat #4 was, like the others, making for Australia. It is with misfortune that they were not seen, given that the Indian Ocean despite its size, spread out over a large area is still a busy shipping lane even in wartime 1944. Making landfall on the remote northwest coast of Western Australia was possible, considering that they were close. Another few degrees and they conceivably could have landed anywhere along the coastline between Broome and Darwin. Despite our own isolated and often dry and inhospitable northern coastline, it would have been preferable to coming ashore here in comparison to a Japanese occupied island only to face further hardship and certain death.

The poor souls, how dreadfully unlucky they were.

Robert Lanning, along with his two other ship mates that managed to survive the journey half way across the Indian Ocean must have been at first overwhelmingly relieved to see Sumba Island come into view. However it was relief that was short lived. It rapidly turned to dread and then finally to despair.

It is a shame that the names of the other two seamen did not survive. We must be grateful that Lanning's did. Spare a thought that on top of the ordeal that they had just gone through they would have endured further suffering at the hands of their Japanese captors, who would have initially no doubt accused them of being spies. Here one could only imagine the relentless and repetitive questioning. "Why have you come ashore on Sumba Island? Where did you come from?

What is your mission?" and suchlike as they attempted to extract more information amongst the beatings and threats.

It was proven that many former Japanese officers and guards continually lied to Allied interrogators throughout their own post war interrogations for war crimes. What is further known is that the Japanese destroyed many records and documents in the chaos leading up to and just after the surrender. On Java somewhere among these destroyed documents were probably the names of our two surviving sailors from Lifeboat #4. The needle in the haystack today would be the overwhelming if not impossible task of exhuming the known areas where unmarked graves are reputed to be in both the Kembang Kuning and Peneleh Cemeteries in Surabaya. Only then to be faced with the massive DNA testing that lay ahead.

Back on Sumba Island is there not perhaps any trace that still resonates today in local village folklore that the supposed remains of an American sailor lay buried? Where would the remains of Lanning be? Would not there be adults today who were only children at the time but still able to recall an incident of this kind? That also fuels the question of what became of the lifeboat.

At the time of writing and also falling short of going there personally of which the budget unfortunately did not permit, the author did commence an attempt to further investigate by seeking assistance from several noted authorities that have knowledgeable expertise of Sumba Island and eastern Indonesian heritage.

The House of Sampoerna Museum in Surabaya, the Asia Maior-Atlas Maoir Publishers and the KITLV-Royal Netherlands Institute of Southeast Asian and Caribbean Studies in the Netherlands and several individuals who possess firsthand experience of Sumba Island were all were extremely co-operative and helpful, not to mention very interested in the story. They all collectively clarified and explained new and important information especially on the Surabaya element of the story. However to date, the results concerning the Sumba Island part, or more specifically the possible whereabouts of Lanning's grave remain inconclusive. Once again, perhaps we will probably never know.

To briefly sum up this tragic and sad chapter is as follows:

Reputedly there were three men remaining in the lifeboat, one of whom has been identified as Robert Lanning when it came ashore on Sumba Island. Lanning died soon after arrival and the last two unidentified survivors in Lifeboat #4 from the *Fort Lee* were captured by the Japanese and taken to Surabaya, only to very soon meet their own deaths after being forced to take part in a gruesome and illegal medical experiment.

Anyone with any empathy can afford to sense the lament felt by the others who were in Lifeboats 1, 2 and 6 that many of them never lived long enough to ever find out what fate befell their shipmates in Lifeboat #4. Former Armed Guard Lyle Atkinson, seriously wounded from his burns, always felt that after swapping lifeboats, his best friend Robert Lanning gave up his life for him.

For many years afterwards, those that had been rescued pondered, and never really found any satisfying closure. For every family that part, they say, is the hardest – plainly not knowing. Both shipmates and families left behind had to be content with the unreassuringly perception that they had just simply disappeared and become lost, never to be seen again, somewhere out there in the vast expanse of the Indian Ocean.

....But they are not forgotten.

Robert Franklin Lanning the 20 year old Armed Guard from Chicago, Illinois, who died on Sumba Island.

The Lanning brothers Harold at left and Robert in middle with best friend Lyle Atkinson at right. Robert Lanning gave up his place in Lifeboat #2 for his best friend the wounded Atkinson and transferred over to the ill fated Lifeboat #4.

Mr and Mrs Lanning of Chicago who lost *both* their sons in the war.

Never seen or heard from again. Two of the 16 men known to have been in Lifeboat #4. U.S. Navy Armed Guards Harold John Holden (*left*) from Rockford, Illinois and Herbert Anthony Eaton (*right*) from Peoria, also in Illinois.

U.S. Navy Seaman 1st Class 19 year old Warren Smith Finch from Saratoga, North Carolina lost in Lifeboat #4. He was one of seven brothers, six of whom went to war – four in World War Two and two later in Korea.
He was the only one who did not come back.

26 year old Merchant Marine Rudolph Edward Broedlin from Bridgeport,
Connecticut seen here with his wife Christine in April 1944. Employed as
an Oiler on board the *Fort Lee* he was lost in Lifeboat #4.

Robert John (Jack) Kelly Craig a 20 year old Merchant Marine Fireman from Fredonia, Pennsylvania. He had only just come off shift when the first torpedo impacted. He was lost in Lifeboat #4.

The last known photograph of Jack Craig taken on May 23 1944 seen here with his Mother and Father and three younger brothers Rich, Charlie and David, just as he is about to board the bus in Mercer, Pennsylvania following leave. This was the last time they ever saw him.

Seaman William Mellert, who has been serving in the Mediterranean theatre of war, is spending a leave with his parents, Mr. and Mrs. William Mellert, 197 Hurley avenue. His brother, P. F. C. Robert Mellert, also has arrived from Fort Hancock to spend a short leave at his home.

Pre-aviation cadet Theodore

From the 'Personal Notes' column of *The Kingston Daily Freeman* in New York dated Thursday, March 2 1944. It makes mention of Armed Guard William Mellert being at home on leave. Nine months later he would disappear in lifeboat #4. A newspaper report (*below*) of the disappearance of Jack Craig. Perhaps he was one of the three that made it ashore on Sumba Island only to later die at the hands of the Japanese in Surabaya. We will probably never know.

"Jack" Craig Is Reported As "Missing" in Action

Mr. and Mrs. Grant Craig, of College Avenue, have received word that their son, Robert John Kelly Craig, familiarly known to his many friends as "Jack", is missing following action.

Neither time nor place was given where the young man disappeared. The last letter received from him was in October from an.

He is a seaman in the Merchant Marines.

No other details were given.

Three Merchant Mariners from New York - Fraleigh, Savolsky and Sorace reported as *Missing* from the *New York Times* dated Friday, January 12 1945.

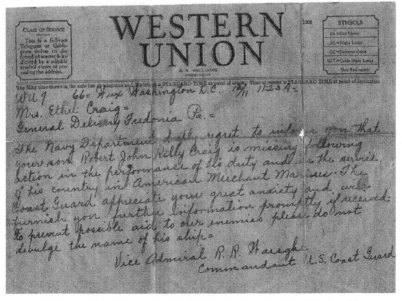

Telegram dated December 11 1944 informing Mrs Ethel Craig of her son Jack's status as 'Missing in Action'.

ADMINISTRATOR

March 22, 1945

Mrs. Christine C. Broedlin
975 Grand Street
Bridgeport 4, Connecticut

Dear Mrs. Broedlin:

By authority of the Congress of the United States, it
is my honor to present to you, the wife of Rudolph E. Broedlin,
the Mariner's Medal in commemoration of the greatest service
anyone can render cause or country.

Mr. Broedlin was lost when his ship, the S.S. FORT LEE,
was torpedoed and sunk by the enemy November 2, 1944. He
was one of those men who today are so gallantly upholding
the traditions of those hardy mariners who defied anyone
to stop the American flag from sailing the seas in the
early days of this republic. He was one of those men
upon whom the Nation now depends to keep our ships afloat
upon the perilous seas; to transport our troops across those
seas; and to carry to them the vitally needed materiel to
keep them fighting until victory is certain and liberty secure.

Nothing I can do or say will, in any sense, requite
the loss of your loved one. He has gone, but he has gone
in honor and in the goodly company of patriots. Let me,
in this expression of the country's deep sympathy, also
express to you its gratitude for his devotion and sacrifice.

Sincerely yours,

E. S. Land
Administrator

Mrs Christine Broedlin receives from the War Shipping Administration news of
her husband being awarded the Mariner's Medal posthumously.

Tarimbang Beach on Sumba Island. Whilst it is a fine example of the tropical idyll, the island itself did not provide sanctuary or liberation for the survivors in Lifeboat #4.

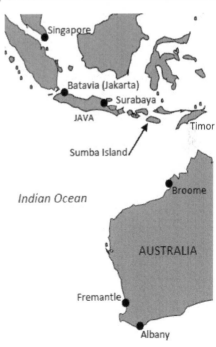

Australian Lieutenant Clifford Perske executed by the Japanese on Java. His file led to the discovery of the sailors from the *Fort Lee*.

The *Darmo Ziekenhuis* (Darmo Hospital) in Darmo Boulevard, Surabaya today. A civilian hospital it was confiscated by the Japanese. It was here that the two sailors and other prisoners met their death as a result of crude Japanese anti tetanus experiments.

With its colonial Dutch architecture one of the verandas of the *Darmo Ziekenhuis*.

Surabaya's *Kembang Kuning* cemetery today. Do the remains of two unidentified sailors from the *Fort Lee* lie buried in here somewhere in an unmarked grave?

LABORATORY OF DEATH

Tetanus Tests By Japanese

LOS NEGROS, March 21 (A.A.P.-Reuter).—A Japanese defendant told the Australian War Crimes Court to-day that Japanese doctors made a "sensational" medical discovery for the prevention of tetanus while conducting fatal experiments on natives in Java during the war.

Former Surgeon-Captain Hirosato Nakamura, who played a leading part in the experiments, said the Japanese Navy in the Dutch Indies had no serums or vaccines to prevent tetanus in 1942, because of the Allied blockade.

So he ordered a naval laboratory to conduct studies in anatoxins (serum modified so as to be no longer toxic).

CHANGED DOSE

Tests on animals gave "splendid results." Then he arranged for tests on 17 natives, who had been sentenced to death by a Japanese court martial.

As a result of the experiment most of the natives died.

"I had no idea the natives would die," Nakamura said. "Anatoxin, as every doctor knows, is not poisonous."

Because of this experiment, he said, he was able to decide the correct dose for the anatoxin, and it had later been widely used in the area with great success.

ADMIRAL ACQUITTED

SENTENCED

A.A.P.-Reuter

LOS NEGROS, Mon. — The Australian War Crimes Court today sentenced two former high-ranking officers of the Imperial Japanese Navy to prison for having illegally killed 15 Dutch East Indies natives by injecting them with a poisonous substance.

Former Surg.-Capt. Nakamura was sentenced to four years imprisonment, and former L.-Cdr. Ei Tatsuzaki to three years.

Court-Martial, and Tatsuzaki had given his permission for the experiment to take place.

Reports of cruel medical experiments began reaching the outside world from Japanese War Crimes Trials. Here two articles from the *Sydney Morning Herald* dated March 22 1951 and the *Hobart Mercury* April 3 1951.

Captain Jack Sylvester. In 1951 he was the officer who interrogated former Japanese officers indicted of war crimes. In the process he came across the oblique reference to survivors from the *Fort Lee* killed in captivity on Java.

Die letzten Tage

[The Final Days]

The *U-181* had used her last two torpedoes to sink the *Fort Lee* precipitating one of the main reasons why she chose not proceed with the pursuit of the unidentified Australian bound ship that was spotted the next day. Despite fixed armaments such as anti aircraft guns, machine guns and if equipped, a deck cannon, a submarine without torpedoes is virtually impotent. It really can only play a defensive role.

Laden with her heavy cargo of precious commodities, along with the mounting anticipation at returning back home to Germany, the *U-181* doggedly continued her journey across the Indian Ocean towards the Cape of Good Hope.

A week after sinking the *Fort Lee* Oberleutnant Otto Giese celebrated his 30th birthday which was honoured with cakes and sherry. Meantime a terrible cockroach plague had broken out on board where seemingly the despicable creatures had managed to permeate nearly every inch of the entire boat. The damned things had evidently originated from amongst some of the older provisions that had been supplied from Batavia. This wasn't helped by the many fouled jars of preserved fruit of which the crew were compelled to just simply throw overboard with disgust.

Averaging 90 miles a day in heavy seas with constant storms they still had 13,000 odd nautical miles to go.

On the morning of Sunday, November 26 1944 increasing engine problems could no longer be ignored. The Chief Engineer reported to Freiwald that slackness in the main bearings of the big twin MAN diesels were beginning to expand themselves rather rapidly. Temporary repair alone could not guarantee that they would hold up and last. Added to their woes the lubricating oil was becoming dirtier by the day. With grim reality the Chief Engineer conveyed that he could not promise the continued operation of the submarine's diesel engines. Simply put, the Babbitt and main bearings and bearing shafts, now running down to bare metal, were completely shot. Not to mention the low oil pressure.

By this stage they were only at the position of 43°05'S– 35°05'E well south from bottom tip of Madagascar with still another 10,000 nautical miles to go. There were the notorious seas off the Cape of Good Hope to navigate first before running the even more dangerous gauntlet back up through the Atlantic Ocean - and all this before negotiating the final leg around to Norway in the colder Arctic Sea.

It became plainly evident that the diesels would not hold. There was only one solution. It could not be ignored.

After much debate Freiwald reluctantly made the decision and announced that they will have to abort the journey, swing about and return back to Batavia. The frustration showed on the faces of the crew. However the thought of falling into Allied hands and spending the rest of the war as POW's even though everyone knew that there could not be that much long of it to go, did not manifest itself as being all that overly desirable. Still held was that small sense of optimism, a perfunctory adhered to more from an unswerving sense of duty, honour and loyalty rather than anything else, despite the defiant propaganda radio reports received from home.

A signal was sent back to BdU headquarters in Germany informing them of the decision and explaining the engine problems. By swinging about now, it was estimated that they stood a good chance to arrive back at Batavia by Christmas. To make matters worse the weather had not improved with increased storms, high seas and heavy swells. Then the port engine finally broke down, leaving just the starboard one barely running.

A signal was received back from BdU HQ acknowledging their plight but requested them to re-supply another *Monsungruppe* U-boat the *U-843* with their surplus fuel. The designated rendezvous point was a position east of the Cocos Islands. Despite the threat concerning Allied carrier planes that had been seen in the area, the changeover was a success. The *U-843* was another type IXD U-boat that was also en route back to Europe. In fact she successfully completed the 16,000 nautical mile journey arriving at Trondheim, Norway on April 2 1945 becoming one of the very few large transport submarines to do so. Unfortunately for her, whilst attempting to undertake the final last leg from Norway down to Kiel in

Germany she was attacked by a British Mosquito fighter bomber and sunk with most of her crew.

For the *U-181* however the return trip back to Batavia was taking a little longer than anticipated. Christmas had come and gone and was celebrated on board with toilet paper painted green serving as improvised decorations and the old gramophone record playing carols over the P.A. system. But the situation personally for Freiwald could not be any worse. For the last two weeks he had been suffering from diphtheria, debilitating enough where he found it extremely difficult to even leave his bunk.

A message had already reached *Monsungruppe* HQ in Singapore informing them of the break down and the decision to return. They were met by an Arado seaplane that was going to help guide them through the Sunda Straits. They were only too well aware of Allied enemy submarines lurking about in this stretch of water.

Finally on January 6 1945 the *U-181* again entered the familiar Tandjok Priok harbour and tied up again alongside the pier. The New Year had been ushered in to the news that the deteriorating war situation for both Germany and Japan had now reached its lowest ebb. Played out in December was the disastrous Battle of the Bulge, where the crumbling Reich threw in the last of her available tanks in a bold plan to seize passage to the English Channel. The operation failed miserably. Russian troops sweeping in from the east were increasingly getting closer to Berlin day by day as Allied forces were confidently making their way up through northern Italy.

The Empire of Japan was faring no better. In October 1944 the massive naval battle at Leyte Gulf in the Philippines, the largest sea battle in history, had left the last vestiges of the Imperial Navy all but depleted. Her once powerful army and navy air forces virtually ceased to exist as a going entity.

As a desperate measure, young inexperienced pilots were now being trained to carry out suicidal kamikaze attacks on Allied warships. Everywhere else her ground forces were being checked or were in retreat. Japan's vital supply lines to her many occupied islands broke down and became non-existent. U.S. and Allied submarines were sinking all their oil tankers and freighters.

The unanticipated arrival back to Java was not only of great concern, but privately for every U-boatman on board it simultaneously engendered a bitter taste in their mouth. Whilst the Far East held exotic temptations and delights, they simply yearned for home, despite the critical war situation there.

Another bitter irony here is that the crew of the *U-181*, whilst it was completely unknown to them and despite now dealing with their own problems, that on Java just short distance away to the east in Surabaya there was held in captivity the last two remaining survivors from Lifeboat #4 from the last ship that they sunk – the *Fort Lee*.

At this stage, late 1944 and into early 1945, only two German U-boats in South East Asia were operational - the *U-861* and the *U-862*. Both were part of the newly created *33rd U-boat Flotilla*, the latter being another IXD type commanded by Captain Heinrich Timm. On November 17 1944 the *U-862* departed Batavia and headed south for a war patrol in immediate Australian waters. After rounding Cape Leeuwin she proceeded eastbound following the Great Australian Bight. In fact her reported position was approximately 100 kilometres south of Albany on November 27. A week later her existence in Australian waters were confirmed when she attempted to attack the Greek freighter SS *Illios* using her deck cannon off South Australia on December 9. Both departed without causing each other any damage.

On Christmas Eve 1945 the *U-862* torpedoed and sunk the Liberty ship *Robert J. Walker* off the southern coast of New South Wales killing two crew, 17 year old Ernest E. Ballard, a Messman from Denver, Colorado and a Chinese-American utility worker Toon Chew from New York. This was the only case of an Allied ship being sunk in the Pacific Ocean by a German U-boat during the Second World War.

The *U-862* continued on its epic voyage crossing the Tasman Sea circumnavigating New Zealand before retracing her course back across the Southern Ocean. On the night of Tuesday, February 6 1945 the Liberty ship *Peter J. Sylvester* was steaming at a position about 1,000 kilometres south west of Perth en route to Colombo. Having departed Melbourne, on board she had a cargo war material including over 300 mules and hay destined for Army units in Ceylon as well as a significant supply of that American staple, Coca Cola.

The *U-862* torpedoed and sunk the *Peter J. Sylvester* killing 32 crew members. A total of 143 survivors in four lifeboats and six life rafts managed to get away. The ensuing search for the survivors still stands on record today as being the longest and largest combined air sea rescue operation Western Australian history. Further tragedy would strike however when a heavily laden B-24 Liberator bomber crashed upon take off at Cunderdin Airfield 120 miles east of Perth killing five of its crew. Belonging to No.25 Squadron RAAF it was participating in the rescue operation as well as out hunting for the elusive sub.

For the SS *Peter J. Sylvester* she stands as being the very last Allied vessel to be sunk in the Indian Ocean during the Second World War. The *U-862* with her crew, suffering from the effects of malnutrition and exhaustion, made for Batavia arriving back there on February 15 after completing a significantly long patrol.

Meantime for the *U-181* new orders were received to head for Singapore which, like Penang further to the north, had both come under recent heavy bombardment by Allied aircraft. It was now dangerous times. Here, she was placed into dry dock where a much needed overhaul of her diesel engines was carried out amongst other repairs including the installation of a *Schnorkel* a device that allows the vessel to remain under water without having to surface to recharge its batteries.

Plans were afoot for *U-181* to undertake another attempt to sail back to Germany on June 1. However events would overtake them. On May 3 Freiwald called the crew together and announced that Adolf Hitler was dead. The following day from Germany came a message from Doenitz informing that he was the successor. Then the two code names *Lubeck* and *Regenbogen* were issued. In an earlier agreement that had come about after the signing of the Anti-Comintern pact between Germany and Japan, if one side should lose the war it would cede its remaining firepower and resources over to the other to continue the battle.

On May 9 1945 Nazi Germany unconditionally surrendered. This now placed not only the crew of the *U-181* but all German naval and other military personnel based throughout southern Asia at the mercy of the Japanese. Former Allies now became prisoners.

Both the *U-181* and *U-862* submarines were handed over the Imperial Japanese Navy and renamed the *I-501* and *I-502* respectively. Neither of them ever saw action again. For a short while, their former German crews commenced training the new Japanese complement until it was agreed that all former U-boat personnel be transferred to the small village of Batu Bahat, actually a former British rubber plantation in the Malayan jungle. Here they became reluctant witnesses to the cruel fights and endless killings in the last days of the crumbling Japanese Empire. Then the two atomic bombs were dropped on Hiroshima and Nagasaki.

Finally the war was over.

In October 1945 the Germans, all 260 of them, were ordered by the newly arrived Commonwealth authorities to leave their relatively comfortable jungle camp. They were marched on foot for interment to the now infamous Changi prison in Singapore, the same notorious facility where only up until just months before it housed Allied soldiers and civilians. The place had already earned its well known reputation for its atrocious conditions and the evil barbarity meted out by Japanese guards.

It was here that Freiwald, Giese and all the rest of the officers and crew from the former *U-181* crew including those from the *U-862* were interned and would call 'home' for the next nine months.

Fortunately, unlike the previous incumbents they were not treated badly by the Allied authorities now guarding the place, often permitting them to work in the garden, grow food and generally clean the place up after the horrific Japanese occupation. The Germans actually began to restore the facility by repairing the plumbing and electrical lighting system. They also constructed a new kitchen and mess area. The only apparent affront was that they were requested by the British officer in charge of their district to remove their Nazi insignias and distinctions that still adorned their uniforms.

In June 1946 all German POW's and civilians in South East Asia were transported to the United Kingdom on board the SS *Empress of Australia* for further internment. After being held in various camps throughout England and Wales, most were repatriated back to Germany a year or so later. Otto Giese finally arrived back to his bombed out hometown of Bremen on August 24 1947. He had been 'lost' for three years.

And what of the *U-181*? Just like her last five victims she never left the Indian Ocean. She never saw Europe again. Instead the U-boat met an inglorious end thousands of miles away in foreign and unfamiliar waters. Under the auspices of Operation *Deadlight* that was occurring in the North Atlantic, she was doomed to oblivion. *Deadlight* was the name given to the plan to sink the remainder of Germany's surviving U-boat fleet.

In Singapore Harbour on the morning of February 15 1946 the *U-181* was hooked up to the tugboat *Assiduous* and towed out into the Straits of Malacca. Accompanying her also was the *U-862* being towed by HM tug *Growler*. For the *U-862* her irony was that it was almost a year to the day after having sunk her last victim.

Under the watchful eyes of two Royal Navy frigates, the HMS *Loch Glendhu* and *Loch Lomond*, Captain Stanley Darling commanding, they were both simultaneously scuttled at the position of 03°05'N–100°41'E.

In her fighting career the *U-181* sunk 27 ships accounting for a total of 138, 779 gross registered tons sunk. Of these, 22 were under her first commander Wolfgang Luth. Under Freiwald she sunk a further five amounting to 35,067 GRT. Her first victim was the 8,159 ton American freighter SS *East Indian* south west of the Cape of Good Hope off South Africa on Nov 3 1942 under Luth. It is perhaps with dark irony that her first and last victims were both American, the last of course, the *Fort Lee*.

Following release from being a Prisoner of War on November 23 1947 Kurt Freiwald was permitted to return to the now divided and occupied Germany. In the 1950's in the new West Germany, he rejoined the Navy and eventually became a Flottillenadmiral [Flotilla Admiral] in the revamped Bundesmarine [Navy]. He retired in 1965 and passed away ten years later on December 12 1975 at age 69 in Stuttgart.

Philip Otto Giese is one of those rare individuals who manage to live and experience full and diverse lives. He was born on November 8 1914 in Bremen. Joining the Navy in 1933 he initially served time on square riggers and merchant ships before joining the Kreigsmarine. After the war and repatriation back to Germany he found his home town of Bremen in ruins. In fact over 4,000 tons of bombs had been dropped on the city alone destroying more than 65,000 houses.

Unperturbed, he went on to successfully achieve his master's licence and establish his own shipping line that operated throughout the North Sea, Caribbean and Asia. He took an active role in rebuilding and re-establishing post war Europe. Having spent much of the war outside of Germany in foreign seas it was during this period of the late 1940's that Giese admits that he discovered for himself the inane and gross atrocities committed by the Nazis in the concentration camps as well as Hitler's rejection to alleviate the suffering of the German people. This led to a remaining lifelong refusal by himself to read any books, articles or watch any movies or documentaries on Hitler. He felt betrayed by the regime.

In another of life's ironical twists he afterwards migrated to Florida in 1964 and later became a citizen of the United States, a country he was already familiar with and had a fond affection for. In 1967 Giese married Vivian an American woman. They raised two daughters, Vivian and Gabriel and two sons Philip and Jon from his previous marriage, one of whom later graduated from the U.S. Air Force Academy and went on to serve in Operation Desert Storm, the first Gulf War in 1991.

Giese and his wife later moved to Sarasota, Florida in 2000. Since 1973 he had been the Pier Superintendent and Manager of the Greenship Steamship Company at Port Pensacola in Florida until retiring in 1981. Afterwards he wrote his memoirs drawing on his experiences as a naval officer from both before and during the war in an autobiography titled *Shooting The War - The Memoirs and Photographs of a U-boat Officer in World War II* a book that has greatly assisted this one in giving an account of the German side of the sinking of the *Fort Lee*.

Too ill to attend a reunion of former *U-181* crewmates in Hamburg in 2000, Otto Giese passed away peacefully on September 29 2001 in Sarasota, Florida at age 86.

The last known survivor of the *U-181* was Leutnant Dietrich Hille an engineer who passed away in 2007.

Otto Giese (*left*) on watch in the Indian Ocean during the homeward journey. With binoculars is Chief Petty Officer Hannes Frohlich.

Days after sinking the *Fort Lee* the crew practice drill with the 3.7 mm anti-aircraft gun that is mounted on the deck of the lower '*Wintergarten*'. The Indian Ocean rages all around them. Soon after this shot was taken the U-boat was forced to return to Java.

The *U-181* laid up in dry dock in Singapore in early 1945 following her abortive attempt to return to Europe. Repairs and the construction of a 'schnorkal' allowing her remain submerged without having to surface to recharge the batteries is seen here.

The crew of the *U-862*......

.....and her captain Heinrich Timm - the last U-boat to operate in Australian waters and to sink a vessel in the Indian Ocean. Like her sister the *U-181* they were both handed over to the Japanese.

The US Liberty ship *Peter J. Sylvester* torpedoed and sunk by the *U-862* south west of Perth. She was the last ship to be sunk in the Indian Ocean during World War II

A lifeboat filled with survivors from the *Peter J. Sylvester*.

Rescue by the battle cruiser USS *Corpus Christi* off Perth in February 1945. The *Peter J Sylvester* was the final Allied ship to be sunk in the Indian Ocean. The SS *Fort Lee* holds the title as the second last. Ironically both were American and both were sunk by German U-boats.

A B-24 Liberator from Number 25 Squadron RAAF based out of Cunderdin, east of Perth in Western Australia. They were involved to find survivors from the Liberty ship *Peter J. Sylvester* and attempt to locate the enemy submarine that sunk her.

The five headstones of the crew that perished in the B-24 Liberator after it crashed on takeoff at Cunderdin Airfield. They are buried together in the Commonwealth War Grave Cemetery in Karrakatta in Perth.

ALLIED SHIP TORPEDOED IN INDIAN OCEAN

Terrifying experiences befell members of the crew of a freighter when she was torpedoed by an enemy submarine in the Indian Ocean some time ago.

When the ship was struck she was plunged into darkness. Men floundered about their quarters, assailed by the fear that they might be imprisoned and go down with the vessel.

Many got away in lifeboats and rafts. The submarine surfaced close by, and attacked the ship again.

The men's difficulties and dangers were not over. For days they were afloat under a pitiless sun; for some freezing nights they were adrift at the mercy of rough seas.

Despite the war coming increasingly closer to cessation the torpedo sinking of the *Peter J. Sylvester* curiously received greater coverage than the *Fort Lee* did several months before.

End of the road – both the *U-181* and *U-862* now the renamed *I-501* and *I-502* respectively seen here tied up alongside the Japanese cruiser *Myoko* September 1945. The *Myoko* herself was also later scuttled in the Straits of Malacca on June 8 1946.

German crew from both the *U-181* and *U-862* now held captive in Changi Gaol, Singapore. At front attired with the apron is the former cook from the *U-181*.

Crews from both the *U-181* and *U-862* line up for a meal in Changi Gaol. At centre is the ex-commander of the *U-862* Heinrich Timm. Note the word 'swill' in English on the side of the drum.

Flottillenadmiral (Marine) Kurt Freiwald in the uniform of the West
German Navy circa 1957. He passed away in 1975 at age 69.

After the war Otto Giese later migrated to the USA. He passed
away in 2001 at age 86.

U-181
Type IXD2 U-boat submarine

Specifications

Crew: 57
Displacement (tons)
    Surfaced 1,616
    Submerged: 1.804
Length: 87.6 metres
Beam: 7.5 metres
Engines: 2 x 2,200 MAN Diesel's
        2 x 580 MAN gen.
        2 x 500 Electric
Fuel capacity: 442 tons
Speed: 19.2 knots surfaced
      6.9 knots submerged
Range: 23,700 nautical miles surfaced
Arms: 4 x bow torpedo tubes
     2 x stern torpedo tubes
     2 x twin guns
Number of torpedoes carried: 24
Emblem under Luth 1941 – 43: Ace of Spades
Emblem under Freiwald 1943-45: Swastika painted on side of
conning tower on journey out to Malaya

Third and Fourth (final) War Patrol
March 1944 – February 1946

Departed Bordeaux, France March 19 1944

3rd War Patrol
Sunk SS *Janeta* – South Atlantic May 1 1944
Sunk SS *Garoet* – Indian Ocean June 19 1944
Sunk SS *Tanda* – Arabian Sea off India July 15 1944
Sunk SS *King Frederick* – Arabian Sea off India July 19 1944
(total tonnage of these four ships 24,869 tons)

Arrived Penang, Malaya August 9 1944
Departed Surabaya, Java October 19 1944

4th War Patrol (last)
Sunk SS *Fort Lee* – Indian Ocean November 2 1944
(10,198 tons)

November 26 1944 developed engine difficulties south of Madagascar and returns to Batavia (Jakarta) arriving on January 6 1945

Taken over and ceded to Imperial Japanese Navy on May 10 1945.
Renamed the *I-501*. Never saw active service again.
Surrendered to Allies in Singapore August 1945

Sunk by Royal Navy in Strait of Malacca off Singapore on February 12 1946

Sic Transit Gloria Mundi

[So passes away earthly glory]

By February 1945 all the rescued survivors from the *Fort Lee* had arrived back in the United States. Some by this stage had already been officially discharged or relegated to be transferred to another vessel. The war was coming to a close and there was not much more of it to go. Nevertheless all were grateful to be home.

The adventure, the experience, the ordeal and or however each and every man individually would wish to personally relate and describe as to what they had gone through would be up to them. For some like Michael Sherry and many others like him, they never talked of the incident, nor really shared their overall experiences with either family or friends. What would be their legacy? What would they do? Would the *Fort Lee* be forgotten and everyone just move on and get on with their lives?

It is doubtful that any former crew member could or would ever forget. In fact it seems that none did. Whilst a lot may never have talked about it publicly to anybody, it was nevertheless an experience that would never leave them.

Lifeboat #3 – destroyed by torpedo during launch

Twenty one year old U.S Navy Armed Guard Herman Claudell Dumas was born on September 20 1923 the eldest son to Herman Clyde and Gordie Dumas in Farmersville, Louisiana. He attended Linville High School before joining the Navy in 1943 undergoing his training at Great Lakes, Illinois and Gulfport in Mississippi.

Dumas was one of six men killed in Lifeboat #3. It was destroyed by the impact of the second torpedo just as it was being launched. At the time of his death besides his parents he left behind a younger brother and a sister Peggy. His mother passed away in 1979 and his father followed five years later in 1984. His brother Ike passed away in 1995 and his sister in 2011. There is now a memorial plaque dedicated to Herman C. Dumas located in the Crossroads, Union Parish Cemetery in Louisiana.

Thirty one year old 3rd Engineer John Frederick Frels was born in Travis County, Austen, Texas in 1914. He was married and left behind his widow Clemmie and their two children, Patricia age 9 years and John Jr aged 6.

The two other Armed Guards Leon L. Carrington and Bernard G. Storm that were killed in the same lifeboat were like Dumas, awarded the Purple Heart posthumously. The bodies of all nine men killed during the attack were never recovered and they were lost at sea going down with the ship.

Young Leon Carrington was a cousin to the Rifenbury family also from Sayre, Pennsylvania who had no less than five sons serving in the armed forces...three of them in the Navy and two in the Army during World War II.

James Louis Arthur age 20 and James William McLamore age 18 were both from Baltimore, Maryland.

Brad Pruitt was good friends with James McLamore and has never forgotten him to this day.

Lifeboat #6

When 19 year old Jim Wilson arrived back in the United States in early 1945 he was granted a 30 day survivor leave which included two weeks at the Naval Rest Centre in Deland, Florida. Afterwards he shipped out on the Liberty vessel SS *John L. Stoddard*. Wilson went on to serve a total of 39 months in the navy on four ships starting with the SS *Exanthia* and then the SS *Jonathon Worth*. It was on the latter whilst anchored in Naples harbour one evening in 1943 and commencing to land troops ashore that she came under attack during a German air raid. It was thought that they were after the cruiser USS *Brooklyn* [CL-40] that was also riding at anchor. Some ships were sunk and others damaged like the *Jonathon Worth* which was taking on water. It sailed back to the U.S. for repairs. After this Wilson joined the *Fort Lee*.

Following the end of the war he married in 1947 going on to have one daughter, four sons and one stepson. Two of his boys later served with the U.S. Army, one in Vietnam and another as a Drill Sergeant. The daughter married a U.S. Air Force pilot. Jim himself worked as a general electrician until retirement in 1987. Today he resides in Troy, Missouri in a street with the delightful name of Shagbark Court. At the time of going to print in 2014 Jim Wilson is still alive and well at the age of 89. He is the last living survivor who was in Lifeboat #6. His contribution to this book has been invaluable.

Michael 'Pop' Sherry was reunited with his family in early January 1945. His three young boys Joe, Don and Jim were playing with toys in front of the Christmas tree which was still up when he unexpectedly walked into the house. Bedecked on his chest were his medals as he sported a new handlebar moustache. His frame filled the doorway. Within days however the ambiguous moustache disappeared as Nancy quietly disapproved of the new look.

Michael Sherry soon after resumed his old role back as a Police Officer in Summit, New Jersey. On the *Fort Lee* where he had been affectionately known as '*Pop*' in the police department he was known as '*Red Mike*'. After retiring in 1958 they moved to Fort Lauderdale, Florida then for short while relocated to New Orleans, Louisiana before finally settling in Pinehurst, North Carolina. Michael Sherry passed away in 1987 at age 81.

His son Jim passed away in 1981 at the young age of 42. He was in the Army National Guard. His other son Don passed away in 1998 at the age of 62. He had spent time in both the Air Force and Army and was also a Vietnam Veteran. His third son Joe is married to Neva. He has three daughters and one son from his first marriage and his wife has two daughters of her own from a previous marriage. They live today in Pinehurst, North Carolina. Michael Sherry and his wife Nancy are buried together, along with their two sons Jim and Don in Pinehurst Cemetery.

Sailor, soldier and airman William [Bill] Francis Mootz was born on January 30 1928 in Kansas City, Kansas. He was one of seven children to Croatian migrants Martin and Mary Mootz. Putting his age up Bill joined the Merchant Marines as a 15 year old and later at 16 was the youngest on board the *Fort Lee* at the time of her sinking. His trip on board the SS *Charles S. Jones* and the *Fort Lee* was his one and only voyage with the Merchant Marines. To go through and survive an experience like this at a young age was the start of many adventures for him. After repatriation back to the U.S. he went on to live a diverse and full life. Adjusting his age again he first joined the U.S. Army serving in Japan and the Pacific with the occupation forces. Discharged in 1947, the following year he then joined the Air Force taking part in the Berlin Air Lift over in Germany.

After military service Bill learnt to become an electrician by attending a local trade school with assistance from a GI program. While he had this knowledge to fall back on, he went to work for Union Pacific Railroad as a switchman. Following this, he too became a police officer with the Kansas Police Department serving with distinction there for 14 years. This was followed by a joint venture with his brother Joe to open B. & J. Appliance where he went on to became a master electrician. Afterwards he started his own company Bethany Electric where he taught and sponsored several future electricians. Married to Betty they both raised six children.

Bill Mootz passed away at home on June 22 2012 at age 84. His ashes are interred at the Veterans Cemetery in Leavenworth. He left behind his wife of 58 years, as well eight grandchildren, 16 great grandchildren and at the time of writing three great, great grandchildren. Bill's stepson Ed Egnatic also went on to serve in Vietnam.

William (Bill) Marion King was born on November 18 1922 in Bluefield, West Virginia. He was awarded the Purple Heart twice. After discharge from the U.S. Navy he married Virginia where they went on to have three daughters and one son. This in turn produced six grandchildren and three great grandchildren. Following a long battle with cancer he passed away in Saffner, Florida on May 17 2009 at age 86.

"We lived next door to Bill for many years in Seffner" writes a former neighbour. "We were friends with him from the day we moved in. He was very helpful to us in so many ways and he usually had a big smile on his face."

Bill King was interred in the Florida National Cemetery with full military honours.

Jack Hennessy was born John Leo Hennessy on July 21 1922 in Mt. Clemens, Michigan. He was the eldest son to John Leo Sr and Lyma Hennessy. His two siblings were younger brother Donald and sister, Martha Jayne. When Jack was only 11 the family moved to Superior in Wisconsin where at 14 he got a job working the taconite docks in the Duluth Harbour. It is here that he first fell in love with the lake that began a lifelong affair with the water, sailing the Great Lake Superior as often as possible. He also loved golf and worked as a caddie saving what he earned so he could to afford to play himself.

The family moved again this time to Minneapolis, Minnesota where Jack attended high school. Here he played ice hockey and baseball, as he did in grade school and actually continued to play hockey into well into his sixties. Afterwards he enrolled at St. Thomas College in St. Paul. Originally wanting to become an engineer, but with the United States entry in to the war he decided to join the Navy instead. At 20 years of age in 1942 he unfortunately could not pass the eye exam due to colour blindness. So he turned his attention to the Merchant Marine where he was readily accepted and signed on.

After the war Jack worked for the local gas utility company Minnegasco, where he stayed until his retirement. He also served as the president of the local gas workers union for many years and passed that legacy onto his son John Jnr, who worked at the same company in various positions also until retirement just three years ago. Jack also worked as a consultant to several smaller gas companies until he 'truly' retired at age 72.

In 1947 he married registered nurse Marjorie Jean Laramie where they went on to have nine children in 17 years – six girls and three boys. Today there are 25 grandchildren and 18 great-grandchildren. Jack worked as a volunteer at the same hospital where his wife worked as a labour and delivery nurse until her own retirement. He remained active with Merchant Marine veterans attending meetings and ensuring later that benefits were being received by other veterans. He golfed for the last time only two months before his death. Jack Hennessy passed away on December 26 2007 at age 85. He is interred in the Fort Snelling National Cemetery in Minneapolis, Minnesota.

For his and Orville Adam's part in aiding the wounded Second Mate both received the following from the Chief of Naval Operations, "Such level headed display of coolness resulting in the saving of human lives, we believe, deserves special praise and commendation."

Robert (Bob) Charles Brookins was born in Sioux City, Iowa on June 11 1925. He joined the Merchant Marines in January 1943 serving until December 1946. Besides the *Fort Lee* he also served on board the SS *Wood Stock Victory, Joseph Wiedemeyer* and the *Santa Fe Hills*. He died in 2011 at Clear Lake, Indiana at age 86.

Zeb B. Page Jr was born on March 8 1919 the son of Zeb Sr and Carrie Page. He was 26 at the time of the sinking and passed away at age 73 on September 8 1993 in Durham, North Carolina.

Augustus Hoffler, at the time a twenty one year old Galleyman from New York lived until the age of 88. Gilbert C. Share passed away at age 86 in Norfolk, Virginia in 2010. Jessie C. Marcum passed away in Richlands, Virginia. Roy Schaffer passed away in 2006 in Seattle, Washington and John Malec passed away in 2011 in Rosedale, Maryland. The remaining four survivors who were in Lifeboat #6 Earl

Smith, John Davis, Francis Smith along with Armed Guard, Orville D. Adams are all now deceased.

Chief Engineer Paul Stauffer passed away in 1979 in Harris County, Houston, Texas at age 86. Sometime between the rescue and the return back to the United States Paul Stauffer presented to Jack Hennessy a transcript of the log that was kept by him in Lifeboat #6. The information that it contained was invaluable. The author is grateful to the Hennessy family for providing a copy of it for research purposes for this book.

Lifeboat #2

After arriving in America from Norway, Ottar Andersen later married and had three children; two daughters and a son Bill who actually had served during World War II as well. After the war Andersen went on to captain other ships, one being the freighter SS *New London*. Ottar Andersen passed away in Walla Walla, Washington in 1968 at age 78.

His grandson Mark Evans from Corpus Christi, Texas attended a reunion of former *U-181* crewmembers in 2000 in Hamburg, Germany, keeping in contact with several of them afterwards. He indicated how the former U-boat men offered their condolences to those killed on the *Fort Lee* as well as to the disappearance of Lifeboat #4.

Able Seaman John Duffy Jr was born in 1921, the son of Amy and John W. Duffy Sr. He attended BMC Durfee High School until 1937. Afterwards he graduated from Fort Trumbull Merchant Marine Officer's School in Connecticut as an ensign. After the war he found employment as a salesman for the Cox Paper Company in Fall River, Massachusetts until retirement in 1980. He married Frances where they went on to have three sons and two daughters.

Duffy became a member of the Fall River Clover Club, a charter member of the Fall River Barber Shop Quartet Singers and also a member of the American Merchant Marine Veterans, New England Chapter [Massachusetts] and the Longboat Key Chapter [Florida]. He died unexpectedly whilst driving his car on May 25 1999 at age 78 just two months shy of celebrating his 50th wedding anniversary to Frances. He is buried in the St. Patrick Cemetery in Fall River. A hardened sailor to the end, he always judged people afterwards as to what it would be like to be stuck with them in a lifeboat for two weeks.

The Duffy family greatly assisted the author by providing an invaluable eighteen page account of John Duffy's personal recollections that he wrote in May 1945 only six months after the incident itself when it was all still relatively fresh in his mind. The document was collated and underwent some minor editing by his nephew Owen Hartnett.

In one passage Duffy wrote, "The ship was going down by the stern rapidly and the seas were beginning to break over the catwalk. I had to pinch myself to make myself believe that it was really happening to us...our good old *Fort Lee* and not some bad dream."

Seaman 1st Class Thomas Charles Swank was born on September 17 1923 in Akron, Ohio. At only 18 he married Odell Hunter who at age 22 was four years his senior. The wedding took place in a small church in Brooke County, West Virginia on July 30 1942. Tom Swank passed away on August 23 1967 at the young age of only 44. He is interred in the Green Lawn Memorial Park Cemetery, Summit County in Akron, Ohio.

Armed Guard Andrew Albert Lemanski was born on February 4 1923. He passed away on April 14 2003 at age 80 and is interred in the Sacred Heart Cemetery in Yale, Michigan.

Purser Robert J. Banks was born on May 27 1916. He was 28 years old at the time. He passed away on May 15 2004 at age 87 in St James, Wantonwan County, Minnesota.

Fellow Seaman 1st Class and Armed Guard Lyle James Atkinson was born on November 28 1925 at the family farm in Dalton, Wisconsin. He was the third eldest born to William J. and Edna Atkinson. Whilst having three brothers and a sister Lyle was the only one to serve his country. He joined the U.S. Navy at age 18 on March 10 1943 attending the training camp at Great Lakes, Illinois. He served on the SS *Newber* and the SS *Sailor Splice* before joining the *Fort Lee*. Following repatriation back to the United States, due to his wounds he spent a short time in a Navy hospital then three months at the Navy Rest Centre in Florida. Whilst at the time he may have been concerned what the burns to his arms may do to ruin his tattoos, later in life he actually came to regret these.

He married Dorothy Douglas of Catonsville, Maryland on January 19 1945. They had met earlier at a USO roller skating party in 1944. "Lyle had purposely tripped me to get my attention," Dorothy later said. Together they went on to have three daughters, Norma, Ginny [Virginia] and Teresa. Lyle was discharged from the Navy on Christmas Eve, December 24 1945.

After managing a dairy farm in Cambria they moved in 1950 to Mauston, Wisconsin where he became a semi trailer truck driver, a job he held for the next 33 years. Yearning to be an auctioneer since attending one as a boy with his father, in 1958 he made his dream come true by attending Reisch's

School of Auctioneering in Mason City, Iowa. Driving his truck during the week he would cry auctions on the weekends. In 1983 he went into auctioneering full time establishing Atkinson's Realty & Auction Service with Dorothy.

A man who was deeply committed to his faith, he always felt that the Lord was looking out for him from being rescued at sea, surviving many miles of safe truck driving and numerous operations. Lyle J. Atkinson passed away on October 13 1996 at Baraboo, Wisconsin age 69 years in the arms of his wife Dorothy who passed away 14 years later in 2010. They are interred together in the Walnut Hill Cemetery in Baraboo, Wisconsin. From their three daughters they have three grandchildren and five great-grandchildren. Despite disliking the water and not ever learning how to swim, Lyle Atkinson had Navy forever in his soul. He was a very neat man and everything had a place. His shoes were always polished with a Navy shine. Daughter Norma fondly recalls, "I remember Dad teaching me to shine shoes the Navy way."

Brad Pruitt was born Bradley Royce Farrington on August 24 1924. Farrington is actually his birth mother's maiden name and Pruitt is his adopted name. After the *Fort Lee* and the return to America he went on to serve on several Liberty Ships including the SS *Winchester Victory* and the SS *Tuscu-*

lum Victory. He served in every maritime war zone except on the Russian convoys to Murmansk before being discharged in December 1945.

After the war his step father found him a job as a water carrier for a brick laying company and also taught him how to lay them as well. Afterwards he went into partnership with the owner where the business itself went onto to become at one stage the largest masonry contractor in Florida called Cook & Pruitt. Here Brad's role mainly involved drafting up the cost estimates on the projects they tendered. He also spent some time in Cuba and later bought a 10 acre mango and fruit nursery farm back in Florida. In 1974 he married Kay which produced a daughter Vicki. In 1989 the family moved from Miami, Florida to Lyons in Georgia where not long after he was diagnosed with inoperable prostate cancer. His wife passed away in 2008.

Today 25 years later since that original diagnosis Bradley Pruitt is still alive and well residing in a VA Medical Hospital in Dublin, Georgia. He is 90 years of age. His contribution to this book has been indispensable. On behalf of the author, his daughter Vicki along with a Mr Greg Rogers conducted and recorded a live interview with him for this book. When asked to look back at his overall time serving in Merchant Marine his reply was,

"I enjoyed every moment of it. It was one of the happiest periods of my life. If I was not such an old man today I would go back and do it all again."

Lifeboat #1

Cecil Burnell 'Tex' Knauth was at the time a 30 year old Oiler on the *Fort Lee*. Born on February 14 1914 in Vernon, Texas he passed away in Washington D.C. on July 31 1963 at only age 49. He is buried in Lawnhaven Memorial Gardens, San Angelo, Texas.

Messman Max John Tarnowski was only 21 years old at the time when the *Fort Lee* was sunk. He was born on July 14 1923 at Garfield, New Jersey the second of three sons and one daughter to John and Margaret Tarnowski. He suffered severely burnt hands during the evacuation of the *Fort Lee* that affected him for the rest of his life. After the war he worked as a chef in a five star hotel but had to prematurely leave as the now sensitive skin on his hands could not bear to stand hot temperatures. Afterwards he went to work for Bendix Aeronautics for 50 years. He married briefly and had one daughter Carole, who was raised by her father and grandparents. He later remarried when Carole was ten. Max Tarnowski passed away on April 18 2004 at age 80 at Elmwood Park, Bergen County, New Jersey. His mother Margaret, a native of Poland predeceased him in 2001 at the grand old age of 104.

Navy Armed Guard Lee Roy Prewitt was born on April 6 1924 in Mercer County, Liberty, Kentucky. He was the son of Zelbert (Jack) and Dora Prewitt. After the war he married Loraine where they had a son Jack. He was also the founder and owner of Liberty Auto Parts and Garrard Automotive Supply as well as past president and director of Farmers Deposit Bank in Middleburg. He passed away on September 14 2009 at age 85.

Signalman 3rd Class Bernard Levin from Philadelphia, Pennsylvania was born on August 24 1925. He joined the Naval Reserve in July 1943. After being repatriated back to the United States he later served at the Armed Guard Centre in Brooklyn, New York until discharge in April 1946.

James Thomas Chaffin Sr was born on October 8 1925 in Jasper County, Georgia. On arrival back in the United States in January 1945 he first went by train from San Diego to Los Angeles. He then took another train to New York then to Kings Point. Afterwards he acquired rest leave in Georgia where he was still having trouble with his feet. He was to later recall, "That there was so much oil all around us. Oil covered the water and everything else - lifeboats, clothes, seamen etc. I could still get oil out of my ears six months afterwards!"

After the war he moved to Atlanta and became an insurance representative for Metropolitan for 35 years. Later he worked for the Georgia Department of Agriculture for eight years. James married Martha Burch of Atlanta and they produced two sons J. Thomas Chaffin Jr. and Robert Burch Chaffin.

James Thomas Chaffin Sr passed away at age 80 on July 2 2006 peacefully at home in Atlanta, Georgia.

His son Tom is a noted author and research professor of history at the University of Tennessee in Knoxville. Based in Atlanta amongst his many works is: *Pathfinder: John Charles Frémont and the Course of American Empire* and a forthcoming book on Frederick Douglass's 1845-46 lecture tour of Ireland. He is also the author of *Sea of Grey: The Around the World Odyssey of the Confederate Raider Shenandoah.* Tom Chaffin greatly assisted the author in supplying a transcript of portions of a recorded interview that he conducted with his father over two days in April 1998.

Joseph William Gorga was born April 22 1923 in Paterson, New Jersey. He attended the East Side High School and graduated in June 1941. Joe played American football and the previous year was a member of East Sides High School's 1940 New Jersey state championship team. He joined the U.S. Navy at age 19 undergoing four weeks basic training at the Naval Training School (N.T.S.) located at Great Lakes, Illinois followed by special gunnery training at Gulfport in Mississippi. In all he served about a year on board the *Fort Lee*. After returning back to the United States he married Margaret Arturo on April 1 1945 at age 21. She too was a local girl from Paterson and had also attended East Side High School. They both went on to produce three children that has resulted in five grandchildren and a further four great grandchildren, the most recent being Emily Ann Berry born on December 20 2013.

Joe went onto serve on board the Liberty ship tank carrier SS *Stephen R. Mallory* before being stationed at Lido Beach, Long Island, New York where he was honourably discharged in 1946.

In war where there is tragedy, there is also often humour.

"People found it hard to believe that I got stuck in that porthole," he recalled later with a laugh.

"But shortly after the war I ran into one of the guys that had to push me through. He had to keep pushing and pulling until I became free. I brought him back home and had him tell my wife and whole family the entire story otherwise they probably still wouldn't have believed me!"

That fellow who had pushed him through the porthole turned out to be one Max Tarnowski. They both kept in touch for a little while after the war then lost contact. That is until by a chance meeting they ran into each other one day at the open air farmers market in Paterson. Tarnowski was with his daughter Carole, only a little girl at the time and Gorga was with his wife's family.

Sadly Joe Gorga passed away on February 25 2014 in Brick, New Jersey just two months short of turning 91 and prior to the release of this book. It was only a week before that I had e-mailed his son Joe Jr to report that it was on schedule and had gone into pre-print. Joe informed me that his father was very excited by this news and it is a shame that he did not live a little longer to see it. I am grateful to the Gorga family that his firsthand account was able to be captured. Like Jim Wilson and Brad Pruitt his contribution to this book has been invaluable. However in the words of Joe Gorga himself no man in Lifeboat #1 could ever forget the efforts of Chief Mate Charles Shenberg. Therefore in his honour this chapter is dedicated to him. I think Joe would have liked that.

Lifeboat #4 – All Lost. No Survivors.

As previously mentioned Robert Franklin Lanning was the son of Robert Brewer Lanning and at the time in November 1944 both his parents were living at 4536 West End Avenue in Chicago, Illinois. Born in 1924, he was only 20 years old when he met his death on Sumba Island. Robert attended Our Lady of Sorrows and Marshall Elementary Schools followed by Washburn Trade School. He enlisted in the Navy after two years working for Western Union. A memorial service was held for him in 1946.

Tragically Robert's brother, Harold McClellan Lanning also serving in the Navy as a Seaman 2nd Class, was killed in action off Okinawa on April 7 1945 while serving as a gunner aboard the USS *Maryland*. He was buried in the Fort Snelling National Cemetery, St. Paul in Minnesota. The Lanning's only had the two sons.

After the war the Atkinson family in Wisconsin remained good close friends with the parents of Robert and Harold Lanning. Mr and Mrs Lanning would send Lyle and Dorothy's three girls Christmas presents every year. By doing this they somehow still felt that they wanted to stay connected, as Lyle was Robert's best friend.

U.S. Navy Armed Guard Warren Smith Finch was born on July 22 1925 in Saratoga, North Carolina. He was one of eight children...seven sons and one daughter born to John William Finch and Myrtle Irene Etheridge Finch. They were brought up on a farm near Saratoga and collected their mail three miles away in Stantonsburg. After attending school in Saratoga, he enlisted in the USNR in 1943. Out of the seven brothers, six served in the armed forces – four in World War Two and two later in the Korean War.

Unfortunately Warren was the only one that was lost. At the time he was just 19 years of age. His nephew, also named Warren Smith Finch is the son of Alton Lawrence Finch and is named in honour of his missing uncle. Today he proudly has his uncle's Purple Heart (awarded posthumously) his 48 star flag and some letters that were written to the family afterwards by former crewmates.

Frederick Royal Clyde Stokely was a 39 year old Messman from Del Rio, Tennessee. He was born on October 10 1904 and was the third son, and fifth born of eight children to Joseph Steven David Stokely and Carrie Ann Sexton Stokely. His mother was only fifteen years old when she married lumberman Joseph Stokely in 1892 in Cocke County. His father went on to forge a successful business in timber industry.

Gunners Mate Third Class William Judson Mellert was the son of Mr and Mrs William Mellert of 197 Hurley Avenue in Kingston, New York. He had a brother Robert who had been a Private First Class in the U.S. Army.

Edward K. Simms was a 21 year old Able Seaman from Lockwood, Nicholas County, West Virginia. He was the second eldest of four sons born in 1923 to farmer Homer H. and Amy E. Simms.

Seaman 1st Class Herbert Anthony Eaton was born in Peoria, Illinois in 1923. He was one of four sons to Mr and Mrs Herbert J. Eaton of 829 West Ayres Avenue in Peoria, Peoria County, Illinois. A 1941 graduate of the Spalding Institute he joined the U.S. Navy in 1943. Two of his brothers, James and Joseph were both in the Navy also, and his other brother Donald served in the Air Force. He is listed on the Tablet of the Missing in the American Cemetery in Manila, Philippines.

Harold John Holden was also a Seaman 1st Class in the U.S. Navy Armed Guard and was the son of Mr and Mrs Chellis Holden from Rochester, Illinois.

Rudolph Edward Broedlin was born on August 29 1917 in Bridgeport, Connecticut. He was the second son to Rudolph J. Broedlin and Grace Morey Broedlin. His two siblings were his sister Eleanor and brother Donald. At age 24 he married 22 year old Christine Carroll Glynn on March 27 1941 and resided at 975 Grand Street, Bridgeport, Connecticut. Prior to joining the Merchant Marine he was a production clerk. On completion of training at Sheepshead Bay he received his Seaman's Certificate only on July 11 1944 whereupon he then signed onto the *Fort Lee* as an Oiler.

Together Rudolph and Christine had only just the one son who they named Dennis Edward Broedlin. Born on October 3 1942 he was only two years old when his father disappeared. After the war Christine Broedlin re-married and went on to have another son and daughter. Today Dennis Broedlin is alive and well and married to Ellen. They reside in The Villages, Florida, a series of several large retirement communities. He has three daughters, Kristen, Jennifer and Sharen from his first marriage. Recently Dennis donated his father's Merchant Marine medal along with some letters to the Eisenhower Recreation Centre located in The Villages.

Robert John Kelly Craig was better known by family and friends as 'Jack' or 'Bobby Jack'. He was born on September 22 1924 in Greenville, Pennsylvania the eldest of four sons to Walter Grant Craig and Ethel Grace Kelly Craig. His brothers were Richard and twins Charles and David.

Jack attended school to ninth grade in Greenville and then went on to finish tenth through to twelfth grade at Fredonia, Pennsylvania until he graduated in June of 1943. Fit, athletic with a crop of blond hair and blue eyes he had a flair for sports excelling at baseball and basketball - playing on the County Class B Championship Basketball team of 1943. He was also the President of his high school senior class.

Jack Craig enlisted in the Merchant Marine a month after graduation in July 1943. Following initial training at Sheepshead Bay in Brooklyn, New York, his first assignment was on board an iron ore boat in the Great Lakes for approximately two months. This was followed by being assigned to Philadelphia to supply Caribbean Army and Navy bases from January to late April 1944. He then took a leave on May 1 returning home to Fredonia for a visit.

At some earlier stage in life Jack had been involved in a serious car accident that left a scar on his face. Whilst home on leave his mother said to him "I wish we had the money to get that scar on your face fixed, you're such a nice looking boy". To which he replied, "That's okay, I don't want it fixed. This scar may help to identify me one day."

On May 23 1944 the Craig family which included his father, mother and three younger brothers' escorted Jack back to the bus station in Mercer, Pennsylvania to return to duty. This was the last time that they ever saw him.

After reporting to the Seaman's Institute in Philadelphia, he was accepted for assignment on board the *Fort Lee* because of his diesel training, joining her at the Baltimore, Maryland shipyards. Over the next several months the family received regular letters from Jack from Panama and Australia up until the time of his disappearance in Lifeboat #4. He was only 20 years of age.

After the war Hugh Johnston, the 2nd Pumpman on the *Fort Lee* from Parkerburg, Pennsylvania visited Ethel Craig in Fredonia. Johnston was in Lifeboat #2 which Jack had originally got in to. He related to her the story and to extend his condolences for the loss of her son. The Craig and Johnston families went on to form a friendship visiting each other several times long after the war.

In late 2013 attempts were still being made to track down other family descendants and or relatives of those who were in Lifeboat #4. The author is grateful to the Finch, Broedlin and Craig families for their kind contribution and involvement in this book.

SS Tumacacori

Sidney Fargo, the Master of the *Tumacacori* was born Sidney Jenkins in London, England on March 12 1891 the younger son of Charles and Lisetta Jenkins who ran a grocery business in Hammersmith. After running away to sea at an early age, purportedly unable to withstand the dominance of his two older sisters Elizabeth and Ada, he changed his surname from Jenkins to Fargo. Joining the U.S. Merchant Marine he rose through the ranks to later become a Captain.

He married twice. His first wife was Connecticut born Ruth Adele Near whom he married in New York. They had one daughter Lisa who went onto have two children Daniel, now head of a structural engineering company in Minnesota and Christie, a teacher who resides today in Bournemouth, England. Ruth passed away in Los Angeles in 1941. His second wife was Hawaiian born Esther Kalani who pre-deceased him in 1975.

After the war Fargo was presented with a 48 star flag for services to the Merchant Marine. He ended up living the remainder of his life in the United States.

Years later, Tony Morgan, a grandson of Sidney Fargo's sister Elizabeth [whom he had visited during the war when the *Tumacacori* was docked in Sydney] had the opportunity to meet him. Tony who resides today in Adelaide, South Australia, met his Uncle Sidney in 1979 whilst working in the U.S. shortly before he passed away. By this stage Fargo was living in a nursing home in Santa Cruz, California. Tony's cousin Ross Morgan stayed with Sidney Fargo in Felton, California throughout December 1964 and January 1965. Ross recalls him relating many of his experiences at sea, none more so than expressing the beauty of the harbour and surrounds of Albany. Sidney Fargo passed away peacefully at age 89 on September 17 1980. His other sister Ada, born in 1881 went on to become Australia's oldest female at the time when she passed away at age 110 in 1992.

In late 1944 after departing Tinian Island the *Tumacacori* sailed back across the Pacific to Balboa in Panama. Whilst laid at anchor there 18 year old Galleyman Elmer Fought severely injured his hand which required him disembarking and spending a week ashore in hospital. Upon release he was re-assigned to another ship the SS *Thomas Kearns* as a workaway until she arrived back in San Francisco on April 24 1945.

In June he re-entered the service and was assigned to the SS *Fire Island*. It sailed down to the Panama Canal and then back up to the Gulf of Mexico where they towed a freighter into Galveston, Texas. After that they proceeded to New Orleans where he was finally discharged on November 14 1945. He returned to Hayward, California on board a Santa Fe Trailways bus. In all he had spent 15 months in the Merchant Marine.

After the war he worked in various jobs, later becoming a machinist until retirement in 1993. He and his wife went on to eventually have seven children which produced 14 grandchildren. They now have 35 great grandchildren which has so far resulted in a further five great, great grandchildren. In 2014 Elmer Fought is still alive and well at 87 years of age residing with his wife Euna in Saratoga, California.

Upon the completion of writing, though every effort was made, it is not known how many more former crewmen there may still be alive who served aboard the *Tumacacori*. The same applies for the British MV *Ernebank*. In the latter stages of research the author received a message from a family relative of a former crew mate from the SS *Mary Ball*. However despite numerous attempts to communicate they did not respond.

Précis

During World War II a total of 144,970 enlisted men and officers served in the U.S. Navy Armed Guard. It has been figured at least 1,810 were either killed or went missing in action. Then there were many more wounded. It is a casualty rate comparable to any of the fighting armed forces.

Up to as many as 250,000 men served in the United States Merchant Marine on board at least 4,221 merchant ships. Of these, variable estimates place that somewhere up to 8,300 merchant seamen were killed or went missing. Furthermore as many as 12,000 were wounded and up to 600 were captured and interned as Prisoners of War. Some sources place the casualty rate of those killed even higher at well over 9,000. This figure does not include those who eventually died from wartime injuries. Their casualty rate was 1 in 26 higher than any branch of the Armed Services. After the war between 1945 and 1950 up to 42 U.S. merchant vessels were sunk by hitting mostly left over undetected mines. The last was the SS *American Planter* that struck a mine in the Atlantic in August 1950. It is unknown how many more may have perished in these post-war misfortunes.

For the men who served on board the *Fort Lee* they received their deserved medals and service decorations. For all the surviving the U.S. Navy Armed Guards they were each awarded the Purple Heart, as well as the Atlantic War Zone medal, Mediterranean & Middle East War Zone medal, Asiatic Pacific Medal with ribbons.

But let's remind ourselves that this particular story here would not have unfolded the way it did if not for the *U-181*. No one is condoning or defending their actions, but for the 57 sailors on board it, likewise, they too were young men at the mercy of not only sea itself but also the demands of war. Their misfortune was being held to ransom for what was expected and insisted of them by an evil totalitarian and despotic regime.

After Germany's surrender and with their vessel confiscated, they were placed in detention by the Japanese who virtually saw them as an embarrassment, if not a liability. Freiwald and Giese in particular, were Navy men from the old school where gentlemanly honour and seamanship existed and was taught, so much so that they attempted to still uphold and cling to those values. It would be charitable to say that they had no time for Nazism and its perverted doctrines.

But the last word has to go to the *Fort Lee* herself. She may have been just another dirty old oil tanker, a rather dull, perhaps unremarkable non-descript vessel that possessed conceivably no exceptional qualities. Perchance to say she was nothing really out of the ordinary and there was nothing particularly romantic about her. But she did have a role to perform and a duty to carry out.

She will probably never be 'discovered'...that is doubtful will she ever be the lucky recipient of some expensive expedition where remote robot submersibles fitted with cameras are sent down just to observe and see how she appears today. Although the thought is welcoming, there will probably never be any memorial dedicated to her, nor to the memory of those who served on board her and lost their lives. That is the other side to the tragedy of human conflict.

The SS *Fort Lee* rests in very deep water, at over some five kilometres or 16, 400 feet down on the seabed of the Indian Ocean. The legacy of her story is the memory of her survivors. For all those who have no known grave but the sea itself, it is they that shall never grow old. The white caps that you see on the ocean are the headstones over their graves.

The sea is eternal.

New Jersey Police Officer Michael Sherry in uniform taken after the war in 1950 and with wife Nancy in the early 1980's in North Carolina.

Jim Wilson former U.S. Navy Armed Guard still alive and well in 2014.

Ottar Marius Andersen, Master of the *Fort Lee* passed
away in the state of Washington at age 79 in 1968.

Bradley Royce Pruitt seen here in 2008 at age 84 with his daughter Vicki. He is still alive and well in 2014.

Thomas Charles Swank (left) passed away in 1967 at the relatively young age of 44.

Andrew A. Lemanski passed away in 2003 at age 80.

Lee Roy Prewitt passed away in 2009 aged 85

Former U.S. Navy *Fort Lee* Armed Guards Joe Gorga (*left*) and Andrew Lemanski (*right*) seen both here together in March 2002. Gorga, the last survivor from Lifeboat #1 passed away in February 2014 only two months before his 91st birthday.

John W. Duffy Sr former Able Seaman from Massachusetts seen here in a pre-war High School graduation photograph. He passed away in 1999 aged 78.

Bill Mootz who had only been 16 at the time on the *Fort Lee* seen here with his grand-daughter. *Inset*: At his sister's wedding in 1956. Bill passed away in 2012 at age 84.

At the helm. Lifelong sailor and golfer Jack Hennessy
who passed away in 2007.

Lyle and Dorothy Atkinson in the
early 1990's. Married for 51 years
he passed away in 1996 at age 69.
Dorothy followed 14 years later in
2010.

Inset: Married in 1945.

Memorial headstone dedicated to Herman C. Dumas in the Union Parish Cemetery, Louisiana today. He was killed just as Lifeboat #3 was being launched.

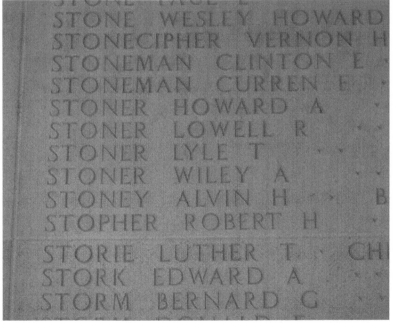

Bernard Gustav Storm, a 19 year old U.S. Navy Armed Guard from Owatonna, Minnesota also killed in Lifeboat #3. His name appears on the Tablet of the Missing in the American Cemetery in Manila, Philippines.

Australian Tony Morgan and baby Gilly with his great uncle Sidney Fargo the former Skipper of the *Tumacacori* in California shortly before he passed away in 1980.

Elmer Fought seen here in 2004 visiting India some 60 years after having first arrived there as a young crewman aboard the *Tumacacori* in 1944. He is still alive and well in 2014 at age 88.

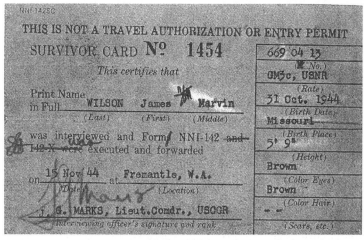

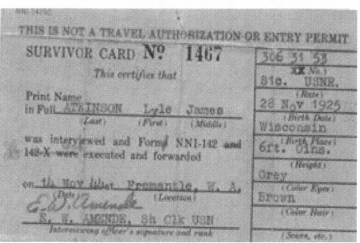

Survivor Cards that were issued to Jim Wilson and Lyle Atkinson and the other Navy Armed Guards when discharged from hospital in Fremantle, Perth and transported back to the U.S. - front (*top*) reverse (*below*). Explicit instructions evidently.

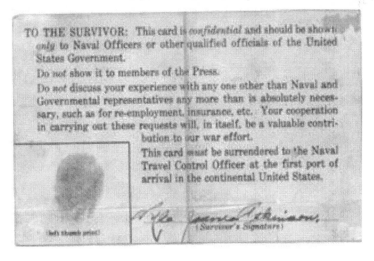

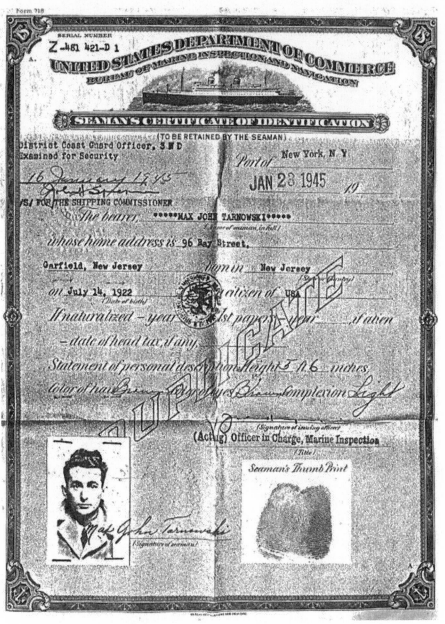

An example of the Seaman's Certificate of Identification issued to all mariners. This one was for Max Tarnowski who was in Lifeboat #2

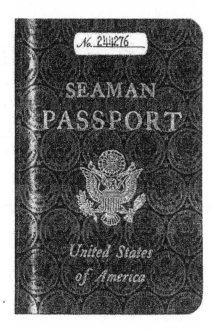

Elmer Fought's Seaman Passport issued to all Merchant Mariners

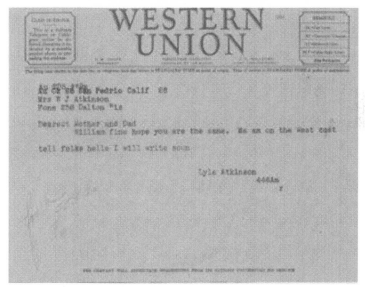

Telegram from S/1c Lyle J. Atkinson back to his parents in Wisconsin

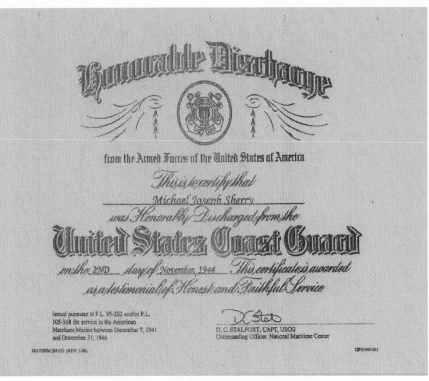

Michael Sherry's discharge certificate issued from the United States Coast Guard for service in the U.S. Merchant Marine backdated to the day of the sinking of the ship.

Bill Mootz's Certificate of Discharge from the U.S. Coast Guard officially signed on January 3 1945 in New York. It is dated from when he first boarded the *Fort Lee* in Abadan until the date of its sinking.

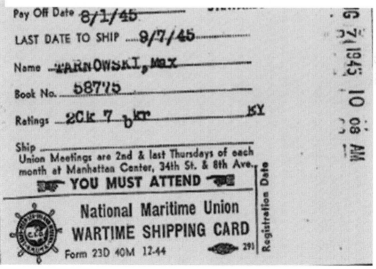

Pay Off Date 8/1/45

LAST DATE TO SHIP 9/7/45

Name TARNOWSKI, MAX

Book No. 58775

Ratings 2Ck 7 bkr KY

Ship _____

Union Meetings are 2nd & last Thursdays of each
month at Manhattan Center, 34th St. & 8th Ave.

☛ YOU MUST ATTEND ☚

National Maritime Union
WARTIME SHIPPING CARD
Form 23D 40M 12-44

Max Tarnowski's NMU Wartime Shipping Card

Rudolph Broedlin's Statement of Service document issued July 11 1944.

Jack Hennessy's framed U.S. flag, bullet shells from his burial at Fort Snelling and his Merchant Marine cap on display in the Hennessy family today.

'In the memory of John L. Hennessy awarded by a grateful nation' signed by the President of the United States.

LEONARD WINN RECEIVES PURPLE HEART

Leonard Winn, Signalman Third Class, U. S. Naval Reserve, son of Mr. and Mrs. David Winn of 23 Bedell street, has received the Purple Heart Medal for wounds received in action against an enemy of the United States last November 2. The presentation to Winn was made at the U. S. Naval Armed Guard Center, Brooklyn, by Lieutenant William L. Musser, U. S. N. R., recently.

Notice that Signalman Leonard Winn who was in Lifeboat #2 receives his Purple Heart. From the *Hampstead Sentinel* Long Island, New York dated Thursday May 31 1945.

Emily Whitney Is Bride on Sunday

Miss Emily Whitney, daughter of Mr. and Mrs. Frank W. Whitney of Willow avenue, Hempstead, was wed on Sunday to Leonard Winn, son of Mr. and Mrs. David Winn of Bedell street, Hempstead. The ceremony took place at the Garden City Hotel.

Mrs. Robert Fitzgerald of Hempstead, was her sister's matron of honor. Bridesmaids were the Misses Jane and Estelle Whitney, sisters of the bride, Mildred Hutzler and Edith Galuba, cousins. Jules Winn served as his brother's best man.

The bride attended Newburgh schools, A graduate of Hempstead high school, Mr. Winn served with the navy during the war. They will live in Hempstead.

Like so many after the war returned servicemen married their sweethearts. Former Armed Guard Leonard Winn married his. From *The Hempstead Sentinel* dated Thursday September 23 1948.

HAROLD LANNING   **ROBERT LANNING**

The body of Seaman 2/c Harold Lanning, son of Mr. and Mrs. Robert Lanning, 4536 West End, will be at the funeral chapel at 3246 Jackson, Monday and Tuesday.

A burial service will be held at Ft. Snelling, St. Paul, Minn. He was killed in action April 7, 1945, off the coast of Okinawa while serving as a gunner aboard the USS Maryland. A memorial mass was celebrated at St. Mel's church shortly after word was received of his death.

An older son of the Lannings, Seaman 1/c Robert Franklin Lanning, was lost at sea aboard the USS Ft. Lee, a tanker, on Nov. 2, 1944. Memorial services were held for him in 1946. He attended Our Lady of Sorrows, Marshall Elementary, and Washburn Trade schools and enlisted in the navy after two years employment at Western Union.

Harold attended Orr, Our Lady of Sorrows, and Marshall Elementary schools. He was attending Washburn Trade school when he enlisted in the navy shortly after his seventeenth birthday. The family has requested that flowers be omitted.

A newspaper report announcing the memorial service for Harold Lanning, the brother of Robert. The Lanning's of Chicago only had the two boys and lost them both.

Descriptions of Rank – Merchant Marine

Master
The Captain or Master is the commander of the ship. Also known as the Skipper he is in charge of everyone and everything aboard ship and must be familiar with the function and role of every task performed on board. He has sole responsibility for the crew, conduct and performance of the vessel. He must know everything about his ship.

Purser
The Purser is responsible for the handling of all money on board and is the officer responsible for all financial administration and supply of the ships goods.

Chief Mate
The First or Chief Mate is responsible for the maintenance of the ship and proper stowage of cargo. An experienced seaman he handles the fore deck in tying up. He is a good navigator in the use of sextants and compasses. He will assume command of the vessel in the event of the Master's death or inability to command the ship.

Second Mate
He is a good navigator and plots courses as well as takes fixes. He handles the after deck when tying up and can also double as the communications officer.

Third Mate
Is the junior deck officer and is responsible for all life saving equipment and assist in the navigation of the vessel and the loading and unloading of cargo. All mates, that is the First, Second and Third stand respective watches.

Bosun
An old seafaring rank that dates from at least the 15th century, the Bosun (boatswain) is the senior crewman of the deck. He oversees freight and cargo being loaded down in to the hold and on board deck. The Bosun also supervises other members of the ship's deck crew.

Able Seaman (AB)

An Able Seaman is expected to perform all deck duties which include but not limited to operating deck machinery such as the windlass or winches, painting, stowing cargo, lookout and handle a lifeboat under oars or sail. He must know lifeboat equipment drill and take command of the lifeboat if required.

Ordinary Seaman (OS)

At the bottom of the ladder in rank. His duties are usually to assist the able seaman.

Wiper

A wiper is the most junior crewmember in the engine room of a ship. The role of a wiper consists of cleaning the engine spaces and machinery and assisting the engineers as directed. In the United States Merchant Marine in order to be employed as a wiper on a ship they need to have a Merchant Mariner's Certificate.

Oiler

The main role of an oiler is to literally oil machinery. From the industrial revolution right through to modern machinery in various industries, oilers were required in maritime, rail engines, steelmaking, and mining. A role less required today due to technological progress and changes.

Galley Hand/Messman/Steward

They are responsible for the daily preparation and serving of meals in the mess room. In addition they can be also required undertake cleaning duties, maintenance and housekeeping duties as well as monitoring food stores, and other utility duties as required.

Pumpman

A Pumpman is part of the engineering department. Mostly they are found only on oil tankers. There can be several titles such as Chief Pumpman and or Second Pumpman. He undertakes all necessary work for the safe operation of the transfer of liquid cargo including the pumps, filters, pipes, valves, deck fittings.

U.S. Navy Armed Guard

S 1/c – Seaman First Class

Carries out ordinary deck duties, including watch duties, messenger and is also member of the gun crew.

GM 3/c – Gunners Mate Third Class

Maintains guns, gun mounts and ports.

SM 1/c – Signalman First Class
Sends signals by semaphore, flags, Aldis lamp, also watch duties

BM 2/c – Boatswains (Bosuns) Mate Second Class
Supervises deck work and manning, operations of loading and unloading and mooring.

SM 3/c – Signalman Third Class
Almost same duties as SM 1/c

RM 2 /c – Radioman Second Class
Transmits and receives radio codes and signals

Lt. Jr. – Lieutenant Junior Grade
Officer of Armed Guard commanding

General Glossary of Terms

USMM – United States Merchant Marines
USN – United States Navy
USS – United States Ship
ONI – Office of Naval Intelligence
SS – Steam Ship
MV – Motor Vessel

Kriegsmarine – German Navy 1933-1945
Bdu – Befehlshaber der U-boote (Commander of the U-boats HQ)
U-boat – *Unterseeboot* (under sea boat)
Ober – higher part of several military ranks
Obermaat – Petty Officer 2nd Class
Oberleutnant – Lieutenant
Kapitanleutnant – Capitan Lieutenant (*lit.*)
Korvettenkapitan – Lieutenant Commander (*lit*) Corvette Captain
Kapitan zur See – Captain (Captain of the Sea)
Konteradmiral – Rear Admiral

SS Fort Lee

Class: T2-SE-A1
Type: Tanker (oil)
Hull laid down: October 24 1942
Launched: February 25 1943
Tonnage: 10,198 tons
Displacement: 21, 880 tons
Length: 523 feet (160 metres)
Beam (width): 68 feet (21 metres)
Maximum Speed: 16 knots
Range: 12, 600 miles (23,300 kilometres)
Propulsion: Turbo-electric 6,000 hp (4,500 kW) Max. 7,240 hp (5,400 kW)
Liquid Capacity: 141,200 barrels of oil.
Constructed by: Sun Shipbuilding and Drydock Company
Location: Chester, Pennsylvania USA Yard #252
Hull No. 327
Entered service: March 15 1943 delivered to Sheepshead Bay, New York
Owner: United States War Shipping Administration
Operator: Bernuth-Lembecke Company, New York City
Crew: 49 Merchant Seamen, 26 Armed naval Guards - Total 75

Sunk: November 2 1944

SS Fort Lee

Convoy USG 9

Departed New York City on May 28 1943

Arrive Gibraltar Mediterranean June 16 1943

Remainder of convoy arrive Port Said, Egypt June 25 1943

Convoy consisting of 79 ships including 14 U.S. Navy destroyer escorts

Convoy MKF 18

Convoy departed Malta on July 11 1943

Fort Lee departs Gibraltar July 12 1943 joins convoy

Arrived Clyde UK on July 23 1943

Convoy consisting of 13 ships mainly British and Dutch registered carrying mainly troops

Departed Liverpool August 1943

Arrived New York harbour August 28 1943

Departed Abadan, Iran on October 21 1944

Sailing alone with no escort. 93,000 barrels Navy C Bunker fuel oil: intended destination Brisbane, Queensland, Australia

Torpedoed and sunk Indian Ocean at position $27^0 35'S - 83^0 11'E$ on November 2 1944 west of Perth Western Australia, Australia

SS Fort Lee

Victims (on board ship)

SS *Fort Lee* Merchant Navy Crew and Naval Armed Guard lost in the explosions of both the first and second torpedoes and launch of lifeboats.

Killed in Engine Room

Name	Age	Rank	Origin
1. VAIN, Thomas Filmore	19	Wiper	Baltimore, Maryland
2. YOHE, Frank Lucian	21	Fireman	Harrisburg, Illinois

Killed in Cabin from Torpedo Impact

Name	Age	Rank	Origin
1. MCCOY, George Alexander		Utility	Baltimore, Maryland

Killed in Lifeboat #3

Name	Age	Rank	Origin
1. ARTHUR, James Louis	20	A.B.	Baltimore, Maryland
2. FRELS, John Frederick	31	3rd Engineer	Austin, Texas
3. MCLAMORE, James William	18	O.S.	Baltimore, Maryland
4. DUMAS, Herman Claudell	21	S 1/c	Spencer, Louisiana
5. CARRINGTON, Leon LeRoy	19	S 1/c	Sayre, Pennsylvania
6. STORM, Bernard Gustav	19	GM 3/c	Owatonna, Minnesota

Survivors

Lifeboat #1

Rescued by SS *Mary Ball* on November 16 1944 and landed at Colombo, Ceylon on November 24 1944.

Name	Age	Rank	Origin
1. SHENBERG, Charles	46	Chief Mate	Baltimore, MD
2. ASHER, Leslie	29	2nd Mate	Baltimore, MD
3. CHAFFIN, James Thomas	18	Midshipman Cadet	Monticello, GA
4. COCHRANE, Lawrence		O.S.	
5. KNAUTH, Cecil Burnell	30	Oiler	Vernon, Texas
6. LOPEZ, Frank	24	A.B.	Waysum, WV
7. REEVES, Ernest		Wiper	
8. TARNOWSKI, Max John	20	Messman	Garfield, New Jersey
9. BIRD, Jerome J.		RM 2/c	
10. CROWE, Rowland R.		S 1/c	Indianapolis, IN
11. GORGA, Joseph William	21	S 1/c	Paterson, New Jersey
12. JOHNSSEN, Gottfried		BM 2/c	
13. KASPER, George F.		S 1/c	
14. LEVIN, Bernard	19	SM 3/c	Philadelphia, PA
15. PETERSON, Russell B.		S 1/c	
16. PREWITT, Lee Roy	20	S 1/c	Harrodsburg, Kentucky
17. MILNE, James W.		Lt. Jr.	

Survivors

Lifeboat #2

Rescued by the British freighter MV *Ernebank* on November 7 1944 and landed at Fremantle, Western Australia on November 14 1944.

	Name	Age	Rank	Origin
1.	ANDERSEN, Ottar M.	54	Master	Houston, Texas
2.	BANKS, Robert J.	28	Purser	St. James, MN
3.	BURIC, I.		Chief Steward	
4.	DUFFY, John W.	23	A.B.	Fall River, MA
5.	PRUITT Bradley Royce	19	Cook	Mt. Rainier, MD
6.	GROVES, Earl A.	18	O.S.	Chanute, KA
7.	HAMILTON, Joseph T.	20	Chief Pumpman	Glidden, Iowa
8.	HART, William	23	Chief Radio Op	Hickory, NC
9.	JOHNSTON, Hugh D.	35	2nd Pumpman	Parkersburg, PA
10.	LEE, Jr., John J.	20	2nd Radio Op	Plymouth, NH
11.	SEARLE, Walter J.		O.S.	Washington, DC
12.	ATKINSON, Lyle James	19	S 1/c	Buffalo, Wisconsin
13.	KIRWIN, James Joseph		S 1/c	
14.	LEMANSKI, Andrew Albert	21	S 1/c	Yale, Michigan
15.	SWANK, Thomas Charles	21	S 1/c	Akron, Ohio
16.	WINN, Leonard		SM 3/c	Hempstead, Long Island NY

Survivors

Lifeboat #6

Rescued by the tanker SS *Tumacacori* on November 9 1944 and landed at Albany, Western Australia on November 14 1944.

Name	Age	Rank	Origin
1. STAUFFER, Paul	51	Chief Engineer	Houston, Texas
2. SMITH, Francis Joseph	43	A.B.	Mathuen, Mass
3. DAVIS, John	38	Messman	Baltimore, MD
4. SHERRY, Michael Joseph	38	Messman	Summit, NJ
5. SMITH, Earl B.B.	19	Messman	Washington, DC
6. SHAFFER, Roy	29	1st Asst. Engineer	Seattle, WA
7. HENNESSY, John Leo	22	Oiler	Minneapolis, MN
8. PAGE, Jr, Zeb	26	3rd Engineer Jnr	Durham, NC
9. HOFFLER, Augustus	21	Galleyman	Brooklyn, NY
10. MARCUM, Jessie C.	22	Bosun	Big Stone Gap, VA
11. BROOKINS, Robert Charles	19	Messman	Sioux City, IA
12. SHARE, Gilbert Carl	18	3rd Cook	Norfolk, VA
13. MALEC, John L.	18	Wiper	Baltimore, MD
14. MOOTZ, William Francis	16	Messman	Kansas City, Kansas
15. WILSON, James Marvin	20	GM 3/c	Troy, Missouri
16. ADAMS, Orville D.	20	S 1/c	Cannelton, Ind
17. KING, William Marion	23	S 1/c	Bluefield, West Virginia

Lost in Lifeboat #4

**Merchant Marine and Naval Armed Guard crew lost at
sea and or landed on Japanese occupied Sumba Island
January 1945.**

Name	Age	Rank	Origin
1. BROEDLIN, Rudolph Edward	26	Oiler	Bridgeport, CT
2. CRAIG, Robert John Kelly	20	Fireman	Fredonia PA
3. FRALEIGH, Harold Robert	18	Messman	Bronx, NY
4. HOFFMAN, Jack Robert	21	A.B.	Wauwatosa, Wisconsin
5. SAVOLSKY, Maxwell	31	Electrician	New York City
6. SIMMS, Edward Kenneth	21	Fireman	Lockwood, WV
7. SORACE, Joseph John	45	2nd Engineer	New York City
8. STINE, Salem Humbleson	35	3rd Mate	Baltimore, MD
9. STOKELY, Frederick Royal Clyde	39	Messman	Del Rio, TN
10. WOOD, Frank Bell	39	A.B.	Edgefield, SC
11. EATON, Herbert Anthony	20	S 1/c	Peoria, Illinois
12. FINCH, Warren Smith	19	S 1/c	Saratoga, North Carolina
13. HOLDEN, Harold John		S 1/c	Rockford, Illinois
14. LANNING, Robert Franklin	20	S 1/c	Chicago, Illinois
15. DELMONTE, Victor R.		S 1/c	Rochester, New York
16. MELLERT, William Judson		GM 3/c	Kingston, New York

All deceased – no survivors.

Total crew on board: **75**

49 Merchant Marine Crew - 26 U.S. Navy Armed Guards

Total Lost: **25** [both onboard ship and in lifeboat #4]

Total Survived: **50**

33 U.S. Merchant Marine Crew & 17 Armed Guards

The badge of the United States Navy Armed Guard

The badge of the United States Merchant Marine

HOW THE MISSION DOES ITS WORK

It provides for the Spiritual needs of seafarers by means of Chaplains, Lay Readers and Seaman's churches.

It ministers to the lonely men in light vessels and lighthouses, linking them with parishes ashore.

It ministers to sick seamen in hospitals especially in foreign ports.

It provides institutions, social life, healthy recreation and outdoor sports for seafarers ashore.

Addendum

A ustralia was certainly by no means geographically isolated during the Second World War. In fact it was during this conflict that for the first time in the nation's history
that she had come under a direct attack by a foreign power.
Australia was actually one of the very few countries to feel
the impact in one way or another no matter how great or
small, by all three principal Axis belligerents namely Germany, Italy and Japan. As there was no direct invasion by any

ground forces, all the attacks were either carried out by air or they came from the sea. For a large proportion of overseas visitors most would still be unaware that Australia was in fact targeted.

Japan carried out almost 100 air raids on Australia, across two states and one territory during World War II. Darwin, the capital city of the Northern Territory is one of the most well known. On February 19 1942 she was hit hard by twin engine land based bombers, Zero fighters and torpedo dive bombers, the latter being aircraft from the same carrier fleet that had struck Pearl Harbour only two months before. In the wake of this first attack over 245 people were killed, the city left in ruins and nine ships were sunk including the American destroyer USS *Peary* (DD-226).

Darwin was the only Australian capital city to come under persistent air attack culminating in some 47 raids from February 1942 to November 1943. In total the Northern Territory underwent some 64 air raids. Millingimbi, Adelaide River and also the town of Katherine which at 300 kilometres (150 miles) to the south of Darwin was the furthest inland air strike on Australia.

Then there is second most devastating air attack to occur on Australia which was at the small pearling town of Broome in the north-west of Western Australia. On the morning of Tuesday March 3 1942 nine Zero fighters destroyed 24 aircraft causing the deaths of well over 100 people. The most southerly air attack conducted by the Japanese on the entire Australian continent was at Exmouth Gulf located only 1,000 miles north of Perth. In all Western Australia sustained 16 air raids on eight different towns and locations of which up to 130 people, mostly civilians including women and children were killed.

Elsewhere Queensland too came under scrutiny and several air raids were carried out on both Townsville and Mossman, near Cairns in the north. Most however were aimed at the Allied airfield on Horn Island in the Torres Strait, the stretch of water that separates Australia from New Guinea.

Additionally there were naval bombardments carried out by Japanese submarines on both Sydney and Newcastle in New South Wales and also at Port Gregory on the coast of Western Australia. Highlighted is the brazen attack carried by three Japanese midget submarines in Sydney Harbour itself on June 1 1942.

With the huge presence of American military might stationed in Australia between 1942 and 1945 there were also many inevitable incidents. These involved not only of those from the United States but also our own fighting men and women as well as those from many other nationalities.

There is the B-24 Liberator that was shot down with up to 33 persons on board including twenty, mostly wounded U.S. servicemen, six miles off Broome's Cable Beach during the first devastating Japanese air attack there. There were only two survivors. After spending over 30 hours in shark infested waters they both managed to swim back to shore where one died soon afterwards from exhaustion. The aircraft has never been located.

Then there was Flight Sergeant Grady Gaston in B-24 Liberator 'Little Eva' that crashed near Burketown, Queensland in December 1942. Remarkably, he ultimately survived after spending the next 141 days in remote bush and mangrove scrub along the shores of the Gulf of Carpentaria before rescue.

These are only but just a few to mention. The list goes on and there are a multitude of many more exploits involving bravery, courage and tragedy. If anything it clearly illustrates and symbolises the strength and co-operation that exists between this great nation of Australia and the sincere hand of true friendship that she extends to all her Allies. In America there is Veterans Day, observed every year on November 11.

It is in the spirit of all good nations everywhere who uphold the causes of peace, democracy and decency that we continue to observe all those who have served and given the ultimate sacrifice. That is why Australia's ANZAC Day, observed every year on April 25, Remembrance [Armistice]
Day...also observed on November 11 and even Australia Day
[January 26] have never been more important for us to ac-
knowledge, pause and remember.

Bibliography & References

Never Seen or Heard From Again by Captain Arthur R. Moore
Merchant Marine Veteran (http://www.armedguard.com/never.html) ©2001

Shooting The War: The Memoir and Photographs of a U-boat Officer in World War II by Otto Giese & James E. Wise Jnr. ©1994 Naval Institute Press
ISBN 1-59114-298-9

U-333 – The Story of a U-boat Ace by Peter Cremer
Triad Grafton Books UK ©1982 ISBN 0-586-06294-7

The Anchor Light – The official paper of the U.S. Merchant Marine Veterans of WWII © August 2008 issue page 2
Interview with James Chaffin by Phil Jordan

Arctic Interlude: Independent to North Russia by Harry C. Hudson
Merriam Press ©1997

Wolf Pack by Gordon Williamson
Osprey Publishing ©2005

Die Ritterkreuztrager der Kriegsmarine by Clemens Range - Stuttgart
Germany Motorbuch Verlag ©1974

Die Deutschen Kriegsschiffe - Biographen Vol. 2, Vol. 5, Vol. 7, by Hans
H. Hildebrand, Albert Röhr, Hans-Otto Stienmetz - Koehlers Verlagsgesell-
schaft Publishers, Germany.

Deadly Secrets – The Singapore Raids 1942-45
By Lynette Ramsay Silver
Sally Milner Publishing © 2010
ISBN 9-78186-351410-1

**In The Shadow Of The Eagle – German Raider and U-boat Attacks off
Western Australia and in the Southern Ocean During World War II** by
Kevin Gomm
Digger Press (formerly Helvetica Publishing) ©2010 & ©2013
ISBN 978-1-4461-7597-2

Lifeboat by John R. Stilgoe
University of Virginia Press ©2003

Thank you to:
United States Merchant Marine Association
United States National Archive – College Park, Maryland
United States Navy Memorial (www.navymemorial.org)
National Archives of Australia (WA branch)
National Library of Australia (Trove)
State Records Office of Western Australia
Rainer Kolbicz - (Switzerland) uboat.net
Ara Saraswati – House of Sampoerna Museum Surabaya, Java
Drs. J. Robert van Diessen - Asia Maior/Atlas Maior Publishers

Drs. Nico A. van Horn, Archivaris KITLV/Royal Netherlands Institute of Southeast Asian and Caribbean Studies, the Netherlands

Battye Library – State Library of Western Australia

Fremantle Historical Society and Library

Red Cross Society of Australia (W.A. Branch Historical Section)

Albany Public Library, Albany W.A.

Albany Historical Society

Vancouver Arts Centre - Albany

Army History Unit - Canberra, A.C.T.

With special thanks to the following individuals and families in the U.S.A.

William (Bill) Hultgren – Maritime Historian

Captain Arthur R. Moore - Maritime Historian

Joseph (Joe) M. Sherry

JoAnne Sherry and the Sherry family

Bradley R. Pruitt

Vicky Wright (nee Pruitt)

Jim M. Wilson

Mark Wilson

Joe W. Gorga Sr

Joe Gorga Jr

Larry Gorga

Carole Urso (nee Tarnowski)

Joan Gottschalk (nee Hennessy) and the Hennessy family

Jonah Berndt (Hennessy family)

Norma Spencer (nee Atkinson) and the Atkinson family

Tom Chaffin and the Chaffin family

John Duffy Jr and the Duffy family

Dennis E. Broedlin and Broedlin family

Warren S. Finch and the Finch family

Erna L. Craig and the Craig family

Joe Mootz
Ed Egnatic
Deanna Mootz
Elmer C. Fought
Micky Fought Lango
Gail Wheeler (nee Baltoumas)
Bonnie Sisson Manning (Ancestry research)
Larry Freeman (Dumas memorial photograph)
Joy Endreshak (Ancestry research)
David Burch – Navy League of the United States
Carl Evans
Greg Rogers (Pruitt interview)

With much special thanks to those in Australia:
Glenice Delpozzo (Jacka family)
Leonie & Brian Copeland (Jacka family)
Troy Jacka
Tony Morgan & the Morgan families for Sidney Fargo
Murphy families for Sidney Fargo (U.S. & U.K.)
Lynette Ramsey Silver O.A.M.
Lt. Sid Henry - D.S.C. R.N.V.R.
Kristi McNulty – Fremantle City Library
Cheryl Hamill – Fremantle Hospital
Roger Cunnington Albany Historical Society
Rail Heritage of Western Australia

Websites
www.usmm.org (U.S. Merchant Marine)
www.armedguard.com
en.wikipedia.org/wiki/SS Fort Lee
www.pacificwrecks.com
www.wrecksite.eu
www.trove.nla.gov.au
www.pub17.bravenet.com
www.clydebuiltships.co.uk

www.clydesite.co.uk
www.combinedfleet.com
www.uboat.net
www.woodmanpointquarantinestation.com
www.warsailors.com
www.mariners-l.co.uk
www.shipsnostalgia.com
www.railheritagewa.org.au
www.findagrave.com

References and Manuscripts

Port of Albany Register of Inwards Movements – From Oct 1 1913 to Mar 1 1962, for the period of November 1944.

Port of Fremantle – Harbour Master Register & Log 1940-1945

National Archives, (U.S.) Washington D.C. Declassified documents, transcripts of eyewitness accounts, crew interrogations relating to the sinking of the Fort Lee.

Dept of the Navy, USNR, USMM – some documents as supplied to the author by James M. Wilson (declassified 1972, papers acquired 1977).

Other associated materials collated by Lynette Silver from Japanese interrogations held in file MP742/1 336/1/1939. National Archives, Melbourne, Australia.

More good books by the same author at
Digger Press.com

Red Sun On The Kangaroo Paw

Very popular - detailing all the Japanese air raids and attacks on Western Australia throughout the Second World War -the 70th Anniversary 1942-2012 Commemorative Edition. From Broome to Port Hedland and from Wyndham to Exmouth Gulf elements of the Imperial Japanese Navy Air Force, Army Air Force and vessels from her naval fleet penetrated the skies and waters of Western Australia. Throughout 1942 and 1943 a total of eight different towns and locations were targeted causing casualties and damage.

DVD Red Sun On The Kangaroo Paw – The Documentary

Now see the book now come to life – featuring interviews and live footage concerning the attacks on WA by the Japanese during World War II. Time 1 hour. Narrated by the author.

In The Shadow Of The Eagle

Besides the more well known *Kormoran* there were in fact up to six different German surface raider vessels that operated off the Western Australian coastline and in both the Indian and Southern oceans during World War II. This does not include the U-boat submarines that arrived later. Between them all they laid mines, sunk shipping and caused casualties.

Beneath Cold Waves

Between 1939 and 1945 over 55 vessels and ships were sunk as a direct result of enemy action in immediate Australian waters. A pictorial glossary covering both the World War I and Second World War period.

Memories Of A Matelot by Lt. Sid Henry DSC, RNVR (edited by Kevin Gomm)

From minesweeping in the North Sea, to naval operations in the Mediterranean Sea and North Africa, including Greece, Crete, the siege of Tobruk, Italy, to the Normandy D-Day landings and finally to Burma. Sid Henry traces his journey from humble beginnings at crafting the art of seamanship in Liverpool to eventually becoming an officer with the Royal Navy Volunteer Reserve [RNVR] and commanding various types of landing craft vessels during the Second World War.

DIGGER PRESS
Preserving Our Heritage

www.diggerpress.com

The Author

Kevin Gomm is the author of the popular *Red Sun On The Kangaroo Paw* that chronicles every Japanese air raid and strike on all the towns and locations in the state of Western Australia during the Second World War.

He is also the founder of Digger Press a small self publishing book business.

An accomplished musician and seasoned traveller, his interests are wide and varied. Writing and researching historical wartime events are just one of many.

Lifeboat #6-The Sinking Of The SS Fort Lee is his fifth book.

www.diggerpress.com

DIGGER

www.diggerpress.com